5/69 (1)

α⌐

ELIZABETHAN WALES

ELIZABETHAN WALES

THE SOCIAL SCENE

By

G. DYFNALLT OWEN

CARDIFF
UNIVERSITY OF WALES PRESS
1964

First Published 1962
Reprinted 1964

PRINTED BY J. D. LEWIS AND SONS LTD.
GOMERIAN PRESS, LLANDYSUL

To

MY WIFE

PREFACE

ALTHOUGH this book is concerned with the social background of Wales during the latter half of the sixteenth century, it is not intended to be a social history of that period. This would have required a more precise chronological framework, a stricter continuity in the presentation of data, and a fuller narrative of events and personalities.

Its object, therefore, is not an analytical study of the particular historical factors which moulded and influenced the social evolution of the Welsh people during the reign of Elizabeth. Rather, its aim is to illustrate the social and economic environment that conditioned the lives and habits of the different classes of Welsh society, their relations with one another, their reaction to the pressure of material incentives and personal ambitions and aspirations, their labour and leisure, the character of domestic and public behaviour, and, not least, the multiplicity of activities which led to the quickening of national life in all directions.

This attempt to reconstruct as authentic a picture as possible of the pattern of life in Elizabethan Wales is primarily based on unpublished documents in the Public Record Office, the British Museum and the National Library of Wales, but considerable use has also been made of the extensive and valuable material which has already been published on this period. Appreciably more data, however, are required to build up in firmer detail a more complete picture of the various aspects of Welsh social life which have been touched upon in this present volume. This will explain why the interpretation of certain facts may seem impressionistic, and why it might be erroneous to assume, in the absence of corroborative evidence, that developments described as happening in one or more localities, occurred generally throughout the Principality. Another point is that, because they deal with specific incidents and social features in time and place, some of the glimpses of Welsh life in this book may suggest that it was static or impervious to change in some respects. Nothing could be further from the truth. In thought and action the Welsh, like other contemporary peoples, were affected by ever-changing forms in law and custom, religion and politics, economic conditions, and home and foreign events. But it is with the daily existence of men and women behind these changes that this work is principally concerned, and it is hoped that it will have succeeded in portraying a little of the reality of that existence.

I wish to express my warmest thanks to the authorities of the Public Record Office, the British Museum and the National Library of Wales for placing their records at my disposal ; to the Readers of the University Press Board for their valuable suggestions ; to the Secretary, Dr. Elwyn Davies, for his kind interest and generous advice during the preparation of the work for the press ; and to my friend Mr. William Griffiths for his ungrudging assistance with reading the book in proof.

G. DYFNALLT OWEN

CONTENTS

ILLUSTRATIONS

A*

I

THE COUNTRYSIDE

THE victory on Bosworth Field and the consequent accession of Henry Tudor to the English throne had imbued the Welsh people with an almost ecstatic feeling of national pride and unity. The House of Tudor was invested with every recognisable virtue until a sense of proportion was eventually restored to the more perspicacious Welshmen. Towards the end of Elizabeth's reign, William Maurice of Clenennau, in Caernarvonshire, had no illusions at least about the lineal antecedents of the Tudors, for he wrote in a letter to a cousin that :

> ' it is not so that our nation came to court in the time of Owen Tudor (Henry VII's grandfather). Owen (Glendower) was a great favourite with Richard II, and that was the cause of his rebellion. His great attempt deserved greater commendation for holding out against a king (Henry IV) fifteen years than the other (Owen Tudor) for holding the favour of a great queen (Margaret), widow of Henry V.'[1]

But there was another consequence of the military verdict at Bosworth and the new order that ensued. The fact that the victor was a Welshman drew the attention of the English people to something that the majority of them had probably long forgotten or ignored. That was the presence of another and different society in the remote highlands of the west. Their interest and curiosity were further stimulated when a stream of loquacious, temperamental and mettlesome Welshmen poured over the border and settled among them, in town and countryside.

To more enquiring minds among the English, the Welsh emigrants excited speculation as to their origin, the kind of civilisation that they had evolved in the seclusion of their mountains, the nature of their country, their manners and mode of living. The ignorance that surrounded their past history was largely dissipated by the appearance of Polydore Vergil's History of England in 1534. Vergil, an

Italian scholar who had settled in England, had been on amicable terms with Henry VII, and had been encouraged by him to compile such a work. The Italian, who had conceived a great respect for the Welsh monarch, found nothing comparable to admire in the half mythological half legendary early history of Henry's countrymen. He dismissed as fatuous the belief that the Welsh had originally fled from the sacked city of Troy, derided the romantic lucubrations of Geoffrey of Monmouth, and did not hesitate to cast doubts on the veracity of the traditions concerning the idolised national hero, Arthur. Having read and edited the censorious works of Gildas, he had no scruples in correcting certain popular illusions about the nation's past. But although his work wounded the susceptibilities of the Welsh and roused some of them to accuse him of prejudice and distortion, it was a monument of creditable research and an authoritative source of information on Welsh history which was extensively used by later historians.

Vergil's History furnished a much needed background knowledge to a closer understanding of the Welsh people. It was to familiarise themselves still further with the country and its folk that some English writers visited Wales during the reign of Elizabeth, noting everything of interest to them and keeping a valuable record of their impressions. One of them, William Camden, a protégé of Gabriel Goodman, native of Ruthin and Dean of Westminster, was an accomplished scholar. His appetite for learning and his inordinate delight in antiquities impelled him to acquire enough Welsh to be able to consult records and manuscripts. But his *Britannia*, a compendium of factual knowledge accumulated over many years, was no academic coagulation of data on these islands. Camden was interested in people, and some of his observations showed that he had sharp ears as well as eyes for their qualities. The folk of Merioneth for instance :

' have an ill name among their neighbours for being too forward in the wanton love of women.'[2]

On the other hand, the inhabitants of the Vale of Clwyd possessed irresistible physical attractions :

' The colour and complexion of the Inhabitants is healthy, their heads are sound and of a good constitution, their eyesight continuing and never dimme, and their age long lasting and very cheerefull.'[3]

Then there was William Harrison who appeared to be particularly impressed by the marvels allegedly to be found in Wales. At Barry Island, he wrote :

' there is a rift or clift next the first shore whereunto if a man doe lay his eare, he shall heare such noyses as are commonly made in smithes forges or clinking of yron barres, beating with hammers, blowing of bellowes and such like.'[4]

It was the testimony of these visitors to, and writers on Wales, that drew increasing attention to the Welsh people. Foreign observers too—the diplomatic representatives of continental states—referred to them in their dispatches, although their comments were based on hearsay rather than on personal acquaintance with the Welsh. In the opinion of a Venetian diplomat :

' The Welshman is sturdy, poor, adapted to war and sociable. The men (of England, Cornwall and Wales) are for the most part tall of stature and robust, and far above all, the Welsh.'[5]

while a Spanish ambassador wrote to Phillip II of Spain in 1586 that :

' the land is rather mountainous, but still very rich in cattle and sheep ; there is plenty of wheat, and the parks are numerous and good.'[6]

Such passing references to Wales and its people were intended for the eyes of governments only, to be tabulated as items of foreign intelligence. But the intellectual public of the continent were not long to be deprived of information about the small nation in the west whose blood was flowing in the veins of the autocratic lady on the English throne. The effervescent patriotism of Humphrey Llwyd of Denbigh could not tolerate that omission, and as a result of his correspondence with the eminent Dutch cartographer, Abraham Ortelius, a grandiloquent description of the Welsh people and their land appeared in the latter's *Theatrum Orbis Terrarum*, published in 1603 and acclaimed as the most authoritative atlas in existence.

There were few landed magnates in Elizabethan Wales whose wealth and pretensions could be compared with those of the higher ranks of the English nobility. Their numbers were as restricted as the extent of their Welsh estates was small, some were more English than Welsh in their antecedents and up-bringing, and for the most part they were more dependent upon and attached to the larger properties that they owned in England. The history of the landowning class in Wales is essentially that of the small gentry, squires of limited means who lived a semi-rural existence, and were sometimes barely distinguishable in their mode of life from the richer yeomen. By skilful manipulation of the English land laws, matrimonial arrangements, selective purchase of property and other, less commendable, methods, some of them were able to accumulate substantial estates before the century was out. But the best part of the Welsh gentry remained relatively poor men whose annual income rarely realised as much as a hundred pounds.

A slender income, however, in no way deflated their self-esteem or acted as a brake on their unshakable belief that they were invested with authority over their inferiors by right of birth. Their ancestors had been the natural leaders of the nation, and they were determined to preserve that position and the social precedence that went with it. It was a feudal instinct that took a long time to die, and it was exercised at the expense of those who, by the same rule of custom and class stratification, were born to serve and obey. A contemporary description of Piers Holland of Abergele, in Denbighshire, portrays this type of Welsh squire, imperious and assertive, who exuded this inherited feeling of domination in word and action. He :

‘ is all in all and rueleth and comaundeth all men as him listeth, usyng his will for lawe and his affection for reason. So as by his wilfull and extorteus dealing in that hundred, he purchaseth to hymselfe greate riches, for within three parishes next adjoynninge there is nether mariage agreed upon nor weddinge concluded betwene riche ne porre gentlemen ne yeomen, servants nor laborers, whereof the said Pieres hath not some rewarde as of some more or of some less, as thabilitie of the person extendeth unto. And that wich is more to be lamented, there is no jurie sworne nor any enquest impanelled betwene partie and partie for any value more or less but the same is ledd by the becke of the same Piers, and where he willeth there it goeth, be hit right or wronge.'[7]

One peculiarity of the gentry, which struck their English neighbours as being excessive and ludicrous at times, was their personal pride and their insistence upon the importance of pedigree as a cardinal criterion of social standing. To the Welsh gentleman, his pedigree was a matter of deep concern. For one thing, it established his kinship and relations with other families pertaining to the squirearchy. This was important, for it very often determined his loyalties and his animosities in the political rivalries and personal feuds which infested the ranks of the gentry. Above all, it justified his social pretensions and self-esteem. The numerous manuscripts of the period, which abound with the detailed ramifications of ancestral descent, show how profoundly attached were the squires to the sentiment of family pride. It was this that impelled Sir William Herbert of St. Julians, in Monmouthshire, to stipulate in his will that his daughter should marry a gentleman bearing the name of Herbert or forfeit her right of succession to his property.[8] And it was pride of family that persuaded the squires in the vicinity of Mold that the best way of perpetuating their memory was by setting their armorial bearings in the windows of the parish church.[9]

The study of genealogy was seriously pursued by gentlemen of a literary or antiquarian bent. For instance, Sir Edward Stradling of St. Donats, in Glamorgan, was a recognised authority on Welsh pedigrees and heraldry, and was often solicited for information on these matters.[10] For some, however, manuscripts were not an adequate repository of pedigrees. They were perishable and only accessible to a few people. A more concrete and durable manual of family descent was found desirable for the edification of future generations, and the choice fell upon gravestones and monuments in churches. The squires of Brecknock specialised in this sepulchral testimony to the excellence and length of their pedigrees, and almost monopolised a descent from the historical and mythological rulers of the ancient lordship of Brecon. One family, in

particular, claimed that it could trace its lineage back to one of
the knights of King Arthur's Round Table who, in turn, was
alleged to be descended from ' Belin the Greate, Emperour of
Greate Brittayne.'[11] It was this obsession with ancestry that
bewildered and amused the English, and stimulated one of
them to compose the following lines in a mock Welsh-English
language :

> ' Pye Got, they bee all Shentlemen
> Was descended from Shoves none lyne (Jove's own line)
> Parte humane and parte divine . . .
> And from Ffenus that fayre Goddesse
> And twenty other shentle poddies (bodies)
> Hector Stoute and comely Paris
> Arthur Prutus, King of Ffayryes . . .'[12]

Such ineffable pride was liable at times to transgress the
bounds of decorum and verge on vulgar self-advertisement.
One such occasion gave rise to much comment along the Welsh
border and, to the obvious satisfaction of the inhabitants,
brought divine retribution upon the guilty party. A gentleman
in the neighbourhood of Presteigne had persuaded himself that
water was no fit liquid to be used for the christening of his son,
and so he :

> ' upon a proud stomack caused the water to be voyded out of
> the font and filled it with wyne, and so caused his sonne to be
> therin christened. After which it is noted by the Countrey how
> he and his grew to decay in substance of Credyt, his race ex-
> tinguished.'[13]

The gentry arranged their marriages with as much foresight
and prudence as they conducted their other affairs. What
primarily interested them was the territorial or financial
advantages that would accrue from a felicitous alliance with
other families of their own class. They rarely went outside their
own social circle, since they had little to gain from marriages
with their inferiors. Money was, of course, always welcome
even from that quarter, but power and influence were of
paramount importance and these resided in their hands. Their
natural inclination to keep things for themselves, and their
appreciation of the position that they gained during the

century, especially during Elizabeth's reign, as privileged servants of the Crown, made them reluctant to open their ranks to members of the commonalty by marriage. They preferred to employ marriage as a restrictive practice in order to coalesce their ranks and heighten the sense of their class unity, and for this reason they evolved a system of alliances which knit much closer than ever before the landed families of North and South Wales. For instance, the Stradlings of St. Donats, in Glamorgan, married the Griffiths of Penrhyn, in Caernarvonshire, and the Maurices of Clenennau in the latter shire allied themselves with the Johns of Abermarlais, in Carmarthenshire. The consolidation of their power and the extension of their influence by these inter-regional marriages had the effect of amalgamating the Welsh gentry into a self-reliant and strongly entrenched class, which could become a potent political—and military—force, and eventually did so.

The actual participants in these marriages—the sons and daughters of the squires, mere fledglings some of them—were, of course, in no position to protest at the way their future was being arranged to fit into some scheme of territorial aggrandisement or adjustment. Maurice Wynn of Gwydir was so determined that his daughter Jane, not yet fourteen years of age, should marry into the Thelwall family that he was prepared to see her coupled with the three sons of Edward Thelwall in succession, if the eldest boy selected as first choice should happen to die.[14] Fatherless daughters were more vulnerable still. When Roger Salisbury died, his three little girls were placed under the guardianship of the family priest and two neighbouring gentlemen, one of whom made a convenient match whereby he obtained his choice of the orphans and her share of the property.[15]

It was a matter for Providence whether business marriages like these prospered or not. No doubt many did, but in the case of another Jane, the daughter of Hugh Owen, a Pembrokeshire squire, it resulted in an exhibition of sheer cruelty. A great deal of land and money had been contributed by the contracting parties to the dower, but the husband, David Lloyd, a Carmarthenshire gentleman, felt that he had been cheated by his father-in-law, and proceeded to take revenge upon his wife. The list of his brutalities was impressive even for those rough days. He had thrown her downstairs, had ' bust ' her head with a cudgel, wounded her with his rapier, knocked out four of her teeth, trampled her underfoot, and wrenched her hair from her head ' in whole lockes.' All this, and probably more, for an alleged non-payment of some three hundred pounds in land promised him by her father.[16] The daughters of the poorer gentry may have accounted themselves fortunate in that the paucity of dowries saved them sometimes from such indignities and acts of sadism. On the other hand, they could only look forward to spending a monotonous life at home, or an unprofitable and negative existence as companions or maids to ladies of quality. Even these posts were not always obtainable unless they could claim to have a practical knowledge of needlework.[17]

Women hardened by the repetition of the marriage vow would, of course, not always submit to a tyrannical or domineering husband, and often gained the sympathetic ear of the law courts to which they took their complaints. Anne Lloyd, married for the third time to the squire of Llandeilo Tal-y-bont, in Glamorgan, left her husband on the grounds of cruelty and claimed maintenance from the property that she had brought him as her dowry. The squire put up a good defence on the grounds that he too was no stranger to the tribulations of married life. His wife had refused to prepare his meals, had spent her money on her children by her former husbands, and had called him rogue, rascal and other offensive names. Nevertheless, he was penitent, regretted having laid his hands on her, wished her back and offered sureties for his good behaviour in the future. The court, however, rejected his petition and legalised his wife's separation.[18]

Separation was one solution to misunderstanding, incompatibility of temperament and strained relations in the marriages of the Welsh gentry. Infidelity, however, could lead to more serious consequences, since it might not only impair marital relations but upset the material arrangements upon which the marriage had been based. Husbands did not consider themselves bound by any conventional standard of conduct in their married lives. It seemed to be the most natural indulgence, after marriage, to enter into illicit union with other women and have children by them. Bastard sons and daughters suffered no harm from the conditions of their birth. They were not socially ostracised nor discriminated against by their reputed fathers. On the contrary, they were publicly recognised, enjoyed the protection of the families into which they had been adventitiously born, and were bequeathed property and gifts like the more legitimate offspring. And no one, not even the Church, showed much disapproval of this behaviour.

But where wives allowed their thoughts and fancies to be distracted by men other than their lawful husbands, or succumbed to seduction, they had to be particularly careful in concealing their indiscretions. Discovery could lead to the death of the lover, and to their own disgrace and humiliation, for no gentleman could stand the opprobrium of being a cuckold. The possibility must have occurred to them many times, in view of their own amatory adventures, and they devised crude and rather naive methods of testing the physical fidelity of their wives.[19]

It was the fear of discovery that induced some wives to adopt desperate measures to avoid it. A case that set the whole of North Wales talking and speculating was the behaviour of Sir Richard Bulkeley's second wife, *Yr Arglwyddes Fach*—Her Little Ladyship, as she was called by the people of Anglesey. It became common knowledge that when the good knight was away attending to the affairs of the realm in the Parliament of 1571, she had committed adultery with a prepossessing young man who used to serenade her under her bedroom window, and—what added a spiritual flavour to an otherwise mundane scandal—with the household priest of the Bulkeley mansion who had made ' diverse rymes and ballads of dishonest love ' to her. Sir Richard duly returned home, and suddenly fell ill. The symptoms were alarming but spectacular :

' purging upward and downward for 4 dayes together, XX stooles in the day and night, extreame tortions in the belly, great ach in the head and in the bones, a shivering cold in the whole body,

and his legges and thighes broken out in botches and boyles as big
as crabbes.'

Not surprisingly poison was suspected, and Sir Richard took a
liberal dose of Mithridatium and unicorn's horn as an antidote.
It kept him alive for some months, during which time the
suspicions of the family and countryside fell upon his wife. She
was imprisoned in her room, accused of introducing mercury
and arsenic into her husband's food, and mercilessly interrogated. Whether she was guilty or not—and few had any doubts on
that point—the case was hushed up, and she was sent home to
her own family after Sir Richard's death.[20]

Encouraged by the example of the English gentry, and
seeking to demonstrate their wealth and rank in a somewhat
more peaceful manner than was their custom, the Welsh
squires turned their attention to the improvement of their
homes. The requirements of comfort and privacy, which
gradually supplanted those of personal safety and protection as
life became more orderly and civilised, persuaded them either
to dismantle the rough and primitive buildings that had
sheltered generations of their families, or to add a more modern
wing to the body of the old house, which they could embellish
and furnish in the latest approved style.

However, the transition from the physical restrictions and
discomforts of medieval homes to the spaciousness and relatively
sanitary conditions of the Elizabethan manor was slower in
Wales than in most other parts of the realm. At first, the
country was not sufficiently law-abiding to allow of a domestic
architecture free from considerations of defence. A gentleman's
home, although it no longer took on the appearance of a
fortified stronghold, was still expected to afford him and his
dependents some form of sanctuary from the violence which
was almost a daily experience before the Welsh submitted to
the over-riding authority of the law and its courts. Where
waterways were available, it was found more practical to
surround the house with a moat. In the absence of this natural
fortification, it became fashionable to build the mansion on to a
courtyard surrounded by walls with corbels and battlements,

and accessible by a defensive gatehouse, an admirable example of which could be found at Corsygedol, in Merioneth.

Almost all these mansions were built of stone and roofed with slates. With their halls, living chambers, kitchens, pantries, cellars, brewhouses, corn chambers—and even prisons, in some cases—they formed self-subsistent little communities, equipped and provisioned to stand a siege, repel an attack and, as was often the case, to launch a raid. But with the normalisation of political and social life after the accession of Elizabeth, and the growing prosperity of the rural economy, the time was ripe for further concessions to the general tendency towards domestic amenities and fashions. It was now that the country mansions began to incorporate the characteristic features of Elizabethan domestic architecture. Ceilings replaced the old open roofs, and were panelled with oak or covered with plaster upon which were traced ornamental designs. This innovation made it possible to add an upper floor, and sometimes lofts, which were used as bedrooms or store rooms, often interchangeable. The hall was converted into a private dining room for the squire's family, and a living room was set apart for them, while the domestic staff was henceforth relegated to the kitchen and ancillary offices. Staircases of oak were installed to connect the hall with the upper chambers, windows were lengthened and mullioned, window seats were recessed, and glass inserted in the window frames whereby the old system of shutters was dispensed with, and the rooms benefited from the full light of day and from a more adequate protection against inclement weather. Large open fireplaces were another feature of the new emphasis upon home comforts, and they were considered to be as necessary to the sleeping chambers as to the hall and kitchen.

Other materials besides stone were used to build houses. Occasionally the walls were made of plastered rubble, or consisted of timber framework filled with clay. Red brick was also often used for their construction, especially along the English border. A few houses, and this applied particularly to the town mansions of the squires, had galleries around the sides of the inner hall, or on the upper floor which could be approach-

ed from the outer courtyard by a stone staircase. The variety
in construction and design of these mansions, many of which
have survived the accretions and renovations of later centuries,
testify handsomely to the efforts of the Welsh gentry to keep
abreast of fashion, and to their pride of home.[21]

Sanitation and the provision of fresh water were still insoluble
problems for most of the occupants of the new fashionable
country mansions. But at Carew, Sir John Perrot had devised
an ingenious and extravagant scheme for modernising the
water supply of the castle. At the head of a fountain near by,
he had constructed a cistern of lead from which water was
canalised to the castle through nine-inch lead pipes. Another
cistern in the kitchen received the incoming water and re-
directed some of it to a conduit in the courtyard, which was
specially built of free stone and lead and equipped with brass
cocks. A number of other lead pipes radiating from the kitchen
cistern supplied constant water to the brewhouse, the bake-
house and even to the stables of the castle.[22] The installation of
this complex system of pipes within and outside his residence
was characteristic of the interest taken by Sir John in experiments, both domestic and political. But it did not long
survive his meteoric fall from a position of undisputed authority
and influence in West Wales. Soon after his death, in the
Tower of London in 1592, Carew passed into other hands and
the pipes were taken up and sold.[23]

The gentry furnished their country mansions with a lavishness that would have astounded their grandfathers. There was
little in the way of fashionable domestic ware that did not
eventually find a place in their homes. Much of it was purchased in London and other English cities, but there were also
Welsh craftsmen at hand to make pieces of furniture from home
grown timber, and to show their skill in emulating foreign
styles, as well as incorporating their own.

Most of the rooms, including bedrooms, were wainscotted
either in full or in half panels, and, as a result, tapestry was
gradually being superseded although pieces of it, especially of
Arras manufacture[24] continued to be used for wall hangings.
Tables and chairs were made of various kinds of wood, partic-

ularly ash and walnut,[25] but an innovation was cupboards of maple tree wood.[26] Beds were generally built of wainscot or walnut, sometimes fastened to the walls, and having canopies and hanging draperies of silk, fustian, velvet or taffeta fringed with lace or gold and embroidered with coloured designs. Furniture of foreign make was much in vogue, and Flanders chairs and chests, Danzig chests and Lisbon stools were placed in halls and bedrooms to invest them with an air of refined gentility. Floors were being gradually covered with a variety of carpets and rugs. Sir John Perrot had a positive passion for them, and was extravagant in the purchase of carpets of Turkish, Dornex and Scottish make and of Irish rugs. In fact, Carew Castle was a veritable showpiece of contemporary taste in home furnishings. Damask cushions, taffeta curtains, sarcenet quilts and holland cloth were only a few of the foreign fabrics that competed in colour, quality and profusion with furnishings of silk, satin, velvet and the more homely fustian and flannel.[27]

Pewter table ware was, of course, still in vogue, but the gentry had an insatiable appetite for silver ware. Basins, bowls, ewers, goblets, salt-cellars and spoons of that metal were to be found in most mansions, and were regarded as a form of realisable wealth, as well as house ornaments, since they could be pawned in a financial crisis.[28] But their reflection in the light of candles placed in silver candlesticks served as a beacon light for too many undesirable characters. Silver spoons, being the least bulky object in a pocket, had a particular fascination for the housebreakers of Elizabethan days.

Jewellery and personal ornaments, as always, were worn to emphasise the grace and beauty of women, to set off the cut and colour of their dress, and, in the case of their men folk, to advertise their wealth and status. As the century wore on, there was a change in certain forms of jewellery which corresponded, in some measure, with the transition from Catholicism to Protestantism. During the early years ornaments such as brooches had been decorated with the image of the Virgin, with relics alleged to have been worn by her, or with pictures of

sacred objects.[29] These disappeared with the suppression of the
old faith, and were replaced by jewels of exquisite workmanship,
which were not identified with any belief except a devotion to
art. Chains, bracelets and rings of gold, pomanders of the
same precious metal, diamonds in the shape of true lovers'
hearts, ornaments of pearls, enriched with rubies and saphires,
and beads of jet and gold were paraded whenever the occasion
demanded that the gentry and their ladies should appear in
their sartorial splendour.

Their clothes often rivalled their jewels in sumptuousness and
extravagance. Gentlemen's wardrobes included coats of black
velvet, satin and cloth, cloaks and doublets of the same
materials, Spanish leather shoes, taffeta garters, silk stockings as
well as those of home spun wool.[30] When he went abroad, the
squire invariably wore a rapier or sword, and added a ruff to
his outfit. At home, he exchanged these for velvet pantaloons,
velvet slippers or a pair of pinsons and a furred gown with,
perhaps, a velvet cap on his head. Young fops, of course,
sported a rainbow coloured attire when they went to town. A
description of one of them says that he rode into Denbigh
wearing a black felt hat with a plume of red and white feathers,
a canvas doublet and breeches of turkey colour fringed with
black velvet, red stockings of kersey fringed with velvet, a
sky-coloured cloak lined with red bays and fringed with blue
taffeta, and a sword and dagger at his side.[31] That he happened
to be paying a visit to the town pawnbroker would, in the
circumstances, cause no surprise. There were some gentlemen,
of the older and more austere generation, who opposed this
servility to fashion. Sir Richard Bulkeley, for instance, would
have nothing to do with it, and invariably wore round breeches
and a black bombast doublet. His reply to a hint that his
conservatism in dress was unbecoming to one in his position
was that, ' people were given to soe much variety and changes
that once in every seven years they would turne to his fashion.'[32]

If the gentry attired themselves in the best of fashion, one can
imagine the pains that their ladies and daughters took over their
dress. Nothing was too expensive for them, and the skill of
English tailors was called into their service. Their gowns were

made of all the fabrics known to the trade—satin, damask, velvet, taffeta, russet, grogram and others. Stomachers, French bodices, petticoats, kyrtels, parkets, gorgets of lawn, white furred gowns, taffeta hats lined with silk—these and many more were the fashionable articles of clothing associated with women of breeding, taste and wealth. Even the wives of the poorer squires wore red flannel petticoats fringed with velvet and edged with silk, taffeta sleeves and stomachers and knitted stockings of various colours.[33] At a time when the extravagance of the English gentry's dress attracted attention and provoked much satire, their compeers in Wales made as brave a sartorial show as any rural squirearchy was capable of doing, and much more than their incomes sometimes permitted.

One indispensable adjunct to their estates, or so many gentlemen thought, was a deer park. It was a fashion much practised in England, where every manor house with any pretensions had a special enclosure for deer. Even the parsimonious Lord Burleigh had been known to spend a great deal of money on them. It meant a heavy outlay, since the parks had to be surrounded with walls or hedges to restrain the deer from wandering, but this consideration did not unduly worry the Welsh squires. The gentry of South Wales certainly spared no expense. Sir John Perrot erected a wall around his park at Carew in which he kept a good stock of fallow deer.[34] Sir Edward Stradling had two parks, one for fallow and the other for red deer. Their meat must have been particularly tasty, for Sir Edward was inundated with requests for venison from his friends, and even from slight acquaintances who had a special reason for titillating the palate of important guests.[35]

In North Wales, deer parks were less common, although Marsley Park in the lordship of Bromfield must have been one of the most extensive in the country. It contained about two hundred deer of all sorts, supervised by two keepers who were allowed quarters and a certain amount of pasture in the park to feed their private cattle.[36] The Bulkeley family kept their two parks, Red Hill and Priestholme, well stocked with red and fallow deer which furnished them with venison every week.[37]

The comparative fewness of such parks in North Wales may
have been due to the fact that there were plenty of red deer to
be hunted in the mountains, and that it was considered a
nobler sport to chase them through the countryside than to
pursue them inside an enclosure.

Although they derived the greater part of their income from
the rents and customary payments of their tenantry, the
gentry maintained a strong personal link with the land which
was the solid foundation of their position and prosperity. Not
only did they fall into line with the new tenurial changes and
reforms which featured Elizabeth's reign and allow their
tenants more latitude in their methods of cultivation, but they
also turned their own demesne land into flourishing farms
which enabled each manor to become a self-subsistent unit. In
this way the gentry were able to live off the land and to use
their property income to modernise and embellish their homes,
support an establishment of servants and estate officials, and
maintain what they considered to be a proper standard of
living, besides meeting the expenses of educating their sons and
marrying their daughters off with suitable dowries.

Some of the home farms were large and exceedingly well
stocked with cattle, sheep and horses. Sir Richard Bulkeley
had two dairy farms in Anglesey, and there was no lack of beef,
mutton, lamb, butter and cheese at his table. As an excellent
horseman and tilter, he had a special interest in his stables,
where he kept a considerable number of horses and mares, for
himself and for some of the twenty four servants who escorted
him whenever he journeyed from home.[38] Sir John Perrot had
large flocks of sheep estimated at many thousands, besides
scores of cattle and horses.[39]   Edward Jones, squire of Plas
Cadwgan in Denbighshire, executed for complicity in the
Babington Plot, although a petty gentleman, had a small but
well-equipped home farm of 40 sheep, 7 calves, a horse, a
gelding and mare with foal, 4 oxen, 4 kine, besides a barn full of
wheat, rye, barley and oats, which were sufficient to maintain
him and his household.[40]   Like most of his class, he brewed his
own beer and salted his own beef, but he was probably one of

the few gentlemen farmers in the district who possessed waggons with wheelbands made of iron.[41] The typical rural squire without any pretensions to wealth or fashion would content himself with a few silver spoons, and, perhaps, one or two pieces of silver plate as sufficient testimony to his rank, and find more solid proof of his real worth in his cattle, sheep, horses, goats, pigs and poultry.

Their expensive tastes and the difficulty of meeting their liabilities, swollen by the inflationary distortion of the national currency during Elizabeth's reign, forced many of the Welsh gentry to develop a partiality for money-making which set a vicious example to the nation. Some thought that they could find solvency in trade, legitimate or otherwise. Sir Richard Bulkeley dispatched a ship regularly from Beaumaris to Greenland to fish for cod and lug, which he bartered in Spain for Malaga and sherry wines.[42] Sir William Herbert of St. Julians, in Monmouthshire, owned a bark with which he conducted a profitable exchange of agricultural produce for continental goods, and which he left as a legacy to his son.[43] But most of the squires were inclined to look for supplementary sources of income nearer at home.

The obvious place to discover them was in the various financial and administrative offices either farmed out or delegated by the Crown. The collection of Crown revenues, for instance, was considered to be a lucrative employment, although there was always a danger that a vigilant but tiresome Exchequer official might insist upon a minute examination of receipts. This placed Sir John Salisbury in an awkward position on one occasion. He had been entrusted with the collection of mises, a customary present made by the Welsh people to a new monarch on his or her accession to the throne. When summoned to surrender his receipts, it was found that some could not be accounted for. Sir John placed the blame squarely upon the ineptitude of his deputy collectors, and tried to wash his hands of the whole business by trying to persuade Sir John Norris to take over the office and the responsibility of finding the lost monies.[44]

It was much safer to exploit the military requirements of national defence. Musters were exceptionally remunerative, since the Lords Lieutenant of the shires and their deputies were authorised to press men for foreign service and to levy taxes to provide them with arms and uniforms. Their dishonesty on these occasions became proverbial, and their treatment of the civil population scandalous. Sir Thomas Jones of Carmarthen-shire specialised in misusing funds collected for furnishing the shire's musters with armour and weapons. He issued instruct-ions that the parishes should purchase armour from him at a higher price than its actual cost, and then proceeded to sell them old armour for new. In this way, it was reckoned that he had increased his private fortune by some £2,000.[45]

It would appear that the Welsh gentry had not heard that Parliament had passed an Act in the reign of Edward VI which expressly prohibited the discharge of able bodied muster men from service abroad, upon pain of a fine of £20 for each person wilfully allowed to evade his military duties.[46] But they had as little respect for the legislation of the House of Commons as they had for the remonstrations of the Council of the Welsh Marches. Informed of the surreptitious pocketing of public defence funds in Caernarvonshire, the Lord President, the Earl of Pembroke, wrote to Sir John Wynn of Gwydir and William Maurice of Clenennau, the deputy lieutenants in 1591, that :

' I wolde have all men know that I do mislike such lewde dealinge, and I will take such order that your credits shall be repaired by their discreditts who have causelessly complained. But if your accompts be injust, then yourselves are like to feele what it is to abuse the trust which on this behalfe Her Majesty hath committed unto you.'[47]

But he might well have expressed his indignation to the moon. A year or two later, a Caernarvonshire gentleman writing to the same Sir John Wynn hinted that it would be advisable to use public money to equip pressed men,

' and not after the old manner used in all our shires—that half the allowance were put in their owne purses.'[48]

Where ancient customs had not entirely lost their usefulness, the gentry did not hesitate to press them into their service as levers of financial extortion. Of these, the *comortha* proved to be the most pliable and productive. Originally it had been a free benevolence to relieve the victims of misfortune and impoverishment,[49] but later it had been applied quite overtly by the contumacious lords and barons of the Welsh Marches to obtain funds for the maintenance and benefit of their retainers and mercenaries. The Act of Union that sealed the fate of the Lords Marcher had tried to deal a death blow to the system of *comortha* by expressly prohibiting it. But a custom that had proved its value as an instrument for raising money was too resilient to be suppressed by an act of Parliament. It assumed another form which, although more innocuous in appearance, was no less oppressive than before. In the hands of the impecunious or greedy members of the gentry, it became simply and solely the means of filling their coffers or advancing the fortunes of their immediate relations. And from the four corners of Wales came revelations of the manner in which the defenceless tenantry were browbeaten into submissive payment of the ' voluntary ' *comorthas* demanded of them.

A request from Richard Price, the all-powerful head of the Gogerddan family, that the men of Cardiganshire should meet him at the parish church of Tregaron on a particular Sunday in 1599, was obeyed with much misgiving. Upon their arrival, the countryfolk found themselves confronted by five hundred armed partisans of the family, who shepherded them into the church to hear divine service. This enforced act of piety was followed by a greater degree of mortification than most of them had expected. When they issued into the open air, they found that a platter had been placed on the churchyard stile, while grouped around it were four Justices of the Peace of Cardiganshire, including Price himself. The squire of Gogerddan proclaimed that a *comortha* should be organised, for which he and his fellow Justices would be duly grateful. He added, however, that anyone failing to show an exemplary liberality would run the risk of being pressed for military service in Ireland. It was a short but effective speech, for it produced a hundred pounds before the last despondent countryman left the churchyard. Encouraged by this, Price arranged that his

wife should initiate further *comorthas* amongst the women of
north Cardiganshire for his own benefit, and was able to add
some £200 to his personal fortune. Other Justices of the Peace
followed suit, and were emulated by minor officials within the
shire who extorted hundreds of sheep and lambs, and gave in
return ' the thanks of the Justices ' who had appointed them.[50]

In Montgomeryshire, John Vaughan of Llwydiarth, with
three daughters to marry off, collected money and cattle to the
value of £300, besides smaller amounts to relieve the pressing
wants of his friends and supporters.[51]   In the lordship of
Gower, the position of the tenantry was pitiable in the extreme
in the face of this predatory practice. There the *comortha* was
inflicted on them some twelve or thirteen times a year, generally
by gentry of reduced circumstances who could barely afford to
marry off their daughters or keep up appearances. Despite the
prohibition of the custom by the Lord of Gower, the Earl of
Worcester, cattle, corn and money continued to pass into the
hands of the impoverished squires through fear of reprisals.[52]

Although the scandals associated with the *comortha* were
common knowledge and eventually forced the Government to
decree its abolition, the custom was too strongly entrenched and
served proprietory interests too well, to die a legislative death.
The most that a shrewd and experienced native critic of
abuses and malpractices in Wales could advocate on this point,
as late as 1575, was that the *comortha* should be prohibited
except for ' fire and mischance.'[53]   But little was done to limit
the excesses of the *comortha*, and the helplessness of the authorities was only too plainly revealed towards the end of Elizabeth's
reign. When a request was made to the Welsh gentry by the
Government that they should voluntarily defray the cost of
equipping a number of soldiers to serve in the Cadiz expedition
of 1596, the Lord President of the Council of the Welsh Marches
added a caustic postscript to the copy of the request sent to the
deputy lieutenants of Caernarvonshire. He wrote :

> ' You have ever been forwarde in comorthas for your owne
> private gaynes, therefore I conceive you wilbe mutch more
> favourable in this comortha for the public good of the whole
> State.'[54]

It was about all he could do or say to show his disapproval of the practice.

Despite the expedients employed by the gentry to enrich themselves and to defray the expenses of a more ostentatious way of living, many were unable to cope with the recurrent inflation of the currency which afflicted all classes. The debasement of the coinage by Henry VIII, and the flow of silver from the mines of the New World, resulted in a steady increase of prices which even Elizabeth's monetary reform failed to check entirely, and the squires of rural Wales were often hard pressed to make both ends meet. The more improvident had to resort to borrowing among themselves, sometimes with disastrous consequences. The usual arrangement was for the lender to offer property, cattle or corn which the borrower would sell on security. Sometimes, however, these fetched a lower price than the money which the latter had signed a bond to repay, so that the unfortunate man found himself liable for additional debts.[55] Other impecunious gentlemen found it less difficult to swallow their pride and pawn their rings or finery with tradesmen in neighbouring towns.[56]

The financial predicament of squires, and of yeomen for that matter, meant brisk business for usurers who had been released from the moral restraint of ecclesiastical condemnation by the consensus of Tudor public opinion that it was no crime to lend money on interest. Free to exercise their profession, a number of these petty financiers sprang up in town and countryside, and they were to be found in all social categories. A typical case was that of a Montgomeryshire yeoman who entered into a transaction with a neighbouring squire by whom he was induced to buy cattle and corn at excessive prices. The debt which he unfailingly contracted increased from year to year, and, upon his death, was assumed by his heir. To avoid legal action, the son agreed to let the gentleman usurer occupy his farm and homestead until the debt had been liquidated. He himself voluntarily became a labourer, and within a few years he had laid aside enough money to pay the debt. The squire

not only refused the money but had the son evicted when he
tried to take possession of his old home.[57]

When even usurers failed to come to the assistance of impoverished landlords and tenants, the dubious precedent of
Henry VIII seems to have recommended itself to many of
them. The forging and clipping of coins had its practitioners in
Wales as in England, and squires as well as yeomen and
tradesmen circulated false coins of tin and copper, or ' did
clipp, impayre and rownde the money.'[58] The lower orders
contented themselves with forging shilling and sixpenny pieces,
but a squire might aim at something higher, like a royal of ten
shillings.

The pretensions of a Piers Holland* were accepted by the
submissive lower classes, but they provided just that challenge
upon which the Welsh squires fed their pride and pugnacity.
Their former undisputed claim to the leadership of the people
soon degenerated into a squabble among themselves for a
preponderant influence in local affairs, fought out with the help
of friends, retainers and supporters, and with a supreme
indifference to the unhappy effects of their intemperate
behaviour upon the conduct of public business and the standard
of public morality.

It became almost impossible to control their feuds and
moderate their passions, since they were permitted by the
Crown to accumulate wealth and power, and to occupy the
principal offices of local administration. The Tudor monarchs,
implacable opponents of the old feudal aristocracy and
territorial magnates, fostered and favoured the squirearchy, in
Wales as in England, as a counterweight to the older landed
families, who were implicated in rebellions against them almost
up to the end of the century. But by doing so, the Crown
created a powerful class whose interests it had to respect, and
whose fidelity and support it had to cultivate. The temptation
to exploit the Crown's dependence upon their good will was
irresistible to the Welsh squires, and although they never
wavered in their allegiance, with the exception of a few in-

* See supra p. 12

By courtesy of the British Museum

HUMPHREY LLWYD

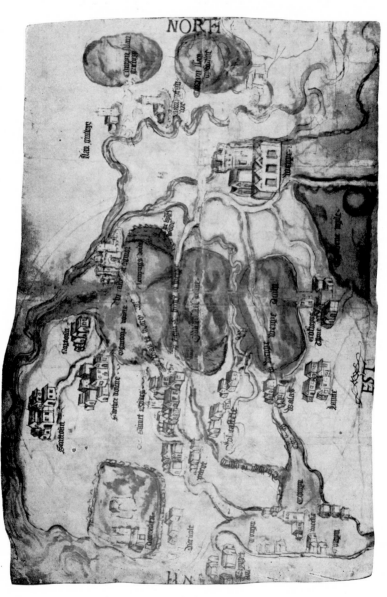

Crown Copyright : reproduced by permission of the Controller of H. M. Stationery Office and by courtesy of the Chancellor and Council of the Duchy of Lancaster.

dividuals, their internecine quarrels and opportunism put a heavy strain upon the tolerance of the central government and its representatives in Wales.

It seemed that little could be done to inculcate a sense of responsibility among them. The law was unable to restrain them, although it did not shrink from imposing the supreme penalty at times. The method was tried of inducing influential and well connected families to mediate and effect a reconcili- ation between parties concerned in disputes, but even that did not always succeed. No doubt, many of the quarrels which disturbed the countryside could be attributed to the normal clash of personalities, ambitions and interests, but they were aggravated by the congenital incapacity of the squires to co- operate among themselves, and by their immoderate sense of pride. It was this that drove a distracted Lord President of the Council of the Welsh Marches to ventilate his irritation with the North Wales gentry in a letter addressed to two of their most prominent members. ' How can your mynds be united in publique defence,' wrote the Earl of Pembroke in 1591,

> ' when they are devyded by pryvalt quarrells ? And what hope of succour in the field may any man have from him who is his professed enemie at home ? Or how shall her Majestys service in this tyme of danger go forwards yf one of you crosse the same because the dealinge therein is comytted to another. All men cannot be deputie Lieutenants, some must governe, some must obey.'[59]

It was the almost insurmountable difficulty of getting the Welsh gentry to recognise this simple truth that perplexed and exasperated the Crown and its officials.

In a private report on the endemic turbulence of the squires, a Welsh observer intimated to the Privy Council that one method of curbing their unruliness would be to force them to disband their retainers.[60] That it should have been necessary to remind the Government in 1576 of the existence of this class of quasi-mercenaries showed how inoperative English law could become when challenged by the tenacious customs of the Principality and the intransigence of the gentry. The first Tudor king had decreed the Acts of Livery and Maintenance

B

which aimed at the liquidation of the private armies of retainers
supported and paid by noblemen, and had enforced them with
stringent penalties. The English nobility, for the most part, had
submitted to the destruction of their military power. The Welsh
gentry, on the other hand, were reluctant to acknowledge that
the prohibition of retainers also applied to them, and continued
to maintain bands of armed men to protect them and to fight
their battles.

For instance, two domineering brothers, Henry and Edmond
Mathews of Cardiff, could rely on a formidable host of gentlemen and yeomen, within and outside the town, to harass their
particular enemies, Sir George Herbert and Edward Lewis of
the Van. They bastinadoed their servants on the castle green,
chased them up and down the streets, and overawed the citizens
generally by their turbulence. Their triumphal march into
Cardiff in 1596 was the climax to a relentless campaign of
provocation. Returning from an alleged business visit to
London, Edmond was met at Pen-coed, in Monmouthshire, by
some 150 of his armed retainers, who escorted him to Cardiff.
On the road they encountered a number of men who had been
pressed for service in Ireland by Edward Lewis. Mathews
peremptorily ordered them to return with him to Cardiff. This
was a deliberate incitement to desertion ; nevertheless they
obeyed and added a little colour to the ranks of Mathews's
retainers as they entered the gates of the town and marched
uproariously through the streets,

> ' to the great wonder and amazement of the people which beheld
> not onelye the trowpes and garrisons whiche the sayd Edmond
> brought with him throughe the streetes of the town of Cardiff in
> battal araye, bothe before him and behind him, but also the
> retorne and callinge backe of the souldiers which that morninge
> were sent towardes Irland.'[61]

Where long standing rivalries and feuds culminated in open
hostilities, the gentry appear to have favoured towns as the
most convenient battlefields on which to settle the issues
between them. They were convenient for the simple reason
that each side could concentrate their forces on a narrow front
and let weight of numbers decide the combat. Moreover, any

material damage which resulted would be at the expense of the unfortunate townspeople, not of the parties involved. And so, Thelwalls and Salisburies clashed at Ruthin, the Vaughans and Prices at Llanfyllin, and the streets of Aberystwyth reverberated with the battle cries of the Prices of Gogerddan and the Lloyds of Aber-mâd. But at no time did these antagonisms erupt more fiercely than during parliamentary elections in the Principality.

The Act of Union had extended parliamentary represent-ation to all the Welsh shires, which henceforth elected a knight for the county. In the opinion of the squires, political life was predominantly an expression of dutiful obedience and loyalty to the Crown. There was no fundamental issue to divide them into contending and fractious parties, each with its notions of how the country should be governed. In any case, to tamper with the established order could be construed as treason, and the few Welsh squires implicated in plots to that end were not represent-ative of their class and mind, and received little sympathy from their fraternity.

With no political theory or constitutional argument to enliven the electoral campaign, the gentry introduced a more combustible element which could be depended upon to set rival candidates by the ears and inflame their supporters. The elections were transformed into trials of strength between families who were competitors or enemies in other fields of activity, and who came to regard a seat in Parliament as a desirable appendage to the offices which they already occupied or to which they aspired. To secure the prize, they were prepared to employ downright disreputable methods, and to engage in pitched battles if necessary. The fact that this was, to say the least, an offence to the dignity of the House of Commons did not perturb the contestants, most of whom would have behaved with exemplary discretion at Westminster itself. But family prestige had to be maintained, especially as there was a distinct inclination in the countryside to equate it with political maturity.

The only persons eligible to vote in an election were the freeholders who could claim to enjoy an annual income of forty shillings from their land.[62] They were summoned by the sheriff to present themselves at the shire hall between 8 and 9 o'clock on the morning of election day. There their qualifications were examined by the same official, and the candidates, in turn, could demand that the voters or ' polls ' as they were sometimes called,[63] should take an oath that their qualifications were genuine and not faked for the occasion. These preliminaries completed, the ' polls ' proceeded to elect the future member for the county, not by ballot but by acclamation. It was the sheriff's duty to judge by the volume of voices which of the candidates had been chosen, and his hearing was reinforced by the knowledge that a mistake on his part might result in a fine of £100. Voting had to be terminated, and the successful candidate proclaimed, before the clock struck nine, otherwise the election was declared void.

These circumstances were propitious for all kinds of abuses and high-handed practices, and no one was more experienced in them than the gentlemen of Denbighshire. When the writ was issued for the summoning of the notable Parliament of 1601, Sir John Salisbury, squire of Llewenni, decided to make a bid for the county seat. His opponent was Sir Richard Trefor, who had the initial advantage of counting the sheriff, Owen Vaughan, among his personal friends. Both parties made no pretence of allowing the freeholders of the shire to judge their respective merits as candidates. They simply terrorised those who were within reach of their strong arm. Trefor used letters of muster to intimidate Salisbury's supporters with the threat of immediate military service in Ireland. Sir John, with a batch of similar letters in his pocket, notified Trefor's adherents that he had exactly the same idea in mind for them.

When election day arrived—polling was to be held in Wrexham—Sir John with an army of retainers marched into the town preceded by a trumpeter who blew his instrument in reckless defiance. The company made for the church with the object of bivouacking there, although Sir John insisted afterwards that it was an irresistible desire to say his prayers that had attracted him to the holy place. The door, however, was locked, and his armed men wandered disconsolately around the churchyard. Meanwhile, Trefor had issued directives to his faction, and among those who hurried to Wrexham to afford him assistance in the impending battle were eighty of the toughest miners in the coalfield of Denbighshire. Fortunately for the town the expected clash did not occur, but the election did not take place either.[64] The matter was reported to the House of Commons by the sheriff, who, not unnaturally, gave a favourable account of his alleged exertions to keep the peace between the two parties. The House expressed due consternation and indignation, but despite the demands of a Welsh backbencher, it would appear that no writ was directed for another election. Denbighshire had the signal misfortune of not being represented in the Parliament which witnessed the first stirrings of opposition against the autocratic powers of the Monarchy.[65]

Another piece of chicanery that commended itself to gentlemen candidates in Denbighshire was to augment the number of freeholders during an election. This was very much in evidence in 1588, when John Almer set himself up against John Edward, who was supported by the sheriff. Both candidates resorted to the indiscriminate creation of new freeholders by temporary grants of land to the requisite value of forty shillings, but they took the precaution of securing the eventual reversion of their property. The Edward faction, however, went a step further. On the day of the election, again at Wrexham, they induced a number of artisans—fullers, tailors and the like, to masquerade as freeholders, shepherded them into a private house and there unanimously elected Edward as the county member. The supporters of his opponent, who had observed the law by congregating in the shire hall, found themselves completely outmanoeuvred, for not only did the sheriff fail to appear there to conduct a properly constituted election, but he most improperly attended the rival and private election and insisted on returning Edward to the House of Commons.[66]

A strain of barbarism was sometimes only too evident in the behaviour of the Welsh gentry, but in an age when ambition and personal advantage were the paramount guiding principles, there was perhaps little room for a more humane conception of social relationships. One redeeming feature, however, proved that the upper class was not entirely occupied with the harsh exploitation of its inferiors. The Welsh landed families had constantly patronised the culture of their nation, and had assisted in preserving the literary heritage and musical traditions handed down from generation to generation. Despite the pressure of public duties and the pardonable attention to their own particular interests, many of them still considered it to be a natural obligation on their part to safeguard and encourage the poetic ebullience of their countrymen.

They did so by extending the hospitality of their homes to bards and minstrels, as their forefathers had done. This was the immemorial custom of *Clera*, whereby accredited poets went from one country house to another, composing laudatory poems in which they praised their hosts, not forgetting their families and pedigrees. In Glamorgan, it was described as,

> ' resorting abrode to gentlemens howses in the loytringe time betweene Christmas and Candlemas to singe songes and receeve rewardes.'[67]

The more affluent gentry could afford to keep their private poets and harpists, who entertained them when they were alive and signalised their virtues in elegies when they were dead. Thomas Richard, the household harpist of Sir Edward Stradling at St. Donats, showed such exceptional talent that many English friends borrowed him to play to their guests in their homes. In this capacity he toured the country mansions of southern England, and had the privilege of demonstrating his mastery of the harp to Sir Phillip Sidney.[68]

The squires also participated in the Eisteddfodau, where poets and harpists assembled periodically to compete for prizes and recognition, and were accorded the right of distributing honours to the victors. It was the family of Mostyn in Flintshire, for example, that had long enjoyed the privilege of awarding a silver harp to the most outstanding player on that instrument.

It is significant that when the Government, alarmed by the disorderly conduct and prolific numbers of minstrels in North Wales, appointed a commission to reorganise the bardic order and eject the less reputable rhymsters from its ranks, no less than twenty one members of the most eminent landed families were selected to sit on it. They were chosen, so the terms of the commission ran, for their ' experience and good knowledge of the Scyence,' an acknowledgment that they were sufficiently conversant with Welsh poetry to be able to judge each candidate for the bardic order on his merits.[69] Yet another revelation of the interest of the gentry in the advancement of their native culture is the fact that when one of them, Tomos Prys—himself a poet—tabulated a list of contemporary Welsh bards, he included the names of no less than fifty four gentlemen and knights in Caernarvonshire, Anglesey and Denbighshire alone, who had mastered the intricate measures of Welsh poetry and composed in them.[70]

Sir Edward Stradling was particularly active in the dissemination of Welsh culture. Apart from his patronage of bards and the accumulation of a library of books and manuscripts on Wales, which he lent willingly to historians like Rice Meyricke—author of a History of Glamorganshire—Sir Edward provided the funds for the publication, in 1592, of the Welsh Grammar compiled by the scholar Siôn Dafydd Rhys. In a letter which the grammarian wrote to Sir Edward, he described how this disinterested financial venture had impressed Court circles in London, for

' there is more worshipfull speeches concerninge youre selfe about the settinge forthe of that booke than about anye one thinge that ever you dyd in all youre life.'[71]

This was no exaggeration. Some 1,250 copies of the Grammar were printed, and, in his will, Sir Edward magnanimously stipulated that, with the exception of fifty copies reserved for the author, they should be gratuitously distributed among those Welsh gentlemen who were as desirous as he to see the language flourish and prosper.

The intellectual activities of the squires were not confined to the study and practice of versification. The secularisation of learning and the spread of the humanities brought within their reach new fields of knowledge which they explored and advertised with the unbounded enthusiasm of the Elizabethan age. No subject was considered too insignificant or recondite for the purpose of study and exposition, and there followed an unprecedented effusion of writing in Welsh upon an equally unparalleled diversity of topics. Planetary influences, medical recipes, astronomy, the art of poetry, the history and topography of Britain, religious dialogues, translations from Latin, Greek and English—these were only a few of the lucubrations of the aristocratic writers of the day in Wales. Practically none of these works were published, but recognition in print was rarely sought after by a people whose traditional literary practice had been oral transmission or, at the best, the circulation and copying of manuscripts.

Not all the Welsh gentry, of course, wrote in Welsh. Their acquaintance with English and continental writers encouraged some of them to try their hand at imitating their style and subject matter, not always with happy results. A cousin of William Maurice, squire of Clenennau, showed quite unequivocally what he thought of his brother's efforts in this field. In a letter to Maurice, he castigated a book which his brother had written as an,

' Italyne ryding tale followinge the vaine of Cornelius Agrippa, being pleased with no thinge and purposinge nothinge but to shoe his owne witt and that without head, tayle or conclusion.'[72]

Some of the gentry cultivated more aesthetic tastes and showed a predilection for prevailing fashions in the visible arts, which they were able to satisfy because of their wealth and their contacts with the world of European culture. Sir George Herbert of Swansea, for example, was the happy possessor of a portrait of Lucrece, painted by a contemporary artist.[73] Sir Thomas Stradling had in his mansion at St. Donats a picture of ' Christ in Resurrection ' by, possibly, a Flemish painter which, however, served not to rouse admiration but doubts about the extent of Sir Thomas's allegiance to Rome.[74] But it was Sir John Perrot's magnificent home at Carew Castle that really reflected the catholicity of culture of the genuine Elizabethan aristocrat. His library contained a number of books in French and Spanish, as well as in English and the classical languages, while his music room abounded with all the known instruments of the age. There were sackbuts, cornets, a flute, two recorders, a violin, an Irish harp, hautboys and a pair of virginals, together with books of music—a rare acquisition which he may have procured through his contacts at Court, and a set of psalm books for singing.[75]

A few years prior to the accession of Elizabeth, a Venetian ambassador wrote in one of his dispatches that :

> ' there was an atmosphere putrescence which produced the disease called "The Sweat", which, according to general report, was never known in other countries and only twice before in England. It commenced in Wales, then traversed the whole kingdom, the mortality being immense amongst persons of every condition.'[76]

The ambassador may have been too ready to accept the public view that the plague had emanated from Wales. But it could very well have originated there, since the conditions in which many of the lower classes in the countryside lived were productive of malignant diseases of all kinds.

Houses fit for human habitation were the exception rather than the rule in the Welsh countryside, although the situation improved immensely during the reign of Elizabeth. Generally speaking, they were not built to provide the occupiers with much comfort, and were usually constructed from the rough and ready materials available in the locality. This was not entirely the fault of the people who built them. The old custom which still permitted a man to establish his claim to a piece of waste land, if he could erect a complete house between sunset and sunrise, scarcely allowed him to indulge in the luxury of designing a home and selecting the best materials.

Usually the walls were made of mud or clay strengthened with pieces of timber, and the roofs were thatched except in North Wales and a few other places where slates had come into fashion and were used both for dwelling houses and farm buildings. In the homes of the poorer rural classes, holes were

B*

cut in the walls to serve as windows which, not infrequently, let in something less salubrious than fresh air. This was a long pole, equipped with a hook at one end, used by ingenious thieves to extract whatever object the hook managed to catch along the walls and floors.

The relatively well-to-do yeomen had more substantial homes with a semblance of privacy and comfort, such as lattices instead of uncovered apertures as windows, and a number of rooms serving as a hall, buttery, parlour, cellar and sleeping chambers. Often these dwellings were divided into an upper and a lower half, the first being used as the general living room and the other as sleeping quarters. The floor was of earth beaten to an unyielding hardness by constant treading, and above there was usually a loft, accessible by a ladder, where cereals, meat and other foodstuffs were preserved by being laid upon green rushes. It was not uncommon for farm animals to be accommodated in the lower end of houses. This was not only a measure of enforced economy ; the beasts also performed a useful function by helping to keep the house warm and countering the dampness of the winter season. But there was one serious disadvantage in that they offered a hiding place for robbers who slipped amongst them before nightfall, and looted the house while the family was asleep.[77]

At the other end of the scale, there was the prosperous farmer who was desirous of modernising his home. Such a one was Thomas ap Robert, a yeoman of the Queen's Chamber, who leased a farmhouse near Abergele, in Flintshire, and undertook to build,

' one good and substanciall double Chymney of stone to serve for the hawle and Chamber over the Hawle of the said farme house.'[78]

Another affluent yeoman in Montgomeryshire developed a taste for domestic furniture more befitting to a squire than to one of his class. His house had a number of upper rooms with bedsteads, chests and cupboards, a hall decorated with pieces of steel armour, headpieces, bucklers, bows and arrows, and, finally, a wainscotted parlour in which a pair of virginals and a copy of Foxe's *Book of Martyrs* symbolised an equitable distribution of favours between artistic and spiritual interests.[79]

The quality and variety of interior furnishings and household goods were dictated by the social standing and material wealth of the householder. Where there was unrelieved poverty, furniture was primitive and sparse, and of doubtful value even to bailiffs—a truckle bed or straw mattress, rough hewed tables and benches, and a few indispensable cooking utensils. The ordinary yeoman class fared better. Some continued to use straw for their beds, but there were an increasing number who enjoyed the luxury of featherbeds, leather beds and bedsteads of board, complete with mattresses, sheets, coverlets, blankets, quilts and bolsters, and used basins, urns and towels to satisfy the requirements of personal cleanliness. They had cupboards, coffers and chests in their living rooms, trestle tables with boards and chairs, and around the fireplace or in the kitchen were grouped kettles of iron and brass, frying pans and bake-stones, tripods, tongs and spits. The richer yeomen had also acquired a taste for pewter dishes, plates and saucers, and for table cloths of linen or canvas on which they served meals to their friends and guests.

These meals were hardly sumptuous, but they showed how far the Welsh rural community had advanced gastronomically since the days when their forefathers had existed on a pastoral diet. Meat had become a common dish, and mutton, veal, beef, pork, calves' feet and bacon appeared regularly on their tables. White bread was not unknown amongst them, but it was more customary for the generality of country folk to eat oatcake, peascake, rye bread and boulted bread—a mixture of rye and wheat. Other familiar dishes were egg-pies, groat gruel with a piece of butter in it followed by a dish of sweet milk, *llymru* and broths or cawdels, for which there was no lack of vegetables such as onions, parsnips and beans. Meals were usually washed down with beer or bragot—mulled ale sweetened and spiced— and sour milk. The poorer class of labourers lived on a meagre and often improvised diet. A breast of mutton boiled in porridge was a delicacy for them ; on the other hand, it was not uncommon for them to relieve the pangs of hunger with turnips or the carcase of goats, one of which at least defied consumption because ' its fleshe did stinck.'

The Welsh countryman had been as modest in his attire as in his diet. He had been satisfied with the minimum of clothing necessary to cover his person without impeding his movements, and nothing could have been more alien to his mode of living in previous centuries than the sartorial trappings of society. This economy in dress had attracted the attention of an Englishman, who wrote of the Welsh in the fourteenth century :

> ' They be clothet wonder well
> In a shirte and mantell,
> A crysp breche well fayne
> Bothe in wynde and in rayne.
> In this clothynge they be bolde
> Though the weder be ryghte colde . . .
> Evermore in this araye
> They doo fyghte, playe and lepe
> Stonde, sytte, lye and slepe,
> Without surcot, gown, cote and kyrtell . . .
> Without lace and chaplet yn here lappes,
> Without hode, hatte or cappes
> And alwaye with bare legges.'[80]

The description here is one of a primitive folk with little pretence to the external refinements of civilisation. For that matter, these were not considered as having any particular value by a hardy, pastoral people, invigorated by the harsh conditions of their life, and whose bellicose temperament allowed them little time or inclination to develop a taste for amenities of any sort. The picture, however, had changed completely by the middle of the sixteenth century, and the reign of Elizabeth saw the Welsh becoming more and more absorbed in their efforts to emulate their English neighbours in deportment and dress.

There was, inevitably, that class of Welshmen who believed that it was imperative to leave Wales and reside across the border in order to become fully assimilated to the English way of life and dissociate oneself completely from the formative environment of Welsh manners and speech. They would have heartily concurred with the opinion of William Jones of Newport, in Monmouthshire, who towards the middle of the century wished his children to be ' browghte up accordyng to the maneres and condicionez of the norture of Inglonde,' and made arrangements in his will for them to live and be educated in Bristol until they came of age.[81]

In no section of the community was this change in attire more evident than among the rural middle class. The barefoot peasant of earlier days completely disappeared, and there emerged instead the tenant farmer and the freeholder with a pair of solid leather shoes, knitted woollen stockings, a hose of frieze or leather, and a doublet or jerkin of fustian, canvas or frieze, the whole attire being set off by a felt hat or a cap. What was quite as striking an innovation was the variety of colours that accompanied these habiliments, and which must have appealed to the Welsh whose natural delight in hues and shades of colour had hitherto been only expressed in their poetry and prose romances.

Doublets could be ' horseflesh coloured ' or russet or a ' gynger ' colour ; breeches and hose yellow or brown ; hats blue or black with band and lined with velvet, silk or sarcenet ; and cloaks ' laid down with lace.' The richer yeomen, throwing restraint and expense to the wind, indulged in shirts with golden bands edged with gold and lined with taffeta, striped canvas doublet lined with orange coloured sarcenet, purple Venetian hose of cloth cut upon black serge, and stockings of white wool.[82] Even the poorest and meanest person, at the bottom of the social scale, would make some effort to equip himself with the minimum of dress and footwear exacted by convention, like the suspected thief in Denbighshire who ' had a bare russet jerkin and a paire of sloppes and a great red nose.'[83]

The wives and daughters of Welsh yeomen were no less eager than their menfolk to gratify their newly awakened interest in clothes. For instance, the wardrobe of a mistress of a Cardiganshire farm contained, amongst other articles, ' one ffrise gowne, one red petticote, one blewe mantle, one whit doblet of ffustian, one kerchief and a band.'[84] Women of this class wore ruffs of lawn around the neck, nets or caps of the same material on the head, and buckled shoes. Even in the less affluent classes, female dress was variegated and colourful. A contemporary description of two women walking along a Welsh country road says that one of them :

> ' wore a flannel pettycoate and upon the same a Savoyard tucked up about her of Buffin [a coarse cloth] pinked and hemmed with Black cotton, a red wastecoate, a black felt hat with a cipres band around it, and a green Lace under the same band.'

Her companion was dressed in a ' red wastecoate, a black Savoyard tucked up about her, an old red petticoat under it, and a kerchief on her head.'[85]

Attached to the residential quarters of the yeoman's house, or standing a little apart from it, were the farm outbuildings usually constructed of wattle and mud, and thatched. There was the barn, where grain and vegetables were stored, and which was sometimes kept in serviceable condition by ' thake and dalbing,' that is by renewing the straw roof from time to time and daubing the walls with clay or some other material.[86] Then came the stables for horses and oxen, the dairy house where cows were kept, the styes, and the kyrdell or ' dortour '[87] which accommodated the poultry, including turkeys.

Although horses were common enough, it would seem that oxen predominated on the farms of the period, and were the principal draught animals. It was they that drew the wooden or iron ploughs and harrows in spring and autumn, and dragged the sledges and waggons filled with corn and hay to the barns at harvest time. Sometimes, the ploughing was done by mixed teams of oxen and horses, encouraged by hired persons or members of the family, armed with ploughstaffs to goad the animals. Where the circumstances of husbandmen did not allow them to own more than one ox or horse, they often pooled their animals to form one team to plough their respective fields.[88]

The richer yeomen depended much upon hired service to maintain their farms in a flourishing condition, and had little difficulty in obtaining all the assistance they needed from an abundant agricultural labour market supplied by the lower classes in town and countryside. The yeoman could hire his labourers at country fairs or, if he preferred it, he could hire those who came to seek work on his farm, paying them a weekly or daily wage. This latter arrangement presented certain advantages in that it enabled an exacting farmer to dismiss his labourers at will, whereas in some shires no employer, who hired servants for a long term of service, could dispense with them without permission of the Justices of the Peace.[89]

Maids were hired in the same way, but for less than half the remuneration given to men. It was not uncommon, however, for a maid of a better class and with some property of her own, to select her employer and to extract more profitable terms from him. One young Denbighshire girl, who owned a cow as well as certain domestic effects such as pewter, clothes and some sheets, hired herself and the use of her animal and moveable goods in return for the use of a piece of pasture ground and preferential treatment in the matter of board and wages.[90] In this respect she was a privileged person, for the majority of farm labourers and maids rarely earned more than 26/- and 10/- respectively during their year's service, were kept on meagre rations, and had to sleep in the stables and outhouses adjoining the residence of their masters, where their coffers and belongings were only too often rifled by passing vagabonds. Their world of hard work and cramped living space was far removed from the servants' quarters in the country mansions of the squires. There, habits were occasionally so informal that even maids were often dispatched on horseback, astride a man's saddle and equipped with spurs and whip, to execute commissions for their masters.[91]

Wood was still the principal fuel for warming houses in the winter months, although coal was tending to supplant it in those districts adjacent to mines and face workings. But there were certain parts of the country where neither coal nor wood was procurable, and the inhabitants had to fall back upon turf. This was extensively used by the people who lived on the moors and bare highlands of Cardiganshire and Denbighshire, and whom necessity had long rendered insensitive to its pungent smell, as one English poet observed :

' Good turffe and peate on mossie ground is won,
Wherewith good fires is made for man most meete,
That burneth cleere and yields a savour sweete
To those which have no nose for dayntie smell.'[92]

In Flintshire too, most homes burned fires of turf, which was
dug in considerable quantities on the many heaths in that
county. Sometimes, the owners of turf plots leased them for
domestic use or to be exploited for sale in neighbouring towns.[93]
It may have been an exceptionally severe winter or high market
prices in 1574 that accounted for the invasion of the common
land of the Rhuddlan burgesses by a number of husbandmen,
who dug up and carried away the turf for their own use.[94]

Like their betters, the ordinary country folk were inclined to
regard marriage as a useful, but by no means sacrosanct,
social institution. Few among them were prepared to concede
that romance and mutual affection should play any part in it,
and even those few would hardly have denied that a marriage
without a dowry would be inconceivable. A typical dowry
between two families consisted, for example, of two cows,
twenty sheep and a mantle. It was customary, in some districts,
to return a part of the dowry to her family if the young wife
died within a year.[95] Members of a family, who had gone out
into the world and made their fortunes, would often—as a
matter of pride or benevolence—help their people at home to
comply with this exigency. For instance, William Evans, a
merchant tailor in London, bequeathed as much as £400 to
provide his poorer relations in Brecknock, within seven degrees
of kinship, with adequate marriage dowries.[96]

The harsh conditions of the age demanded that marriage,
like so many other forms of human relationships, should be
exploited to the full by the ordinary countryfolk. Little
latitude was allowed for disinterested love-matches. A bold
young man might, occasionally, defy censure and convention
and persuade his sweetheart to elope with him ; and her
parents would, in accordance with imprescriptible custom, cut
her off without a penny. Like Evan Guto, a fiddler of Genau'r-
glyn, in Cardiganshire, who eloped with the daughter of a rich

yeoman near Towyn, in Merioneth. In this case, however, the romantic young lady eventually returned home in a penitent mood, was forgiven and inherited her father's property.[97]

Such adventures were rare. It was more in the spirit of the times that eligible young ladies should be harassed and victimised by suitors who could appreciate the financial advantages of marriage, and deluded by dishonest proposals to that effect. A bitter lesson in misplaced trust was administered to a girl from Brecknock, who allowed a certain Humphrey Lloyd to protest his attachment to her in a letter, and seemed not to have doubted his intentions when he proceeded to borrow from her not only sums of money, but such articles as a taffeta scarf, a hat and girdle and a ring of gold, which he conveniently forgot to return when he transferred his attentions elsewhere.[98] His action was deplorable, but not extraordinary. The young lady may have had good reason to be thankful that he had not subjected her to more physical pressure, since the abduction of girls and their enforced marriage through rape or terrorisation was a common occurrence in the countryside.

Even families would sometimes employ the most objectionable methods to browbeat their womenfolk into marriage against their will. A young girl of the parish of Betws Bledrws, in Cardiganshire, was approached by her uncle as she was winnowing corn in the loft of his house, and told that he had decided to marry her to a man in the neighbourhood of whom he obviously approved. She obviously did not, for she refused to entertain the suggestion, whereupon her uncle locked the door and bullied and badgered her until midnight. Finally, she was forcibly placed on the back of a horse, taken to a neighbour's house and put to bed with his wife. In the early hours of the morning, her bed companion was surreptitiously replaced by the suitor who had been chosen for her, and it was only her struggles and shrieks that saved her from being outraged. In the meantime, the sheriff of Cardiganshire had been notified of the abduction, and was in hot pursuit. The girl was rescued and escorted to her mother's home. But no sooner had the sheriff turned his back than the uncle reappeared, abducted her for the second time, and had her conveyed to a friend's house in

Carmarthenshire, where she was held *incommunicado* for some time. That she brought a case against her uncle shows that she had eventually been released, but her experiences, unhappily, were only too common in Elizabethan Wales.[99]

One reason for this violent attachment of, or rather to, a lady's person, may have been the privileged position enjoyed by Welsh women in society. Unlike English women, they had never been relegated to an inferior status, but had exercised certain rights of property and of indemnisation for wrongs committed against them which, as formulated by the Old Welsh laws, had been far in advance of any recognition extended to women by contemporary legal codes. The substitution of English for Welsh law did not materially affect or modify these rights, which were often protected and enforced by the customs of various shires. For instance, the custom of Caernarvonshire dictated that half the goods of a deceased husband should go to the wife, after the discharge of all debts and funeral expenses, and no legacy was permitted to nullify or interfere with this practice.[100] In Montgomeryshire, she was to enjoy the third part of her dead husband's goods while she lived.[101]

The advantage of marrying widows, by fair means or foul, was patently obvious in this case, and it may explain why some jealous husbands inserted a condition in their wills that the'r wives should only inherit their property if they ' avoided mens company.'[102] In Pembrokeshire, would-be claimants to the favours of women of wealth were stimulated by the knowledge that the goods of a girl betrothed in marriage were, by custom, to revert to the fortunate suitor in the event of her death before their union was solemnised, if she had given them to him.[103] There was incentive enough, therefore, to precipitate marriage by abduction or other means, if the ordinary and mercenary business of arranging dowries became too protracted or threatened to favour one suitor more than another.

Child marriages were not uncommon. Girls were often led to the altar at the age of thirteen or fourteen, and boys of fifteen could be forced by their parents to take a wife. This was perhaps not so extraordinary when it is remembered that children of eight years of age were liable to be mercilessly interrogated by law officials with the object of incriminating their parents.[104] Among the richer yeomen, dowries consisted of sums of money, which were sometimes produced and placed ' on the book' at the time of the ceremony,[105] or of live stock and land. Not that these arrangements were always strictly observed. When Ifan Lloyd met Edward Deye of Denbigh to arrange a marriage between his daughter and Deye's son, he promised to bestow £100 upon her if Deye conveyed 60 acres of freehold land to the young pair after marriage, to enable them to begin life in propitious circumstances. The acres failed to materialise, for Deye treacherously divided them among other members of his family, and then hurriedly left the country, forcing the young people to return to the house of an infuriated Ifan Lloyd and live on his charity.[106]

Where money was rapidly becoming the operative motive of so much human action and endeavour, it was not surprising that it should also dictate the emotions of the heart. For instance, at Carmarthen, it encouraged young people to precipitate their marriages, for it had long been the custom that any pair joined in wedlock in St. Peter's Church received a *comortha* from the kind-hearted townspeople, who were present at the ceremony, to assist them to set up their home. This generosity had been very much abused—even persons outside Carmarthenshire were known to have arranged to be married in St. Peter's Church in order to qualify for the *comortha*. The result was that many respectable families refused to attend divine service or appear in the church rather than be subjected to forced contributions from importunate couples. The Corporation eventually suppressed the traditional custom, although it allowed gifts to be bestowed upon those newly married, but only outside the precincts of the church.[107]

It would have been too sanguine to expect that marriages arranged on every basis except that of mutual love should always be successful. Women of resolute character might create conditions for contentment by carrying out their domestic obligations and bringing up large families. But for many wives such natural activities as these were circumscribed very often by the fact that they had to spend much of their married life with their in-laws. This was particularly true of the poorer classes who did not have the means to set up their children independently, and were often predisposed to regard their sons' wives as little more than extra domestic help to cope with the task and drudgery of making both ends meet. Relations were bound to become exacerbated, and mutual dislike was sometimes aggravated by the latitude allowed to husband and parents to beat and maltreat the daughter-in-law. One way of escape was to flee the house and find service in some other part of the country. Another, which appealed much to disgruntled wives, was to poison their tormentors. Ratbane, put into pottage, was the remedy of Brecknock and Radnorshire women who wished to liquidate obnoxious husbands, while a Carmarthenshire wife experimented with quicksilver introduced into her husband's milk.[108] It was a dangerous bid for freedom, since the dreadful penalty for poisoning was to be boiled alive in oil.[109]

Failing this desperate remedy, consolation was only too readily found in adultery. With so little store set by reciprocal affection, it is not surprising that infidelity and promiscuity were vices that almost attained the recognition of being fashionable, and certainly over-rode all class distinctions. In fact, rural society had become so inured to them that one of the customs of the lordship of Denbigh, for instance, allowed that the goods of a dead man should be divided in equal portions between his widow and his children, whether the latter were legitimate or not.[110] In the diocese of St. David's alone, five hundred persons were forced to do penance every year in market place or church, clothed in sheets and blankets and carrying papers tabulating their acts of immorality.[111] The Church, which regarded itself as the custodian and tutor of public morals, was visibly disturbed by the laxity of laymen in these matters, but some of its own members were only too guilty of the same misconduct. Moreover, many of its practices discredited rather than encouraged the belief in the sanctity of marriage. In the Welsh dioceses, it was the custom for every man and woman, upon the occasion of their marriage, to pay individually a tenth of their goods to the curate performing the ceremony, whereas only two shillings a year were demanded as fine from those who committed adultery or co-habited as man and wife. As one indignant critic observed, this

'causeth matrymonye to be litle sett by and much refused in those quarters.'[112]

To put infants out to nurse was an approved custom in the Welsh countryside, as well as in towns, although the results were not always felicitous, for

'commonly in taking of nurses, men are driven to take such as they can find, and not such as they would wish to find.'[113]

But side by side with this, there persisted the custom of fosterage, which had been a peculiarity of early Welsh society, whereby male infants were entrusted at a very tender age to the care of people outside the immediate family circle. On the face of it, this seemed an unnatural practice, for it tended to replace the normal affection of brothers for one another with the attachment, often deeper, of foster-brothers brought up under the same roof. The relationship between foster-sons and those who had nursed and mothered them during their impressionable years was akin to that of adopted children, and it was reflected in the loyalty and partisanship of the foster-brethren. This was especially true of the gentry, and much of the discord and lawlessness in Wales during the reign of Elizabeth was attributed to their maintenance of foster-brothers who attended upon them as squires and flung themselves enthusiastically into their quarrels and intrigues.[114]

Old age was not without its problems for those who had little to fall back upon when advanced years incapacitated them for work. Parish relief and almshouses, where they existed, shared the burden of maintaining many of them, but, in general, the family spirit was strong enough to accept the responsibility of providing a home for aged people. In some cases, this obligation took the form of an agreement between the aged person and one of his kinsmen, whereby the latter undertook to keep him during the remainder of his life and give him a decent burial in return for the surrender of all his property or goods.[115]

When death took place, it was customary for neighbours or friends of the bereaved families to watch over the body during the nights or night preceding the funeral. If there existed any suspicion that death was due to other than normal causes, the corpse was buried between boards so that it could be exhumed and subjected to an autopsy by the local surgeon, if necessary, before decomposition had advanced too far.[116] Otherwise, the dead were generally buried in winding sheets within the parish churchyard[117] or in former monastic cemeteries, or within the church itself if they were socially qualified to lie there. This sometimes tempted necessitous people to commit wilful acts of desecration, as, for instance, at Llanilltud in Brecknock, where the wife of a local gentleman had been buried in a linen sheet. It could only have been extreme poverty that drove the wife of the vicar of the parish to enter the church during the night and open the grave in order to steal the sheet.[118]

Funeral ceremonies were usually very simple, but it gradually became the fashion among the upper classes to organise them into public demonstrations of grief, complete with a lengthy procession in which mourners, sympathisers and super-numeraries were ranked according to social precedence or dramatic effect. A Monmouthshire squire, for example, stipulated that at the time of his burial, the cortege should be escorted by six poor men in black gowns and an equal number of women in white gowns.[119] Funerals also provided an opportunity for the manifestation of repressed religious beliefs and customs. At Beaumaris, lighted candles and psalm singing were reported to have accompanied one funeral service despite the express ordinance of the Bishop of Bangor that such Catholic practices should be vigorously condemned and rooted out.[120]

Few people in the Welsh countryside could complain that they did not dispose of sufficient leisure time to relax from the daily obligation of having to earn a living. In fact, one English poet would have had the world believe that earning a liveli-hood was of secondary importance to the Welsh :

' But most of Wales likes better ease and rest
(Lives meat and mirth and harmlesse quiet daies)

Than for to toyle and trouble brayne and brest
To vexe the mynd with worldly wearie waies.'[120]

The problem was to devise forms of amusement which would enable them to enjoy their liberty without transgressing the susceptibilities of the guardians of the law, since the paternal concern of the Government for the welfare of its subjects had resulted in a series of restrictive decrees, which may have been well-intentioned, but must have seemed exasperating to many loyal citizens. The attitude of the authorities towards gambling, for instance, was deeply resented. It was partly actuated by ethical considerations, but more by a desire to restrain men from running the risk of financial ruin and becoming a liability to the community. All games of chance were declared illegal ; but what provoked opposition, and tended to make the prohibition inoperative, except spasmodically, was the fact that the gentry could exclude themselves from the provisions of the anti-gambling laws.[122] This on the grounds, presumably, that they could afford to lose, refrained from cheating, and possessed controllable tempers when luck turned against them. In any case, the Government did not wish to antagonise them or deprive them of one kind of gambling which was happily disassociated from politics.

The most popular games of chance with the privileged and the disenfranchised classes alike, were cards and dice, familiarly known as ' the tables,' and ' shuffle boarde ' for which, in one case at least, a shilling piece beaten hollow was used.[123] They were usually played in alehouses, which became notorious for their rowdiness and sharp practices, and were eventually made subject to a decree which declared it to be an offence for an alehouse keeper to permit gambling on his premises. The interdiction was promptly ignored, and the incidence of court cases in all parts of Wales, especially in Denbighshire, showed that gambling was rapidly becoming endemic. It was not confined to the taverns of those days. Markets and fairs were the chosen hunting grounds of card and dice sharpers, who exercised their prestidigations under the nose of the law. Griffith ap Tudor, arrested at Wrexham fair in 1590 with a pair of dice concealed in his codpiece, was only one of the wandering band of tricksters who frequented these places and had no difficulty in finding victims to play with them.[124]

The anxiety of the Government was justified, on moral grounds at least, and the social repercussions of gambling were well illustrated by a case of juvenile delinquency at Denbigh in 1579. There a law-abiding citizen, John Barber, had his hands full with a young son who was not only stubborn and vindictive, but had suddenly developed an extravagant taste in clothes totally disproportionate with the money doled out to him from the family funds. A little investigation showed that he was in the habit of spending his time drinking and gaming in the taverns of the town. A threat to make him mend his ways by a thorough thrashing with ' staves ' fell on deaf ears, for strolling along the streets a little later, Barber saw his son sitting at a gaming table in a house. He rushed through the door, but the boy was quicker than he, for when the irate father reached the table another person had slipped into his seat and was coolly playing his hand. Retribution, however, possibly in the form of unpaid bills, stepped in and the harassed youth was driven to break into a mercer's shop and steal some money.[125]

Those who were not addicted to gambling had a choice of other distractions in which to expend their energy or while away their hours of relaxation. For the gentry and yeomen there was tennis, which had been introduced from France and popularised by no less an august and agile an exponent than Henry VIII. It was a recognised pastime in countryside and town alike ; for instance at Swansea, in Denbighshire parishes where betting on the players was a concomitant feature of the game, and at Cardigan where it was played with perhaps more vigour than grace. It was here that a group of gentlemen and yeomen proceeded one afternoon, in 1580, to give a public exhibition of tennis in the parish churchyard. Their cries and exhortations became so deafening that the Justice of Cardiganshire, who was trying to sift evidence in the Assize Court near by, lost the thread of his forensic argument and his temper, and ordered that proceedings should be instituted against the players for disturbing his and the Queen's peace.[126]

Some members of the landed classes showed greater interest

in hunting with dogs, ferrets or sparrow-hawks. The private breeding of birds of prey for the purpose of hunting was solely reserved to them by law. Sir Edward Stradling had a well-stocked eyrie, and was as generous in his gifts of hawks as in his presents of venison.[127] William Powell, a Monmouthsire gentleman, was also a keen breeder of sparrow-hawks on his estate, and obliged his tenants to keep a tender watch over the nests, particularly as there were many experienced hawk thieves in the neighbourhood who stole the young birds to sell them to poachers, and who invariably wrung the neck of the haggard or female hawk after rifling the nests.[128]

The more progressive among the gentry were not averse to using fowling pieces in this sport. Much dexterity and care were called for in the manipulation of sixteenth century guns, and the slightest negligence might have fatal consequences. One unhappy tragedy took place in the grounds of Denbigh Castle in 1589, when a party of friends went there to shoot pigeons. The owner of the sole sporting gun among them, having reset the flint, nonchantly held the gun with the muzzle pointing backwards and discharged it accidentally at one of his companions, hitting him in the throat with ' hails of lead ' from which he died.[129]

Fishing also had its attractions, but hardly of the sort that inspired Isaac Walton centuries later. It was not a question of a meditative cast of the line, but rather of a clandestine disturbance of the water. In Radnorshire, a gentleman did not conceive it below his dignity to fish for trout by the illegal method of ' groping ' or tickling,[130] and in Denbighshire poaching was practised by those who were officially expected to treat it as an offence against the propertied classes. A number of squires were actually charged in 1590 with using powler nets for catching ' spawnders ' and ' small frie of salmon,' and selling them in Wrexham market.[131] Encouraged by the laxity of his superiors, it is not surprising that a yeoman of Radnorshire broke into the park of a local baronet in broad daylight, hunted the deer there with a greyhound, struck down a doe and carried her off in triumph to his house.[132]

The common folk preferred, or were naturally inclined to,

more vigorous games. While the elders of the community found it more consistent with the dignity of age to play bowls, their sons and grandsons would congregate after divine service on Sundays and on church holidays or public festive occasions like the First of May, to compete in wrestling, running and jumping. But priority was unquestionably accorded to football. It was a sport which allowed for the greatest possible number of participants in a collective effort, and the greatest possible latitude in the exercise of physical strength, the effervescence of local passions and the settling of personal scores. It was frowned upon by the law, but there was little danger of interference except in the event of fatal accidents.

These, unfortunately, were only too common, especially when rival parishes were matched against each other. Llangatwg and Crickhowell were noted rivals in Brecknock, and it was during the course of one game in 1579 that a Crickhowell player was thrown so heavily to the ground that he died of the concussion.[133] A fatal collision at Tregaron, in Cardiganshire, between two contending footballers, who were sturdy husbandmen by occupation, frightened the survivor to such an extent that he chose to flee the country rather than face the inevitable inquiry.[134] It was not unknown for some players to equip themselves with pikestaffs and other weapons, to deposit them within reach during the game, and to use them when quarrels became too bitter to be settled by the arbitration of others or by fisticuffs.[135] In these circumstances, the authorities could hardly be blamed for their critical attitude. But they seem to have overlooked the more muscular game of *knappan*, which was the favourite out-door sport in Pembrokeshire. It was commonly played between parishes, and the general procedure was that two contending hordes of half-naked youths and men, on foot and horseback, should fight for possession of a ball up hill and down dale until one side or the other had safely lodged it in what served as the goal.[136]

Archery was a sport which, in South Wales at least, had an intrinsic right to respect and affection. The professional skill and precision of the Welsh bowmen during the Anglo-French wars of the preceding century had redounded to the military reputation of Wales, and they were still regarded as being of the utmost importance in the defence of the realm, despite the gradual encroachment of firearms and artillery as superior weapons of war. The Government not only encouraged archery ; it made it a compulsory exercise, and took pains to see that any infringement of its decrees in this matter was reported and punished. The fact that as many as 150 perons were presented, on one occasion, at Presteigne for breaking the relevant Statutes proved that the authorities were determined to enforce this dispensation, however much they might turn a blind eye to other irregularities. And so the ' pricke ' or target became a common sight on the parish greens of Wales, and men were taught to handle the long bow with the assurance of their forefathers. Not all the arrows, however, found their prescribed target. Spectators were apt to be suddenly transfixed in the head or neck, and to die of their wounds, more particularly in North Wales, where the inhabitants felt more at ease in wielding the pike, the traditional and cultivated weapon of the ancient principalities of Powys and Gwynedd.

Physical sport and open air recreations were, no doubt, immensely popular in the Welsh countryside, but not to he exclusion of other forms of social distractions which reflected a deep-seated attachment to cultural traditions. The love of song and poetry, and the predilection for string accompaniment which had won for the harp its reputation as the national musical instrument, were as much in evidence as they had ever been. The art of playing the harp was by no means confined to the itinerant musicians, who were often arbitrarily classified and treated as vagabonds, or to the family harpists of the gentry. Many Welsh yeomen possessed, and practised, the harp in their homes, and it would appear that the appellation ' harpist ' was mainly reserved for the professional players who earned their living by this instrument. The *crwth* or violin was another instrument much in demand, and often rivalled the harp in popularity since it demanded less executive ability and was more suitable for convivial meetings. It was the melodies of the *crwth* that brought people together during the dark winter nights and long summer evenings to sing Welsh rhymes and popular songs.[137]

Other festive occasions called for lighter music. Where there was dancing on the village green or around the maypole, the piper with his repertory of simple tunes was in as much demand as the *crwth* player. Dancing, indeed, acquired a distressing popularity in some localities, or so the authorities contended, especially in Denbighshire, where the gay ladies of Bromfield would hire a piper every Sunday to play for them during divine service in the afternoon. Even in the early hours of the morning many Denbighshire parishes would resound to the gay music of pipe, *crwth* and harp, for it was the common custom for crowds of countryfolk, including some squires, to enjoy themselves in this manner.[138]

It was also the custom in North Wales for multitudes of men, women and children to congregate on Sundays and holidays, and make their way to the summit of neighbouring hills or to mountain sides. There they were entertained by harpists and crowthers, who sang to them of their ancestors' exploits in the wars of independence against the English kings, extolled their pedigrees, and declaimed the prophecies of Taliesin, Merlin, Beuno, Cybi and other eminent saints and prognosticators of the past.[139]

There were times when the natural exuberance of the people had to find some outlet other than its expression in emotional singing or nocturnal dancing. The rougher element discovered it in the form of practical jokes, which were designed to cause as much amusement to them as discomfiture to the victims. So it happened that on New Year's Eve in 1574, at Llanfair Tal-haearn in Denbighshire, two respectable parishioners were inveigled, on different pretexts, into going to the local alehouse where they were seized by a group of their acquaintances, forcibly held down in a chair, and their beards and hair shaved completely. The fact that the parish priest himself took part in this horse-play did not commend it to the two shorn members of his flock, who sought some restitution—a financial one, of course, in the circumstances—by legal proceedings.[140]

The agricultural and pastoral occupations of the majority of the Welsh people would seem to have endowed them with the robust vitality which had been characteristic of their ancestors in medieval times. This is evidenced, in some measure, by the many examples of unusual longevity amongst them. Nonagenarians were by no means uncommon in Elizabethan days, and had sufficient control over their faculties to be able to produce coherent and acceptable testimony in disputes concerning the possession of land, the delimitation of estates and the validity of customs. A surprising number lived to the advanced age of seventy and eighty years, and it would appear that the physical endurance needed to exceed the span of life allotted by the Scriptures was transmitted from generation to generation in the case of some families.[141] Fresh air unadulterated by the smoke and grime of industry, active rural pursuits, a simple but wholesome diet, and regularity of domestic habits were pre-eminently conducive to good health, and most of the nation were in the happy possession of these requisites. It need hardly be stressed that this was providential in a country where medical knowledge and practice were essentially limited and hospitals non-existent, and where ill-health was a social and economic disability which allowed of little amelioration and often brought ruin on both sufferers and their dependants.

When diseases did claim victims, there was practically no remedy to counteract them. This was certainly true of the affliction known as the ' stytche,' which can probably be identified with appendicitis ; of fevers of the liver, and of a particular ailment described as an ' ynward burning distaste,' which may very well have been a stomach or duodenal ulcer.[142] These disorders were expected to be borne with fortitude, or at least with resignation, since public opinion was inclined to attribute them to Divine intervention, and the death of the sufferers, when it did occur, was judiciously recorded as an act of God. But not all those afflicted were prepared to endure years of agony or growing debility. They preferred to commit suicide, despite their awareness that they would thereby incur the posthumous reputation of having been instigated by the devil, and forfeit the right to be buried in consecrated ground.

For lesser and more tractable disorders and complaints, the treatment was rough and ready. Offending teeth were usually extracted by the doyen of muscular operations, the smith, who had an instrument for the purpose.[143] Digestive troubles were assuaged with a mixture of powder and ale, and if the pain refused to respond to this panacea, a pot lid or plate was heated at the fire and applied to the abdomen with conflicting results.[144] If it proved to be a case of what was called ' ympostume ' or internal abscess, the results might be fatal, and since there existed no means of diagnosing the trouble, the patient simply had to take his chance. For wounds and serious cuts, turpentine was commonly used as a dressing, and here the odds between an eventual cure or septic poisoning were decided by the state of health of the person concerned.

There were few doctors available, and their practice was generally confined to the towns where their services were in greater demand. Within the walled boroughs and ports, insanitary conditions, the presence of overcrowded public institutions like prisons, and the attendance of so many people at fairs and markets were a positive stimulus to the circulation of infectious diseases. Dysentry, the ' hot ague,' the ' blacke syckness ' and the ' newe syckness ' were some of the contagions which made their periodic visitations to Brecon and struck down many of its burgesses.[145] Another fatal complaint was academically known as *Morbus Gallicus* although less sensitive people roundly referred to it as the ' Ffrenche pocks.' It made its appearance in the border towns of Wales towards the middle of the century and spread into the countryside. Mindful of their duty to society, some doctors made creditable efforts to deal with it. One of them, who was resident at Welshpool, may have recalled to mind some of the herbal concoctions of the Meddygon Myddfai, the eminent Welsh physicians of the thirteenth century, for his prescription for the dread disease was a salve of oldbane, oil of roses, quicksilver, bitterage of gold and turpentine.[146] In Montgomeryshire, the daughter of a country priest acquired a dubious reputation for her expertise in treating this and other repellent diseases, although some sufferers, rather than consult this eminent 'woman surgeon,' preferred to seek relief by visiting the allegedly healing well at Holywell, in Flintshire. The well had long been credited with extraordinary medicinal attributes, and as one observer of those days described it :

> ' This water, besides that it bredeth Mosse of a very pleasant savour, is also most holsome unto mans body, both for washyng and drinkynge and of verie good tast, in so much that many beinge washed therin were cured of divers infirmities wherwith they were borne.'[147]

Tales of its healing powers spread far and wide, and it was constantly being visited by the sick and disabled, English as well as Welsh,[148] while a bathe in its waters was considered a refreshing, and possibly curative, relaxation by the gentlemen of Flintshire.

To subject their patients to surgical treatment was much too hazardous for most doctors, in view of the unselective instruments at their disposal, and their rudimentary knowledge of anatomy, which some of them had only picked up on the field of battle in France, Ireland and the Low Countries. An exception was Griffith ap Rees of New Radnor, who was approached by a neighbour in 1593, and requested to alleviate the pain caused by the ' falling down of his loigns.' This was his first introduction to hernia, and it was with reluctance that he agreed to operate ' scdm scientiam suam,' according to the knowledge he possessed. It proved to be of little practical use. He made an incision with an instrument in the lower part of the abdomen, but within three days his patient was dead.[149]

It was inevitable that quackery should flourish in an age when credulity matched medical ignorance. Wales, no doubt, had more than one David Powell, who practised surgery when he was not engaged in peddling non-therapeutical goods, and of whom a sarcastic but convincing description was given by a person who had every reason to ridicule his pretensions, since one of Powell's concoctions had killed a relation of his. Powell, he wrote :

> ' havinge upon his back a portmantno or capcase, after the manner of a horse leeche, taketh upon him to be a notable

surgeon and perfecte Chirugeon, and in this dyvelyshe and cosoninge sort wandreth upp and downe the contrey amonge women and silly simple folkes, begildinge and deceavinge her Mats subjects of cheese, wole and such odd stuffe, and nowe lastly the said (David) beinge newly come home from Egypt conversinge among the Egiptians (gypsies), as he affermed, whome he had gotten exquisitte knowledge and perfect skyll in the arte and scyence of phisicke, as the said (David) most falsely gave owt, and caryinge about hym a lytl baskett with a urinall therein prognosticating the same (David) to be an excelent phisicyon amonge the simplest sorte that gave credite thereunto.'[150]

Yet it would be true to say that, despite the lethal prescriptions of quacks, Welshmen in general had an inordinate respect for the mysteries of medicine and considerable aptitude for suggesting and applying remedies. Their abilities were commended by no less a distinguished Englishman than Sir William Hare, Master of the Rolls, who while in Wales learnt of a remedy for strongury from which he was suffering. He applied it to himself successfully, and testified that ' never any medicyne did him so much good.'[151] It is also interesting that it was an unknown but inventive Welshman of Elizabethan Wales who devised one of the first deaf and dumb languages, in which the main features of the face—eye, cheek, chin, as well as the fingers of the hand, were used to indicate the letters of the Welsh alphabet.[152]

Those present in the Great Sessions at Denbigh on 15 October, 1570, must have regarded one prisoner in particular with mixed feelings of compassion, scepticism and furtive credulity. He was Hugh Bryghan, from the village of Pentrefelin, and his crime was that of dabbling in occult practices in direct contravention of the legislative wisdom of Parliament and the established monopoly of revelation by the Church.

In reply to a number of questions put to him by the Deputy Justice of Denbigh, Hugh disclosed the mysteries of his magic which, he maintained, were beneficial to the inhabitants of Denbighshire, since they had been directed for some twenty years to identifying thieves and locating the repositories of stolen goods. Expatiating a little further under pressure, he

Vera effigies Clariss:Do.ⁿⁱ Iohãnis Wynn de Gwedir in
Com Carnarvon Equitis et Baronetti &c.
Obijt primo die Martij 1626 Ætat: 73

Honoris ipsius causa   R. vaughan sculp   Prostant D.V.

By courtesy of the British Museum.

SIR JOHN WYNN

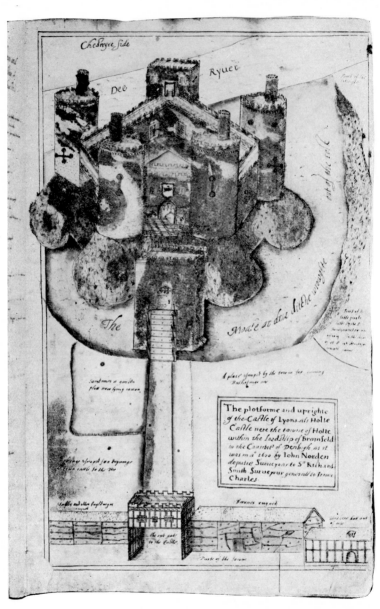

HOLT CASTLE

confessed to having imbibed the secrets of his craft from a deceased uncle, Rhys Bryghan, who had instructed him in the use of a crystal stone. He had undeviatingly followed these instructions, in the following manner. Whenever he was approached by someone whose household goods or cattle had been stolen, he would lead him to the crystal, pronounce certain formulas in the name of the Father, the Son and the Holy Ghost, make a sign of the cross above the crystal, and ask his client to gaze into it. If all went well, the likeness of the thief would be revealed to the aggrieved party, and he himself would feel justified in accepting a small financial token of appreciation and gratitude.

Hugh had to admit, however, that the potency of his magic did not always function. For some reason or other, it was rarely that the men and women who solicited his help could discern any resemblance to human features in the crystal. It was children under twelve years of age who had the gift (or more correctly, the imagination) to see faces where there were ostensibly none, especially those of them who had never received Communion. Such an avowal probably produced much consternation in court. There may have been ugly whispers, if not downright charges, of a pre-arranged understanding with the devil to delude the innocent boys and girls, who had not been officially received into the protective bosom of the Church. Hugh went out of his way to deny vehemently that he had conjured up spirits or ' familiars,' and his expostulations that he would never dream of collaborating with the Father of all evil to lay some of his progeny in this world by their heels, appears to have made a favourable impression. He was released on the condition that he would never again meddle with his crystal.[153] He probably did not. A second offence might have entailed imprisonment for life.[154]

The law might denounce and castigate any manifestation of wizardy of this kind, but the yeomen and peasants of the Welsh countryside were too strongly attached to, and entrenched in, their superstitions to be deflected from them by official reprobation. Hugh Bryghan was obliged to renounce his crystal, but there was no lack of other practitioners in sorcery. Beggar

c

women were congenitally addicted to a mild form of prescience, particularly where people were unduly anxious about the state of their health. One of them distinguished herself in Denbighshire by foretelling who would become the victims of dropsy, a most distasteful prophecy since it was regarded as an incurable disease.[155]

Some mysteries certainly lent credence to the prevailing notion that supraterrestial elements were busily at work and could literally push a finger into people's affairs on earth. A case that defied explanation at the time was that of the wife of a Denbighshire squire, Elen Myddleton, who was expecting a child and had gone to her mother's house for prenatal advice and companionship. She was sitting one evening before the fire and conversing with her sister and some maids, when she felt a violent blow in her side. She accused the maids of ill-timed playfulness, which they all denied. Later she went to bed, but was horrified to find that the spot where she had been struck was discoloured yellow and bore what seemed to be the imprint of a hand. Two days after the birth of her child she died, and a further examination showed that the imprint was unmistakably that of a human hand.[156]

As for ghosts, the atmosphere of Elizabethan Wales was most congenial to their purposes, sinister or otherwise. A positive invasion of them took place in Denbighshire in 1602, which struck terror into the hearts of the inhabitants, some of whom were so affected by their appearance and ' chatter ' that they took to their beds and died, mouthing horrible blasphemies and displaying all the signs of being possessed by evil spirits. The success of the spectres was generally attributed to the iniquity and profligacy of the times, but it was soon overshadowed by an incident which was considered important enough to be discussed in private correspondence. A friend of the secretary of Sir Thomas Parry, a Welshman born and Elizabeth's ambassador at Paris, wrote to him in that same year that :

' we have much talke of an apparition in Wales not far from Chester, of great troupes of horse and foot in battle aray, seen upon a mountaine by sixteen or eighteen persons of credit, but when they came to discover what they were, sodainly vanisht.'[157]

From another source it appears that the strange sight took place near Nant y Ffridd, between Wrexham and Treuddyn, and those who witnessed it estimated that there were two or three thousand men on horseback and foot, with banners unfurled, marching in warlike manner through the dusk.[158] The phenomenon was interpreted as a forewarning of some dire event, and the Queen's death a few months later probably satisfied public opinion and speculation on this point.

This was not the only communication on the subject of Welsh spirits. Sir William Cecil, later Lord Burleigh, must have been amused by a petition forwarded to him in 1589, in which he was informed that Skenfrith castle, in Monmouthshire, contained a treasure closely guarded by a ' dyvell ' who sat on a hogshead of gold, and his ' dame ' who sat likewise on a hogshead of silver. Tradition or the ' voice of the country ' prophesied that there was little likelihood of their ever being disturbed, but the petitioner intimated that he was quite prepared to remove both guardians. With a tactful regard for Cecil's proverbial parsimony and conservative views on national expenditure, he added that he would do so ' without any charge to the Queen and your Lordshippe.'[159] Such disinterested patriotism would undoubtedly have commended itself to Sir William if the petitioner had not been a prisoner in the Tower of London and was obviously tired of the place.

The country fair in Elizabethan Wales was not only an occasion—rare enough, no doubt, in some districts—for enjoying a welcome respite from the dull cares of every day life. It was also a factor of economic importance in the transition of the countryside from a state of bare self-subsistence to that of a productive agricultural community. Before the development of speedier methods of transport and of more reliable communications, and prior to the advent of the commercial traveller, it offered the only satisfactory means for the exchange of goods, and assured the slow but steady circulation of money and commodities, even through the most isolated rural parishes.

In the fair, the shrewder and more practical Welsh countryman, in disposing of his produce, could learn in time to ascertain the comparative value of wares, the requirements of customers from near and far, and the fluctuations of demands dictated by fashion and need. This knowledge of market practices would teach him to utilise his farming resources to the best advantage, and enlarge the compass of his husbandry. On the other hand, he would have the opportunity of realising the progress made in other industries and crafts, attested by the wares displayed in the fair, and which he now had the money to buy for his family and home. Moreover he could satisfy his interest in news from the outer world, and improve his contacts with it, for the country fair, like the town market, generated and disseminated genuine and false information on all manner of subjects, and sometimes functioned as an improvised post office. At Caergwrle, for instance, it had become the custom to entrust letters to people riding thence to London, and to receive communications from those who had come from the capital to attend this Denbighshire fair, and were bearers of written or verbal messages.[160]

The crowds that frequented the country fairs were not all attracted to them for social or commercial reasons. There was a turbulent element that was always ready to disrupt the peaceful proceedings and provoke quarrels with the public. At Ewenny, in Glamorgan, where an annual fair was held for eight days, ' savage and disorderly ' people, some of whom were gentlemen bearing the honourable names of Stradling and Turberville, acted boorishly towards the public, and, on one occasion, assaulted the officers of the Crown who were responsible for maintaining order.[161]

It was equally exasperating to discover that private quarrels between squires might explode into a skirmish on the fair ground or result in a forced levy on the owners of stalls and standings. Those who had long been accustomed to set up their ' polles ' or booths at Llandaf fair, in the Carmarthenshire parish of Llanboidy, had paid regularly a nominal sum of money to the representatives of John Morgan Wolfe of Whitland, who had leased the fair, together with other local sources of income, from the Crown. They were disconcerted one fair day in 1590 to see about a hundred armed men, led by John

Read of Laugharne, descend upon them and demand the same
dues. The hostility between Wolfe and Read was well known,
and it was evident that the fair ground had been chosen as the
stage for a trial of strength. Loyalty to Wolfe may have
galvanised some of the boothkeepers into a show of resistance,
for Read decided to waste no further time in parleying with the
public. He ordered one man, who had set up his booth in the
churchyard, to remove it outside, ' thinkinge ' or so he alleged
later, ' it inconvenient to sett pooles where people are buried.'
Actually the law was in his favour, for it was forbidden by Act of
Parliament to hold fairs in churches and churchyards. But it in
no way exonerated his next action, which was to threaten to
pin the man's hand with a nail to his booth, and then wound
him severely in the arm with his dagger. In the meantime, the
rest of his company had scoured the fair exacting dues on all
sides—some onions here, a little garlic there, a few apples
yonder, a felt hat from a haberdasher, a loaf of bread from a
confectioner, and soap from a vendor of sundries. When they
withdrew with their spoils, the fair proceeded merrily and
busily as it had done ever since it had first been organised by
the abbot and monks of Whitland Abbey.[162]

A familiar figure on Welsh country roads was the pedlar or
chapman, who carried an assortment of wares on his back and
hawked them from door to door, or displayed them for sale in
the parish churchyard. He had to procure a licence from a
Justice of the Peace before he could follow this profession. It
was a valuable certificate, for it elevated him above his fellow
traveller, the vagrant, and afforded him a certain immunity
from the petty persecution directed against the much suspected
beggar and tramp. Without it, he was liable to be arrested,
and not for vagabondage alone. Many pedlars were accompanied by women who shared their fortunes, and although con-
cubinage was discreetly ignored in the highest circles of the
land, it was frowned upon by authority when it was too
overtly practised on the public highway.

No fair, of course, was complete without the presence of the
pedlars. Here families or groups of them would gather and

compete in self-advertisement and salesmanship with traders from all parts of the country. They could do so with some degree of confidence, for their wares were often superior in quality. Some pedlars retailed glassware, shirts, bands and collars, cakes of white soap and acquavite, which they had previously bought in English border towns like Shrewsbury. Others offered useful things like straw baskets, beehives and domestic implements made with their own hands.[163] But it was an exacting and often unprofitable occupation, and like much else open to depression and stagnation in times of war. The military commitments on the continent and in Ireland spelt bankruptcy for one unfortunate Ewenny pedlar. So many of his clients in Monmouthshire had been pressed into foreign service that he found himself encumbered with bad debts and at his wits' end to pay for his goods.[164] Yet some of the fraternity were able, thanks to a herculean constitution, to weather the rigours of their itineraries and the hardships of their calling, and reach the ripe age of a hundred years.[165]

The movement of Welsh people across the English border gathered impetus during the reign of Elizabeth. Actuated partly by dissatisfaction with working and living conditions at home and partly by the material attractions and novelties of another civilisation, there was a large scale migration into the variegated social and business world of England, particularly in and around London.

In the febrile world of commerce and trade, there was hardly one sphere of activity into which Welshmen did not penetrate. The various guilds of merchant tailors, drapers, glovers, coopers, dyers, haberdashers and others, contained a strong Welsh element, which made its presence felt in the animated life of the city and became an integrated part of the community barely distinguishable except perhaps by its accent. The more industrious were able to compete successfully with their English rivals and make substantial fortunes. In commerce, too, there were London Welshmen who quickly perceived the advantages of foreign trade, and entered into transactions with commercial circles in Antwerp or prosecuted their interests as far afield as Danzig.[166]

Many of this colony came up as youths from Wales and were apprenticed for the customary period of seven years before being allowed to exercise their chosen professions. For some the initial years of training proved a stepping stone to prosperity and to all the privileges associated with the status of a freeman of London, which was granted them upon the satisfactory completion of their apprenticeship. But not all were fortunate in their masters, and the inhumanity with which some of the latter treated their apprentices came to light in the case of Charles Jones of Wrexham.

An orphan boy, he had been apprenticed by his elder brother in 1596 to a London merchant tailor, upon payment of £10 for clothes and instruction, supplemented by a bond that he would faithfully execute all contractual obligations. In return, the tailor bound himself to observe the London custom of supplying him with apparel, meat and drink, and to pay him a subsistence allowance of 6/8 a week whenever he despatched him overseas on business. Within a short time, however, the boy found himself leading a dog's life without any means of protection, since the physical treatment of apprentices was not subject to any control outside the guild. The day came when he was accused of stealing his master's goods. He vigorously denied the charge, whereupon the tailor, assisted by his wife, tied the boy to a post and whipped him unmercifully. To escape further torture, the lad confessed to the theft, and was expelled from the house, but to satiate his detestation of him, the tailor contrived to have him impressed for the Queen's service and shipped him off to the Irish wars.[167]

The drift of Welshmen to England did not entirely gravitate towards the capital. Montgomeryshire girls served as maids in Chester and other towns, Welsh craftsmen settled down as weavers in Berkshire, clothiers in Somerset, tanners in Shropshire, coopers in Suffolk, well-to-do yeomen in the Home Counties, and opportunist purveyors of goods to the continent in Kent.[168] The town of Shrewsbury particularly attracted Welsh youth who became apprentices to those engaged in the wool trade, and who later became masters in the various crafts associated with it.[169]

From time to time, many would return home impelled by a bout of longing for the land of their birth, although the welcome they sometimes received considerably dampened the joys of homecoming. So Richard Davies discovered when he appeared at Wrexham in 1589, after an absence of seventeen years and was incontinently arrested for horse-stealing. It was only the testimony of his friends in Suffolk to his integrity that saved him from having to prolong his visit to his native town under the close supervision of the local gaoler.[170] And it was, no doubt, out of respect to the good name of family and parish—or to avoid disparaging remarks about his appearance after a long sojourn in England, that William ap Richard, before returning home to Anglesey, judged that his clothes were not respectable enough and was tempted to steal a coat and doublet of superior quality to replace them.[171]

But with the emigration of Welshmen to England, there went a steady but smaller movement of English people into Wales, few of whom were attracted there by the magnificence of its wild scenery. Wales had the reputation of being one of the most fertile provinces of the realm, and the newcomers, for the most part, had every intention of taking up permanent residence and leading a more contented existence. Many were industrial workers drawn by the new lead, copper and mining enterprises financed by the perspicacious capitalists of London. But the rich arable and meadow lands of the border shires and South Wales also appear to have induced a number of English yeomen to cross the border and settle with their families as far west as Cardiganshire and Carmarthenshire. In their wake came the landless labourers as well as the vagabond and unemployed element, who drifted aimlessly in their search of work or charity from as far afield as Sussex, Yorkshire and Devon. They were to discover that the Welsh Justices of the Peace were as unrelenting in the application of the penalties of the law against the ' sturdy beggar ' as any local government official in England.

The more choleric Welsh, with their deep-rooted attachment

to tradition and custom, were apt at times to resent the intrusion of the phlegmatic Saxon, who made little effort to learn the language spoken around him, but who, nevertheless, was prepared to acclimatise himself to the habits and unpredictable humours of his neighbours. But this resentment occasionally erupted into violence. At Llanelly, in Carmarthenshire, a Lincolnshire yeoman and his wife were forced to barricade their house against an assault by a group of local farmers, and were happy to retrace their steps over the border after a violent pummelling and many uncomfortable hours in the stocks.[172] But worse was to happen in Montgomeryshire, where an Englishman was killed and his murder traced to a neighbour who had been heard to declare that ' it was an ill time or world when the knave, John Jevons, being an Englishman, should master or control us in the parish of Castell Caereinion,' and had never concealed his hatred towards the man.[173] It was disclosed that, during the year 1602, some forty houses belonging to Englishmen had been attacked at night and destroyed by hostile neighbours within the relatively short period of five years. This outburst of anglophobia can be explained, perhaps, by the fact that the English who settled in Montgomeryshire were industrious people and that their success excited jealousy. A hint to this effect was made by a Welsh writer, who usually took no pains to conceal his partiality for his countrymen. The men of Montgomeryshire, he confessed :

> ' are addicted unto idleness and unprofitable games. Whereby it cometh to passe that you shall finde many ritche Englishe farmers amongste them whereas the Landelordes themselves, which will take no paynes, do become very poore.'[174]

The daily problems of the Welsh countryman were aggravated by the ever recurring threat of military conscription. The protracted war in Ireland and the interventionist policy of the Government on the continent could only be carried on by pressing men for the armed forces of the Crown. Gradually the selection of able-bodied labourers and husbandmen for overseas service became a part of the routine duties of the Lords Lieutenant of the shires, their deputies and the Justices of the

c*

Peace. It was not always executed with exemplary impartiality and a sense of responsibility. Too often the richer yeomen were able to purchase their release from compulsory service or to hire a willing substitute, while the poorer husbandman, even the father of a large family, had no option but to accept ' press money ' and resign himself to a lengthy separation from his home.

It was also a subtle method for bringing matrimonial schemes to fruition, and breaking down the resistance of unwilling parties. At Llangennech, in Carmarthenshire, a Justice of the Peace forced a wealthy neighbour to take his daughter to wife by the simple expedient of confronting him with the alternative of an indefinite period of service in the Irish wars.[175] Some shires attempted to rid themselves of beggars and vagabonds by impressing them, but the Government got wind of their machinations and declared it compulsory that only able-bodied men should be selected. The shire authorities were not entirely to blame, for the constant conscription of men was draining the countryside of its best elements. In Caernarvonshire, for example, there was a serious shortage of agricultural labourers and farm servants due to the manpower exigencies of the Irish wars.[176]

The pressed men were given weapons supplied by their respective shires, and a brief initial training in their use. They were then despatched to join their commanding officers at some Welsh or English port. The men of Brecknock were furnished with breastplate, gorget and helmets ; the men of Cardiganshire with muskets and calivers, provided by London and Chester merchants, as well as with pikes, halberts, swords with basket hilts and Turkey blades, and other arms. They were also given a complete set of clothing—coats, doublets, hose, stockings and shoes, and advanced a week's wage while they were en route to Milford Haven, the port of embarkation. In Carmarthenshire the press was conducted along unusually humanitarian lines. Married men were exempt from military service abroad, and replaced by ' sole ' men. Anyone infected with venereal disease was immediately discharged, and so was the fortunate person who could complain of a ' grief ' in one of his legges,' which might have been anything from an ulcer to varicose veins. Flintshire men appear to have been parsimoniously treated, for they only received fourpence as 'press money,' and were invariably directed to the fighting in Ulster. On the other hand, the Glamorgan conscripts could pride themselves upon their distinctive battle dress, for they marched to deal with the enemy in blue coats lined with yellow cotton, or in red coats with a lace of green.[177]

In this way, Welshmen found themselves engaged on a far-flung battle line, and fought and died in the bogs of Ireland, on the sand dunes of the Low Countries, under the walls of French and Breton towns, and in the harbours of Spain and Portugal. But the conditions of service and warfare could and did have a demoralising effect upon the least resistant amongst them. Diseases were rampant and lethal, the ubiquitous dysentery being the most deadly of them all. Where it was not possible to be invalided out of the service, the most reckless of the pressed men were prepared to forge passes in order to escape the torments of camp and campaign.[178] The question of pay was a further source of discontent. Its irregularity was an accepted feature of the chronic mismanagement of national funds, and even when it materialised some of it failed to reach the pockets of the rank and file owing to the dishonesty and embezzlement of officers and officials.

Very often, especially in the case of the expeditionary forces to Portugal and elsewhere, remuneration was postponed until their return to England. But there was no guarantee that the soldiers would receive their back pay. The alternatives facing them were either to walk to London to demand their pay or to find their way home consoled by the thought that to regain their liberty was worth the loss of any gratuity. Thomas Richard of Denbighshire chose the road to the capital in the hope that he would be fairly rewarded in the matter of pay after serving in Sir John Hawkins's ship on the Portuguese expedition of 1590. All that he received was 2/6 from the city's benevolent fund organised and distributed by the Lord Mayor. The disillusioned Welshman, like many other soldiers abandoned to their own devices after being discharged, lived on alms until hunger forced him to steal some clothes and delivered him into the hands of the constable of Llangollen.[179] Yet another rude awakening for some pressed men was to discover that their absence abroad—sometimes deliberately engineered for the purpose—had enabled unscrupulous landlords and avaricious neighbours to terrorise their defenceless families into surrendering inherited or leased property.

There was no lack of incentive, therefore, to avoid the rigours and dangers of overseas service, either by bribery or by failing to answer the roll-call. Desertion could be punished by death, but many took the risk of withdrawing surreptitiously from the ranks of pressed men and retiring temporarily from public view or fleeing the country. Some were actuated by political rather than by physical considerations, particularly in North Wales where loyalty to the Catholic faith was still strong and fed upon a smouldering resentment towards the Protestant policy of the Government. When the constable of Hope, in Montgomeryshire, presented a warrant to David ap Roger which authorised him to search for two of the latter's sons who had been selected for service in the Irish war, he was informed by the father in terse Welsh that in no conceivable circumstances would they fight for the Queen.[180]

The constable of Llandybïe, in Carmarthenshire, engaged on a similar mission, met with something more than verbal opposition. Having received strict injunctions from the authorities to apprehend a certain Morgan Harri, a poor labourer of some fifty-five years of age, he had secured his person and was conducting him to the muster point, when he was attacked by a group of local people sympathetic towards the pressed man, manhandled by them and forced to release his victim.[181]

These, however, appear to have been isolated cases of an indisposition to serve the Crown abroad. The generality of the pressed countrymen of Wales carried out their exacting military duties with the doggedness and intrepidity that were characteristic of the Elizabethan soldiers and sailors who crossed the sea on the Queen's business.

The succession to property in Wales had been governed by the traditional custom of gavelkind, whereby land was divided equally between the male heirs. But it was an anachronistic form of tenure in the aggressively individualistic age of the Tudors, and the Act of Union which completed the fusion of Wales with England, made short work of it. The House of Commons substituted for it the English principle of primogeniture, which dictated that land was not partible but was to descend to the eldest living heir. The abolition of gavelkind was undoubtedly welcome to the generality of Welshmen, since it removed the one restriction that militated against the concentration of land in the hands of one person and its disposal by him at his own will.[182] It also extended the opportunity of increasing the size of individual properties without the danger of an eventual disintegration through subdivision, and it was probably this aspect that commended it to the Welsh.

The English jurists who carried the change through were little concerned with its economic or social repercussions. They considered it their business to bring Welsh tenurial customs within one category or other of English law. But there was one argument in favour of the suppression of gavelkind which could not fail to recommend it to the Government. It was summed up by an attorney at the Court of the Welsh Marches who, after lamenting the impotence of the Council to deal with the disorders in Wales, underlined one incontrovertible reason for this unruliness and adumbrated the one apparent and effective solution. He wrote :

' For further suppressynge of the enormyties forseid, if it were orderd that the eldest sone shulde enherit in every place in Wales, it shuld avoyde moche evyll ffor those as pretend to be gentylmen and have lands departed amongs them. Although every mans parte be but XId by yere, they will reteyne theffs and harlotts to them so that one of them will have XXti or XXXti watyng uppon hym in a ffayre or markett. No such rule is in North Wales where the eldest sone dothe inherytt.'[183]

The Government may have hoped that primogeniture would gradually displace the immemorial ties of tribal kinship and weaken the ties of personal loyalty, dependence and service by reducing the number of people who profited by them, and so contributing to the pacification of the Welsh countryside.

All these considerations accounted for the fact that gavelkind was suppressed with small regard for its possible effects on the material situation and domestic arrangements of the people affected by it. This was not the case in England. When a bill was introduced in the House of Commons in 1601 to abolish gavelkind in Kent, it was rejected on the grounds that the Crown would suffer a financial loss. The opponents of the bill argued that many yeomen in that county enjoyed an annual income of £10 from their land and were accordingly taxable for subsidies ; the Exchequer obviously stood to lose if their numbers were reduced by the abolition of gavelkind. The counter argument that the unification of subdivided properties would prove more conducive to prosperity in Kent failed to convince the majority of the House.[184] There is no evidence that the desirability of preserving gavelkind in Wales on economic or any other grounds was ever discussed by Parliament. The custom was simply abolished by the Act of Union of England and Wales.

But not altogether. It survived in certain localities, for example, on the manor of Trelech in Monmouthshire, much to the irritation of the gentry who were enthusiastic abolitionists since they hoped to profit by its liquidation, and made every effort to discredit the custom. One of the manor's tenements had been divided between the son and the nephew of a deceased tenant. The nephew had agreed to sell his half to Sir Walter Herbert, who wished to acquire the other half as well. He assaulted the son, evicted him and arranged with a compliant jury of the manor to deny that the property had ever been partible by gavelkind. The custom also survived in the lordships of Elfael and Cyfeiliog, in Radnorshire and Montgomeryshire respectively, and there was a quixotic situation at Monmouth. Whereas in the town itself customary lands descended from father to son by the law of primogeniture, in the manor of Monmouth which included some property in the town, they were subject to gavelkind and divided equally between male heirs or, failing them, between daughters.[185]

As a consequence of the abolition of gavelkind, it became imperative to reduce the ancient forms of Welsh tenure to an orderly system, and to approximate them to those which obtained in England. It took many years for the Crown lawyers and the law courts to disentangle and simplify them, and, in general, the descendants of the former free tribesmen were accorded the status and rights of freeholders. The successors of the non-tribesmen, on the other hand, were treated as tenants eligible to hold land on renewable leases for lives or for terms of years. Certain traditional and intermediary tenures, like that of copyhold, were recognised and tolerated, and the manorial customs which dictated their application were allowed to persist.[186] Yet even these were gradually relaxed as the century wore on. For example, on the Stradling estates in Glamorgan, the old custom enforcing residence on a copyhold tenement was mutually ignored by landlord and tenant, and the latter was given leave to live elsewhere provided he paid his dues and kept his house in a habitable and well repaired condition.[187]

Of all tenures, leases offered the best advantages to tenants who were not recognised as freeholders. They stabilised the relationship between them and their landlords, and strictly defined the conditions on which they held their land. But there were inherent disadvantages as well. With the rising cost of living, landlords came to regard leases as a lever to extort higher rents and fines, and adopted the expedient of issuing short-term leases for that purpose. Since there was no lack of applicants for leaseholds—there being a shortage of land to meet the exigencies of a growing rural population, the tenant, faced with the prospect of a higher rent at the expiration of his lease, had either to exploit his land more thoroughly or make way for another who would do so voluntarily. From the economic point of view, there may have been much to justify this policy, since there was little doubt that much of the land in Wales was undervalued. Nevertheless, it was the beginning of the pernicious system of rack-renting, which often drove Welsh tenants to despair and compelled many of them to leave their homes. The situation of the unfortunate leaseholder, who found himself at the mercy of an extortionate landlord, was graphically described by the Pembrokeshire squire and historian George Owen, in 1603 :

> ' For now the poor tenant . . . is taught to sing unto his lord a new song, and the landlords have learnt the text of the damned disciple, "quod vultis mihi dare, et ego illum vobis tradam", and now the world is so altered with the poor tenant that he standeth in so bodily fear of his greedy neighbour, that two or three years ere his lease end he must bow to his lord for a new lease and must pinch it out many years before to keep money together, so that in this age it is as easy for the poor tenant to marry two of his daughters to his neighbours sons as to match himself to a good farm from his landlord.'[188]

Money was, of course, the principal object of this unscrupulous rack-renting, but not all Welsh landlords had their eyes glued to the money-bags of their tenants. Some still preferred to receive their rents in kind, and to encourage their tenants to attend to their own interests and prosperity by co-operating with them. A Flintshire landlord, for instance, demised a tenement for four years on condition that the rent for the first two years was half the corn harvest, and two-thirds of it for the last two years.[189] A similar but more comprehensive contract was devised on the Gwydir estates, where Sir John Wynn showed himself uncommonly liberal. The tenant agreed to surrender half the corn harvest as annual rent. In return, he was given two oxen and two steers as draught animals. In exchange for the use of eight cows, he was to yield to Sir John half the cheese produced, a certain quantity of oatmeal, butter and milk, and a stipulated amount of hay and grass for his landlord's stables.[190] This type of lease seems to have redounded to the benefit of both parties, and may explain how some of the gentry, like John Trefor of Trefalun (Allington), in Flintshire, became involved in the illicit export of corn.[191]

However the new leases, in general, were drawn up on a cash basis, and few of them included any payments in kind which had been a feature of the old manorial and tribal tenures. Most of these were now commuted into money payments which, in view of the constant increase in prices, benefited the tenants.[192] There were, of course, some exceptions. Tenants were sometimes obliged to find a reaper or a labourer to work at harvest time on the landlord's private estate,[193] or were expected to bring gifts in the form of poultry at certain times in the year, as did the tenants of Gwydir when they were invited to dinner at that mansion on Christmas Day.[194] In Anglesey, there was a tendency to bind tenants to undertake one day's reaping and one day's transport of corn with horse and drag to the landlord's barn.

It was in this shire too that one opportunistic squire granted a tenement for twenty-one years to a tailor, who wished to exchange his profession for that of farming, on the condition that he should work all the clothes needed by his landlord's family.[195] Other calculating squires inserted a proviso in their leases that the tenant should pay a sum of money to his landlord upon the marriage of his daughter. It was a less cumbersome way of extracting a *comortha* from the unfortunate man than subjecting him to open violence.[196]

The enhanced value of land, the introduction and exploitation of the leasehold system and the need for greater productivity to feed a growing population were all factors that stimulated a more systematic cultivation of the land. Where traditional methods of farming had sufficed to provide a pastoral people with a subsistence diet, the realisation that agriculture could be a profit-making concern, and the general desire for a higher standard of living on the English model, convinced the Welsh husbandman and yeoman that the time had come to revise their agrarian operations. The key to prosperity lay in the more intensive raising of cereals, particularly wheat, which enjoyed priority among all agricultural produce and guaranteed substantial returns whether it was exported abroad or canalised into the home market. And so the process began whereby arable farming established itself on a firmer footing in the rural economy of Wales.

Not only was much newly enclosed land turned over to the plough, but increasing attention was paid to the problem of converting derelict soil and rough mountain pasture into a suitable state for corn growing. It was a task that called for

much ingenuity and perseverance, but the Welsh farmers
showed unusual diligence and initiative in the work of re-
clamation. In West Denbighshire, for instance, with its
extensive moors and bare uplands, they employed an arduous
but effective method for preparing the soil :

> ' After they have with a broad kinde of spade pared away the
> upper coat, as it were, or sord of the earth into certaine turfes,
> they put them up artificially in heapes, put fire to them and burne
> them to ashes, which being throwne upon the ground so pared
> and flayed, causeth the hungrey barrainesse thereof to fructifie
> that the fields bring forth a kind of Rhie or Amel corne in such
> abundance as it is incredible.'[197]

Travelling through Wales, the English poet Churchyard was
impressed by the progress of Welsh agriculture, and the energy
displayed by the Welsh husbandmen in bringing the rich
resources of their native soil to light :

> ' They have begun of late to lime their land
> And plowes the ground where sturdie okes did stand,
> Converts the meares and marrish everywhere . . .
> They teare up trees and takes the rootes away,
> Makes stonie fieldes smooth fertile fallowe ground,
> Brings pastures bare to beare good grasse for hay . . .
> Wales is this day (behold throughout the sheeres)
> In better state than twas these hundred yeares.'[198]

Besides corn, many farmers produced a sufficiency of
vegetables, like beans, peas, leeks and onions, and of fruit—
apples, pears and plums—for their own table, with a surplus
that they sold in the local market towns. Apiculture was
another sideline in which some of them specialised, since sugar
had not yet replaced honey in food and drink. When encouraged by enthusiastic and less conservative landlords, they
were prepared to venture on the cultivation of new products.
It was Sir John Wynn of Gwydir, for instance, who tried to
introduce hop-growing on his estates. He entered into an
agreement with one of his tenants that twelve acres of land on
his tenement should be set apart for the purpose. Sir John
undertook to find the requisite number of poles for the hops, to
construct a warehouse for their storage on the tenement, to
provide the necessary manure—two loads of muck for each

acre—and the wood for drying the hops. The tenant, for his part, was to be responsible for setting, dressing, weeding, pruning, harvesting and drying the hops, and contracted to deliver half of the annual harvest as rent.[199]

Welsh husbandmen had long been engaged in the raising of sheep and cattle, and although they now began to pay more attention to the cultivation of crops, pastoral farming still retained its ascendancy during this century. Apart from the nature of the country which encouraged this type of farming, the breeding of live stock was easy and very profitable. There was a ready market in England for the wool, hides and meat of the Welsh countryside, which was either bought by English purveyors at Welsh fairs and markets, or despatched across the border in the form of herds of animals under the guidance of Welsh and English drovers. And in the local market towns, the sale of butter, cheese and milk was a reliable source of income that enabled the Welsh husbandman to shoulder the burden of rents, taxes and tithes which tended to increase with the rising cost of living. It is for this reason also that, while shortages of corn gave rise to much anxiety and corrective legislation, they were partly compensated by an unfailing supply of other agricultural produce in Wales.

The immense stretches of open mountain pasturage upon which countless sheep and cattle maintained themselves from spring to autumn, and from which they were driven down to the shelter of valleys and farm stables or folds during the winter, presented the Welsh farmers of Elizabethan days with much the same difficulties that their descendants of today have to face occasionally. The main problem was how to prevent sheep and cattle from straying and losing themselves among neighbouring flocks and herds, or wandering into dangerous places or into the hands of undesirable persons who had even a less settled occupation and abode than the animals.

Some of the richer sheep farmers hired a shepherd or *bugail* to guard their flocks, but a more universal custom was to use sheep markings for identification purposes. These showed a surprising variety of slits, cuts and patterns inflicted on the

nostrils and ears of the sheep, from the ' figure like unto the
Sign of Seven in Algorism '[200] to the ' thong cut from under-
neath the right ear, and idem from above the left ear, and the
top of the right ear cropped off' used in Brecknock. Wool
markings were also used extensively, prior to and after the
washing and shearing of the sheep twice a year, in May and at
Michaelmas, and imprinted on various parts of the sheep with
the help of red or black ochre and tar. But despite these precautions, sheep and cattle were inclined to wander or be
stolen, and many stratagems were devised in the hope of laying
the thieves by the heels. At Llangollen, for instance, sheep that
had been recovered but found with false markings super-
imposed on the original ones, were tied in the open street in
the belief, sometimes justified, that they would induce the
thief to fall into the trap of claiming them as his own property.[201]
On the other hand, a favourite device of sheep stealers to
escape detection was to impersonate drovers. When sheep and
cattle, however, were genuinely believed to be lost, a detailed
description of the missing animals was announced at the market
crosses of the neighbouring towns and in the parish churches all
around. And there was no lack of willingness to help in the
search, on foot and horseback, even if it entailed many days of
patient investigation of contradictory rumours and nebulous
information.

  The pasture land of the Principality enjoyed a reputation for
its nutritive qualities which extended well beyond the border,
and opened up a further avenue of income for the more
business-like yeomen. Many of these concluded agreements
with livestock breeders in England to pasture their cattle and
sheep on their grazing grounds for a certain period, and to
return them fattened and in a more marketable condition. For
example, a Middlesex farmer despatched some forty lambs to a
Montgomeryshire yeoman at Llanfair, to be put out to ' haulfs.'
According to this agreement, the latter was to depasture the
lambs on his land, and in return was to retain one-half of their
wool, delivering the other half together with the lambs to their
owner at the expiration of the time period.[202] Abuses, of
course, were inclined to creep into profitable exchanges of this

kind, and two Radnorshire yeomen, who tried to earn a little extra money by pasturing a herd of English cattle on the common land of their township, were accused of ' oppressing ' the common and were indicted for the offence.[203]

In some measure, this transaction was an extension of an old custom whereby husbandmen with more pasture land than they could use allowed the animals of less fortunate neighbours to graze on them, or agreed to keep them throughout the winter months. It sometimes took the form of a charitable gesture, particularly in the case of widows who were entrusted with the care of sheep and cattle, and were remunerated in money or gifts. Where it was a strictly business transaction, the guardian could claim one of the animals as payment. In Cardiganshire, it was understood that a calf born in these circumstances was to be retained by him.

The growth of London and the gradual concentration of population within and outside its walls, were creating a demand for meat which could not be met by the available livestock in the vicinity, already attenuated by the development of sheep farming for the production of wool. The purveyors of the London markets had therefore to seek supplies further afield, and those who ventured to Wales found a partial solution to their problem in its abundant herds of cattle.

The cattle markets of North Wales, in particular Denbigh, Ruthin, Llanrwst and Oswestry, attracted large numbers of English buyers and drovers, who selected their animals with great care and often engaged Welsh labourers on the spot to drive them to England.[204] Being at first unaware of the prevalence of cattle stealing in those parts, they often acquired beasts which had been filched from their rightful owners and had no option but to surrender them. Experience made them suspect any person who offered to sell cattle at exceptionally low prices, and it became a common practice with them, especially those who attended Wrexham fair, not to purchase any animal without first finding a native of the locality who knew the vendor personally and could vouch for his integrity.[205]

Other English dealers preferred to hire Welshmen to buy

cattle from their countrymen on the most profitable terms. One such Kent dealer despatched his Welsh representative to the fairs at Llannerch-y-medd and Newborough in Anglesey, where he bought animals on the open market and enlisted the services of local drovers to help ferry them over the Welsh rivers and drive them safely to his employer's farm in Kent. His reputation for honesty was unimpeachable, for he was granted credit for the balance of the purchase money which he could not produce at the sale.[206]

In time, the profession of drover was adopted by many Welshmen, who wished to see a little of the world or exercise their dormant business faculties. It was necessary to obtain official recognition from the shire authorities before they could set up as cattle dealers, but once this was granted, they were free to travel from market to market and enter into transactions. Some continued to combine farming with droving, and rarely extended their activities beyond the limits of their native shires. Others became professional drovers, and set out periodically with thirty or more head of cattle on the long and arduous journey to Barnet, Brentwood and other well known fairs in eastern England and to the cattle markets of London.

The less vigilant amongst them were sometimes exposed to the knavery of disreputable elements in urban society. Richard Hebbe, a drover from Old Radnor, was told by a London weaver that he intended to marry his sister, who was in domestic service there. Hebbe offered to provide her with a suitable dowry, but the wily Londoner turned down the first offer of £20 and then married the girl secretly. When Hebbe appeared with a drove of cattle at Bartholomew Fair, he had him arrested and entered an action of £100 against him for alleged breach of dowry contract. It transpired that the weaver's intention was to force the drover to pay whatever sum he demanded of him, or be denied entry to London's cattle markets and thus lose his livelihood.[207]

Wales was inevitably affected by the enclosure movement which caused so much distress and complaint in England, and resulted in the depopulation of some parts of the English countryside. As in England, the movement took various forms : the consolidation of scattered pieces of land into compact holdings separated from each other by hedges, fences or ditches ; the conversion of arable into pasture land ; the engrossing of tenements ; and the occupation of waste and common land which gradually diminished the immemorial rights of the tenantry to pasture their flocks and herds on them. All these processes were applied with varying degrees of success, but while some parts of the Principality felt their full effects, others remained comparatively immune to their influences, and preserved their old methods of land cultivation.

The fusion of separate pieces of land into compact holdings made little headway, although it would undoubtedly have promoted a better and more economical use of land, and saved an appreciable amount of time and labour for those husbandmen who had to divide their attention between their scattered fields. A step in this direction was taken in Carmarthenshire, where the freeholders of the royal manors in the north of the shire were permitted to have their tenements strictly divided from one another and their boundaries permanently fixed. But there is little evidence of any corresponding reform elsewhere, and even the gentry were constrained to abide by the old arrangements. In the lordship of Denbigh, some had to ride or walk along a maze of circuitous paths whenever they wished to inspect their property which was dispersed among that of their neighbours.[208]

On the other hand, the old open-field husbandry was beginning to disappear behind an assortment of hedges and other artificial boundaries. Wherever it was possible to erect landmarks to distinguish his tenement or property from that of his neighbours, the Welsh husbandman employed every means and materials to do so, even when his acres were intermingled with theirs. The cheapest and quickest method was to plant hedges of quickset, but in default of this, stakes, mounds of turf, walls and ditches were built or dug to delimit individual holdings. In Anglesey, where the inhabitants had formerly refrained from setting up boundaries,

' now they digge stoney hillockes and with the stones thereof they make rude walles much lyke to those of Devonshire.'[209]

In some places, there was a tendency to enclose plots of arable land, leaving pasture unencumbered with boundaries : in others, the predominance of pastoral farming dictated that meadows should be surrounded with hedges. In West Wales, this practice became so integrated with large estate economy that leaseholders in Pembrokeshire were forced to repair hedges and fences on their tenements, and were threatened with eviction if they tried to evade this obligation.[210]

The conversion of arable into pasture land did not invariably accompany the extension of the enclosure movement in Wales. In reality, there was little call for the substitution of pasture for arable to meet the exigencies of intensified sheep farming and greater production of wool, which was the cardinal motive behind the movement. The mountain and moorland in all quarters of Wales provided a superabundance of pasture for sheep, and the problem of extending the limits of grassland at the expense of land under the plough rarely entered into the calculations of the promoters of enclosures. The development of sheep farming and breeding in the Principality was not hindered by a shortage of pasture but rather stimulated by the availability of sheep-walks. That is one reason why so little was heard of the progress and fortunes of sheep farming in Wales. If it had led to the eviction of tenants and to rural depopulation, there would probably have been as great an outcry as there was in England at the time. It would be truer to say that the enclosure movement in Wales was largely directed towards a more progressive husbandry, and not towards the replacement of tillage by sheep farming. There was neither depopulation nor a campaign of eviction in favour of an expanding woollen industry. Rather the yeoman and the smallholder classes fixed their roots deeper in the soil owing to the gradual debilitation of many of the communal features of land cultivation and ownership, which the enclosure movement did much to expedite.

The concentration of tenements in the hands of fewer cultivators—the third feature of the movement—made uneven progress in Wales. It was limited by the fewness of freeholders, the only class that could dispose of its property as it wished, by the availability of land for the creation of new tenements, and, occasionally, by the opposition of Crown officials. For instance, in the lordship of Haverfordwest, the royal commissioners sent to investigate the material circumstances of the Crown's tenants there in 1577, were informed that many of them were prepared to pay higher rents in return for permission to buy up two or three holdings which they proposed to convert into large dairy farms. After much deliberation, the commissioners rejected their request on the grounds that it might result in the depopulation of the countryside.[211] But further north, in the lordship of Cemaes, a different process was going on. There the movement for the accumulation of tenements found some of its most enthusiastic adherents. By the end of Elizabeth's reign, many yeomen had increased their patrimony by acquiring additional parcels of land, sometimes as many as eleven, either from impoverished neighbours or from those who had abandoned agriculture for some other occupation.[212]

It was the encroachment on common and waste land that called attention to the worst features of the enclosure movement, and generated hostility towards it throughout the Principality. For, above all else, it threatened the ancient rights of the tenantry to pasture their sheep, cattle and pigs on these lands, and to gather timber and other materials for domestic use. As in England, it became a pernicious form of land grabbing, but it was by no means confined to the landlords who were popularly accounted the principal villains. Like Sir John Wogan, who enclosed pieces of Crown waste at Narberth for his own use, a precedent zealously followed by the mayor of Tenby,[213] or the squires of the lordship of Gower who, at an inquest held in 1590, were found to have enclosed many hundreds of acres of common belonging to the constituent manors of the lordship.[214]

The fact is that the ordinary tenant of all classes rarely missed the opportunity to enclose any land that was held in common, or, for that matter, any parcel of land that could be surreptitiously filched without exciting too much publicity. Tenants on royal and lay manors appropriated pieces of the home farm and forest land, in addition to pieces of the waste upon which they sometimes built cottages in order to establish

a permanent claim to them.[215] The following description of
what happened in the lordship of Kidwelly could be applied to
any other manorial properties in North and South Wales :

> ' It appeareth that anncyently there were very lardge and greate
> Commons and Waste within the sayde Lordship out of which it
> should seeme greate Inclosures and Incroachments have byne
> made by the Tenants borderinge uppon them by which his
> Maties Rents oughte to be improved. But it havinge byne donne
> longe since it seemeth not possible to discover them.'[216]

Municipal corporations, like that of Carmarthen, found
nothing objectionable in the idea of enclosing large portions of a
common in the vicinity that belonged to a neighbouring
lordship.[217]   And so insatiable was the land hunger of some
Welsh husbandmen that they ploughed up and enclosed parts
of the Queen's highways.[218]

But it was natural for the majority of the rural inhabitants of
the Principality to regard the enclosure of common land with
anxiety.   They were essentially a class of farmers, owning
small tenements, in which arable predominated over meadow
and pasture land. The common and waste were indispensable
for the good tillage and husbandry upon which their economy
depended, especially in the mountainous districts where the
soil could only be cultivated at a great expense of time and
labour. All accessible and suitable soil was ploughed with the
exception of a few acres of meadow whose hay crops were
needed as winter fodder. The remainder of the land, which
stretched on all sides of the cultivated fields, was regarded as
absolutely necessary for the maintenance of the tenants' horses,
oxen, sheep and cattle, and to deprive them of their common of
pasture by enclosing this land was tantamount to a threat to
the existence of their live stock and draught animals.

Just as the enclosers sometimes entered into a mutual undertaking to sabotage any attempt, especially by the Crown, to
force them to reveal and surrender the acres they had taken,[219]
so the husbandmen and yeomen initiated collective action to
defend their rights of common against the rapacity of fellow
tenants and landlords alike. The brunt of their indignation fell
upon the latter, since the enclosure of common land was only

one of a long series of injustices which they had suffered at the hands of the squires. And so when Gruffydd Nanney, squire of the estate of that name in Merioneth, enclosed a portion of common woodland near Dolgellau with a stone wall, it was immediately thrown down and he was warned of more unpleasant consequences if he dared to rebuild it.[220] Hearing that a park in which they enjoyed common of pasture was being ditched by the squire, the men of the forest of Fynnant, in the lordship of Dinas in Brecknock, assaulted the workmen engaged by him and threatened to tie them to horses' tails if they did not desist.[221] On the common of Cors y Felin, formerly belonging to Neath Abbey but leased to a London Welshman, John Price, who had partly enclosed it, a band of yeomen destroyed the hedges and,

> ' did then and there make greatt rejoysinge and tryumphinge with greatt and lowde voyses sayinge that they would not decist from there saide Ryotous and wicked enterprise so longe as one hedge or mounde were there standinge, growinge or beinge.'[222]

Similar destruction of hedges and ditches made by the gentry was committed in many North and South Wales shires, and at Ystrad Marchell in Montgomeryshire, the irate yeomen seem to have anticipated, in 1569, the methods of the Rebecca Rioters by more than two hundred and fifty years.

Here a piece of common land, formerly in the possession of the now dissolved monastery, had been enclosed by the Crown lessee. The countryfolk around had retaliated by destroying the ditch which had been set up as the boundary. To avoid the expense of litigation, the landlord offered to submit the dispute to the arbitration of two Justices of the Peace of Montgomeryshire. But on the day appointed for discussion between the two parties, his opponents dressed in women's clothes and armed with all manner of weapons invaded and occupied the common. To show that they were, as they declared themselves to be, ' Lordes and Rulers here,' they cut down a number of oak trees, and to the remonstration of the Justices of the Peace they returned the blunt answer that they would ' hewe theym as small as herbes to the potte.' The helpless Justices retired and the yeomen, masters of the common, proceeded to plough it taking care to post sentries in the trees around to warn them of any impending counteraction. Their final ultimatum, which proved the intensity of their feelings and the seriousness of their resistance, was contained in a report which declared them to have stated that,

' whosoever doe meaine to inclose or occupy their soyle, which is the said CCCC acres as they pretend, that they will die uppon them.'[223]

THE TOWN

B Y far the greater part of the population of Elizabethan Wales lived in the countryside and was exclusively engaged in arable or pastoral farming. But a small minority led a sheltered and more corporate existence in towns. The history of these towns during the past two centuries had been a chequered one. Originally they had been built around the castles of the Crown or of the Norman Lords Marcher, and populated for the most part with people of English speech and habits.[1] Although they enjoyed similar privileges of self-government and municipal jurisdiction to those of English towns, they were an alien element in the life of the native inhabitants, and were treated with hostility and suspicion which they reciprocated in full measure. It was a situation that had entailed certain disadvantages for the towns. Not only was their scope for trade limited by this mutual dislike and by the perpetual state of disorder, which disturbed Wales until after the accession of the first Tudor king, but they were often the first targets in any Welsh revolt. Their resistance and survival therefore had depended as much on military as on civil organisation, and the fact that the Crown maintained perm-anent garrisons in many of them had created a feeling of resentful subservience towards the soldiery among the civilians. Their presence might be necessary in a well-nigh lawless country, but it was also an exasperating reminder that the preservation of municipal liberties depended on a nice adjust-ment between the policy of the castle and the interests of the town.

The establishment of law and order under the early Tudor monarchs was the first step in the emancipation of the towns from their status as semi-military institutions. And with the definitive abrogation, by the Act of Union, of all laws prohibiting Welshmen from residing and acquiring property in towns, the problem of security was no longer the first or decisive consider-ation of the municipal inhabitants. Gradually the walls that

enclosed many of the towns began to act as a greater restraint
on the activities of the people within them than on the movements of the native population outside. The desire to improve
trading facilities and to exchange their insanitary and cramped
living quarters for healthier homes impelled many families to
move to the open spaces outside the town gates. Suburbs
spread rapidly, were joined together and eventually grew into
towns which were called New Towns to distinguish them from
the abandoned and half ruinous habitations inside the walls.
The New Towns marked the emergence of a new type of urban
society and culture, which, despite the fires and plagues that
harassed them, continued to increase in prosperity and number
throughout the century.

Denbigh may be cited as a typical example of this development. The incentive to construct a new town originated from
periodic conflagrations, the lack of fresh water, and the fact that
the steepness of the ascent to the old town made transport
impracticable and deterred traders from frequenting the
market there. The new town was carefully designed and built
to obviate this obstacle, had ample wells of clean water,
was surrounded by beautiful parks and had the advantage of
good road and river communications. It is not surprising that,
within a short time, it had grown to be three times the size of
the old town where only a handful of the original inhabitants
still remained to maintain a semblance of life.[2]

But whereas some towns showed unmistakable signs of
revitalisation and progress, others were fated to witness a slow
decline in their fortunes during the century. No longer regarded
as indispensable to the maintenance of the King's peace, or
deprived of their former importance as centres of baronial
authority and jurisdiction by the destruction of the Welsh lords
marcherships under Henry VIII, they slowly degenerated into
insignificant rural towns. Cricieth, for instance, had decayed to
such an extent even in the reign of Henry VIII that it only
possessed two or three houses, while Mold, a market town, had
only forty inhabitants.[3] The same melancholy story was true of
South Wales, where towns like Hay, Trecastle, Llandovery,
Cardigan and Aberystwyth were suffering from the unforeseen

consequences of the demilitarisation of Wales, and were probably very much in the mind of George Owen, the Pembrokeshire squire and historian, when he wrote towards the end of the century that most Welsh towns were ' meane,' ' porre ' or ' ruynous.'[4]

A more far-reaching result was the gradual Cymricisation of the towns. Before, and particularly after, the lifting of restrictions on residence by the Act of Union, there was a steady flow of Welshmen into urban centres. The newcomers lost no time in qualifying for various crafts and professions, enrolling themselves as members of guilds, establishing flourishing businesses and infiltrating into the most influential municipal posts. It would be true to say that they were attracted more by the New Towns than by the older castle-dominated boroughs. It was here that the commercial impulse of the age was making itself felt, and where the political and social environment was conducive to a more vigorous municipal life.

The Welsh language also gained from this migration to the towns. Where English had been exclusively spoken, the native tongue now enjoyed an unaccustomed degree of equality, even to the extent of appropriating an honourable place as a suitable language for commemorative inscriptions in town churches, side by side with Latin and English.[5] The people of Denbigh were versed in both Welsh and English, and honours seem to have been equally divided between them on important public occasions. When the accession of James I was proclaimed in the market square, the Mayor did so in English, and no less a distinguished church dignitary and scholar than Bishop Morgan, the translator of the Bible into Welsh, made an identical announcement in the vernacular.[6]

At Abergavenny, despite the proximity of the English border and the concentration of trade which earned for the town the epithet of ' another Bristowe,' Welsh was more extensively used than English. It was the fact that ' the main or principall language was the Welsh or Brittish tongue ' that induced a prominent citizen of Abergavenny to send his son to London to perfect his pronunciation in English, and so speak it,

'without any corruption from his mother tongue, which doth
commonly infect men of our countre, that they cannot speak
English but that they are discovered by their vitious pronounci-
ation or idiotisms.'[7]

If the language was so firmly entrenched in a border town like
Abergavenny, it may be legitimately assumed that its position
in the smaller and more inland towns was well-nigh im-
pregnable.

The Welsh towns varied considerably in size and population.
For example, Pembroke had only one main thoroughfare
without any intersecting streets,[8] and the same feature was true
of Llandovery and other towns. On the other hand, Cardiff
stood within a wall that was estimated to be a mile in circum-
ference.[9] The disparity between populations was more pro-
nounced. Whereas the inhabitants of Denbigh numbered some
three thousand,[10]—a high figure for a provincial town of those
days—places like Beaumaris, Haverfordwest, Carmarthen and
Brecon averaged between a thousand and fifteen hundred
people, while smaller towns such as Cardigan, Conway and
Pwllheli would probably have no more than five hundred souls
within their liberties.[11] And there were still smaller towns—
Newborough, Harlech and Fishguard, for instance, which had
a mere handful of inhabitants. Sometimes there would be little
to distinguish them, except possibly a municipal building, from
the rural communities around them.

The castellated towns still preserved the walls which had
formerly been built for their protection against the insurgent
Welsh, but these now served little purpose except sometimes as
convenient quarries of materials for the erection or repair of
local buildings. Neither were the castles, to which some towns
owed their importance, treated with much more respect. The
disintegration and dilapidation of the ancient strongholds of
Monmouthshire filled the English poet, Thomas Churchyard,
with regret. He was particularly saddened by the derelict
condition of the medieval fortresses of Abergavenny and
Monmouth, and sang,

> 'A number more in Monmouthshire I finde
> That can not well abyde a blast of winde.'[12]

Where castles were used to accommodate itinerant Justices of Assize, some effort was made to maintain a part of them, like the great hall, in a habitable condition, and to equip it with a modicum of comfort for the dispensation of justice. At Haverfordwest, however, the Justices were obliged to hear trials in the Shire Hall, in default of any semblance of a hall in the castle, although they continued to observe the traditional custom of proclaiming their verdicts in the open air on the castle green.[13]

Very often the local corporations appropriated some portion of a castle and converted it into a gaol, leaving the rest to fall into decay or suffer depredations at the hands of those who could put centuries-old stone and iron to practical use. There were certain risks, of course, but not of a legal nature, as one necessitous citizen of Denbigh found to his cost when he climbed a decayed tower to steal a weatherboard and fell to his death.[14] But vandalism and neglect were allowed to proceed unchecked, to the irreparable damage of some of the finest examples of medieval military architecture in Wales. By the end of the century, for instance, the magnificent defensive walls and towers of Denbigh had been so thoroughly stripped and allowed to fall into ruin that a conservative estimate of indispensable repairs amounted to £5,000.[15] Caernarvon castle was in an almost irremediable condition of decay, but the damage was not confined to masonry and timber. The tower known as Treasury Tower had long been used to house the records of the shires of North Wales, but the insecurity of the walls had at last forced the authorities to remove them to safety. Many records had been damaged during the years prior to this belated decision, others irretrievably lost, and the remainder placed in a temporary but unsuitable repository in Caernarvon town where they were in the process of rapid disintegration.[16]

Within the walls, there was little evidence of that hideous conglomeration of houses which was, in later centuries, to accompany the growth of towns. With the exception, perhaps, of the main street, most houses were detached, each standing on its own plot of ground, surrounded by a garden, orchard or courtyard, and separated from its neighbour by a lane leading

D

to the ' backside ' of the residence.[17] Some of the castellated towns, in fact, took on the appearance of a number of rural habitations enclosed within walls. For instance, it was the common practice at Denbigh to pasture flocks of sheep here and there inside the town to the undisguised delight of the local dogs who chased them indefatigably.[18] At Chepstow, most of the town area inside the walls had been converted into meadows and gardens,[19] and at Usk, flax and hemp were grown in gardens which sometimes extended to one acre or more.[20]

The open towns, freed from the restrictions of space imposed by mural defences, were even more rural in their aspect, and consisted of private dwellings and shops intermingled with farms and small holdings. Very often there was little to distinguish the smaller towns from the surrounding countryside. On fair days, in Llanfyllin, the town was transformed into one collective farm, for there was sufficient pasture on all sides of the houses to maintain and feed the droves of animals driven there to be sold.[21] And there were few towns up and down the Principality which did not possess a penfold to accommodate stray cattle.

The rural economy of the towns was further exemplified by the commons and waste land which they owned, and upon which those of the inhabitants who had cattle and sheep depastured their animals. Conway burgesses appointed special officers known as Drovers of the Marsh, who were responsible for limiting the number of beasts allowed to each burgess to four. Any one who attempted to pasture more than that number on the town marshland faced the prospect of a fine of twopence and the temporary loss of the supplementary beasts.[22] The burgesses of Caernarvon owned a piece of heath where they pastured their cattle, and had to use force and litigation to prevent it from being invaded and appropriated by their neighbours in the countryside around.[23] At the other end of Wales, the number of animals which the burgesses of Newport in Monmouthshire were allowed to put on the town common corresponded strictly to the number of burgages held by them.[24] Trade was not the sole source of sustenance and wealth to the townsman of the Elizabethan age, in particular the Welsh townsman who inherited the traditional computation of a man's estate in terms of cattle, and instinctively realised the dangers of becoming too divorced from the land and its produce.

Town houses varied in style and materials from those of stone, or lime and stone, construction—usually the residences of gentlemen and the richer citizens—to the fashionable timber and lathe associated with this period. In addition, there were the humbler mudwall and thatched cottages where the poorer classes of the urban community lived. Most of the houses of the affluent inhabitants had chimneys, since coal was gradually ousting wood as fuel, and cellars specially built to preserve perishable provisions, and occasionally used as a home bank where money was concealed in bladders and other unusual receptacles. Usually the ground floor consisted of one or two living rooms, a hall and a kitchen, while the upper floor —if the house possessed one—was reserved for the sleeping chambers, sometimes reached by a flight of stairs from outside the house.[25] Some houses, in particular shops, faced directly on to the streets, others were separated from it by an outer gate, while a wicket gate led to the back of the house often designated as the ' mydenyard.'

Many of these houses were furnished in a style which showed how the increasing prosperity of the burghers was being used to improve and embellish domestic surroundings. Carpets now covered the floor instead of straw, iron grates were installed in the halls, and the firelight was reflected in the wainscot which had become fashionable. Leather chairs stood about the rooms, while in the upper chambers featherbeds with linen sheets had replaced the old straw mattresses. Eating vessels were either pewter or brass, were placed on the table with knives and spoons of the same materials, or of tin. Light was provided by candles in brass candlesticks, and a welcome touch of colour and fragrance, in those days of insalubrious smells, came occasionally from flowers in pots distributed about the living room.[26]

The intimate relationship between town and countryside dictated, to an appreciable extent, the occupations of the urban inhabitants. Many were engaged in agriculture, either as hired labourers or as owners of freehold and leasehold tenements. Where sheep farming predominated, it was not unusual for town dwellers to own considerable flocks which they pastured on the town common or on the slopes of the neighbouring hills. Trade was complementary, in a high degree, to the requirements of the rural population in the vicinity, and, in return, the artisans and craftsmen of the towns depended in great measure upon the farming community for their supply of raw materials. Without the animal products of byre and sty, of fold and yard, the glovers, shoemakers, chandlers, saddlers, tanners and other professional artisans would have led an extremely thin life, and the towns would have consequently declined since they depended upon these trades for much of their rents and revenues.

Apart from individual transactions, the main emporium of sale and exchange was, of course, the market and the fair. Most towns had market days two or three times a week, as well as a biannual fair held on a saint's day or during one of the recognised holidays of the Church. In the larger towns, the market was divided into smaller units, each specialising in some particular commodity such as fish, cloth, wheat or cattle, an arrangement which simplified and expedited trade. In the smaller towns, it was concentrated in the main street, principally around the market cross which became the veritable hub of activity on these occasions and the recognised rendezvous, not only of friends and business partners, but also of pickpockets, each with his own method of pilfering goods or emptying the pouches of unsuspecting neighbours. Not the least ingenious of these was the stratagem devised by a thief at Ruthin who would approach a lady, accost her as if she were an acquaintance of his from the same part of the country, apologise profusely for his mistake, and retire with his victim's purse which he had cut from her girdle during the conversation.[27]

Many towns considered it more expedient to erect market houses or halls for the purpose of trade. They were encouraged to do so partly by the obvious advantages of concentrating business under one and the same roof, and partly by the generosity and municipal patriotism of local successful business men or of those who, having made their fortunes in England, wished to become public benefactors to their native towns. A Welsh grocer of London, returning to his old home in Abergavenny, contributed two hundred marks towards the construction of a market house which was to be modelled on the one that he had already erected in Monmouth town.[28] At Grosmont, in Monmouthsire, Thomas Scudamore displayed an exceptional devotion to the best interests of the town by undertaking to build a number of shops for craftsmen in order to attract trade. He purposely went to London to purchase silk and haberdashery goods to provide stock for the yeomen whom he proposed to set up as mercers, but his enthusiasm and lack of experience led him into being tricked by a Lombard Street merchant, who sold him inferior velvet, satin, fustian and other wares, and ruined the whole scheme at the outset.[29]

Markets and fairs presented colourful and exhilarating scenes, for not only did the towns spring into life, but there was an influx of strangers and visitors from distant parts of the country, and from across the border, with goods to sell, money to spend, and news or rumours to circulate. The town authorities were naturally zealous in providing facilities for these potential customers, since the sale of goods constituted one of the principal sources of revenue for municipal administration. Apart from the toll books, in which all sales of animals had to be recorded by law—partly to counteract the prevalent habit of selling stolen cattle and partly to swell local funds—some towns had evolved their own financial devices for extracting direct contributions from those who transacted business in their markets. At Cardigan, for instance, a common balance and weights were maintained in the Town Hall and small dues levied on every commodity weighed during market hours. In addition, the bailiffs were authorised to demand from every stranger who set up a standing in the street and market place the sum of one penny. This was called the ' pitching penny ' and the proceeds were earmarked for the repair of street

pavements, the market cross and the town bridge, whereas the
dues from the common balance were expended on a variety of
municipal accessories, including the purchase of ' two maces of
silver for the Town.'[30]

At Machynlleth, again, all those concerned in the sale of
grain, salt, apples and seeds on the streets paid a certain per-
centage of their goods to the Sergeant at Mace, whose duty it
was, on behalf o the Corporation, to clean the market place,
convey the refuse away, and supply the vendors of commodities
with all the vesselage they needed for their business. Apart from
covering the expenses of their appointed scavenger, the authorities also imposed a toll of one penny at the town gates upon
each buyer and seller, which they generally farmed out at a
profit to the Corporation's funds.[31] Where such variants of
local taxation did not exist, there was always the probability
that plenty of transgressions would be committed on market
and fair days—petty thieving of goods, non-observance of local
weights and measures, dishonest dealing and so on, to direct
a steady flow of fines and amercements into the hands of the
town authorities.

On non-market days, when business affairs might be expected
to take a more quiescent turn, the trading fraternity were
permitted very little relaxation by the perennial problem of
guarding the safety of their commodities and preserving the
stability of their professions. The fight against thieves called for
unending vigilance, and although shops were generally erected
near or under the Town Hall, as if huddling there for protection, not even that venerable building, which invariably housed
the town law court and sometimes the gaol[32], could deter
hardened malefactors from breaking in. Larceny was not
always the work of individual shopbreakers. Denbigh traders
were plagued by a gang of youths who were adepts at cutting
holes through walls, or slipping into shops and hiding under
the counter at lighting-up time, when the proprietor moment-
arily turned his back to fetch candles. All the penalties
sanctioned by the law—whipping, the stocks, the pillory,
branding with hot iron, the gibbet, seemed powerless to reduce

the incidence of petty thieving in the towns, amongst old and young alike.

A further annoyance was the infiltration of unqualified people into the jealously preserved occupations of craftsmen and tradesmen. The Statute of Artificers, passed in 1563, had expressly decreed that no one could exercise a craft unless he had studied it as an apprentice for seven years. And certain towns had added the corollary that no person could enter a profession within their liberties without the licence and authority of the burgesses. Both decrees were ignored to the consternation of the local tradesmen, who discovered time and time again that their ranks contained glovers, tailors and particularly alehouse keepers carrying on their business without the slightest pretence to legality. The unlicensed tavern keepers were the objects of bitter resentment, for they were responsible more often than not for selling bread and ale at enhanced prices, thus infringing the Assize of Bread and other statutory regulations which aimed at stabilising the cost of living.

Yet another and more troublesome problem was the reprehensible practice of some tradespeople themselves to corner the market in some important commodity and inflate prices by organising an artificial scarcity. The Government regarded this ' forestalling ' of goods as a heinous crime against the welfare of the country, but despite many Parliamentary statutes and penalties the municipal authorities were helpless to prevent it. Newport and Tenby were but two of the market towns in Pembrokeshire where hides were sold at exorbitantly high prices before the culprits were brought to heel,[33] and Holt, in Denbighshire, seems to have been the scene of considerable engrossing of corn and victuals.

In Wales, as in England, the towns continued to preserve the tradition and, to some extent, the substance of that local autonomy which they had enjoyed in the Middle Ages. The military and political events of the past two centuries had undoubtedly left their imprint on the urban communities established in Wales to serve as bases for the extension of Royal authority, but they had not impaired the outward forms of municipal government and the special privileges associated with them. The pacification of the country, followed by the Act of Union and the liquidation of the remnants of a super-annuated feudal order in the Welsh Marches, restored their old sense of freedom to the towns and encouraged their inhabitants to make fuller use of the organs of self-government in their own interests.

Municipal authority resided in a compact hierarchy of officials, composed of a mayor, aldermen and bailiffs, supported by a common council. These dignitaries were chosen annually by the burgesses or, where the corporation was a close, co-optive oligarchy, selected by members of that body from amongst themselves. The method of choosing burgesses also varied from town to town, but most of them were drawn from the more reputable and wealthier class of tradesmen and free-holders. Occasionally they represented a mere minority of the townspeople, a situation which often fomented internal discord and an estrangement between the privileged and non-en-franchised citizens.[34]

The jurisdictional powers exercised by the mayor and his officials were quite extensive, and there was a variety of municipal courts to deal with offences committed within the town liberties, and to enforce the fulfilment of civic duties by burgesses and other classes. At Haverfordwest, for instance, the mayor was empowered to hold two ordinary courts every fortnight, and a third—the ' Pie-Powder Court ' on special occasions to supervise the activities of strangers and to control transactions whenever fairs were held in the town.[35] A similar accumulation of legal functions was attached to the office of Bailiff of Brecon, which approximated in dignity and influence to the mayoralty of other towns, if it did not actually exceed it, since its holder was also Escheator and Treasurer of the borough.[36] Aldermen, too, were invested sometimes with legal powers, as at Denbigh, where they had the right to interrogate transgressors and commit them to gaol upon suspicion,[37] and where custom dictated that aldermen retiring from office should be elected coroners for the following year.[38]

A number of responsible officials existed to attend to the routine of local government, and to maintain the proper measure of municipal ceremoniousness. Amongst others, there were the Recorders and Common Clerks or Chief Notaries, who were expected to be qualified lawyers and to assist the mayor in trying cases ; there were the Constables who kept the peace, arranged the nightly watch and undertook other police duties ; there were the Sergeants at Mace who executed verdicts and arrests and attended upon the mayor and the council, carrying their maces engraved with gold or silver and adorned with the arms of the realm. All had their specific and regulated duties to perform, although these did not conform to one unchangeable pattern. The coroner at Machynlleth, for example, was charged with the extra responsibility of seeing that the stallholders at the fairs used the correct yard measure to sell their goods. And at Cardiff, the bailiff was called on to act as town crier, and to proclaim at the market cross the quantity of wares for sale and the prices fixed for them.[39]

The many gradations of town officials were not a dispendable luxury of the Elizabethan age. They reflected, and corresponded to, the multiplicity of duties imposed by local government. As an autonomous unit, the town was responsible for the efficient operation of every form of public service conceivable in those days. The constant repairing of roads and bridges, the upkeep of town mills and common bakehouses, the removal of garbage and the maintenance of a civic charnel house or morgue, the provision of an adequate force to deal with thieves, the control of gaming houses and the prevention of too blatant prostitution, the regular supply of essential foodstuffs, the employment of the poor on useful work—these were some of the daily problems calling for the attention of the town authorities. Their energy in dealing with them was manifested in a plethora of measures controlling and regimenting the lives of their co-citizens in every possible sphere, and culminating, at Carmarthen, in what must be one of the first recorded Sunday Closing Acts. In 1582, the publicans of that town were forbidden to serve customers or to allow tippling on their premises during the hours of divine service.[40]

D*

A problem that was never far from the thoughts of the urban officials was the constant danger of plague and how to moderate its lethal effects, since its prevention was considered totally unrealistic. No one, not even the most practical-minded Government official, had thought of adopting an Italian regulation noted by the Welshman, Robert Parry of Denbighshire, during his visit to Italy in 1600. The Italians refused to admit travellers and strangers into their city states unless they had ' bulletins,' which testified that they had come from places free of plague. Visitors without these bulletins were put into quarantine, and obliged to lodge for forty days, at their own expense, in houses or hostelries outside the city gates. The idea, said Parry in his diary, would have seemed strange to people in Britain. No doubt, but it might have saved many lives.[41]

As it was, the inhabitants of the Welsh towns had to suffer the visitations of the plague with resignation and apply the remedies best known to them. When even densely populated towns like Denbigh permitted open middens at the back of houses, and the accumulation of dirt and garbage in the streets, there was little hope of evading the pestilence. But some towns made an effort to combat the deadly disease. At Beaumaris, for instance, the town council had realised that public sanitation was the key to sound public health and the best antidote to plague-breeding conditions. Unlike some other authorities, they took practical steps to improve it. Officials known as scavangers were appointed to survey the streets at least once a week, and to note whether they were in good repair and kept clean. In the case of dirty streets and lanes, they were authorised to summon the residents to clean them and to report any negligence on their part.[42] At Conway, too, it was part of the duty of the aldermen to examine the state of the streets and to see to it that they were not over-encumbered with filth.[43]

Carmarthen Corporation was particularly vigilant in the matter of public cleanliness, and some of its measures bordered on the draconic. When the least responsible section of the citizens took to washing coal and culm, as well as filthy buckets and barrels, in the water of the town conduits, which had been reserved for victuals, the populace were forbidden to wash anything with this water upon pain of imprisonment. The prohibition bore hardly on the housewives who had been accustomed to wash the family laundry and dinner vegetables, parsnips, carrots, beans and so on at the conduits. Other measures were directed towards preventing swine from running about the streets or rooting in the mounds of filth exposed there. And carters and carriers who transported victuals to the market on horseback were ordered to take their animals outside the town as soon as they had unloaded their wares, in order to avoid adding to the sounds and smells which were prejudicial to the nerves and health of the inhabitants.[44] In Haverfordwest, too, the authorities were not unmindful of the dangers emanating from refuse heaps, and paid men regularly to clean the shambles or meat stalls under the Shire Hall.[45]

George Owen described some Welsh towns as being ' indifferent for intertaignements.' The studious squire ot Henllys, in Pembrokeshire, was probably lamenting the inadequacy of comfortable lodgings, and the difficulty sometimes of finding any accommodation at all. In such an emergency, it was customary for travellers to request a night's lodging in private houses, and the traditional hospitality of the Welsh generally overcame the lurking suspicions that the innocent looking stranger might turn out to be a thief, which was only too often the case.

But other forms of entertainment were conspicuously lacking. Unlike English towns, for instance, there was a singular absence of organised pageantry and presentation of mystery plays and interludes based on scenes from the Holy Scriptures. The town of Wrexham was an exception, since it had its company of interluders who not only entertained their fellow townsmen, but occasionally performed before audiences at Shrewsbury, where they were paid for their acting in money and wine.[46] Haverfordwest Corporation also was activated by a sentiment of sympathy for its citizens who were at a loss for distractions. It maintained a company of waits to entertain them with music and song, and clothed them at the public's expense in liveries of grey frieze faced with green taffeta and ornamented with green moccado and green buttons.[47]

Sometimes the soporific atmosphere of a Welsh town would be disturbed by the sudden appearance of a menagerie. At least, the visit of a camel to Newtown in Montgomeryshire, in 1601, seems to have created a commotion, for people streamed in from the countryside to view the strange animal that was kept in a room at the local hostelry, and to sit on its back.[48] Occasionally, bands of itinerant musicians and jugglers would perform in the streets, but apart from fortuitous visits of this kind, it would be true to say that the townsman relaxed or sought his entertainment in drinking with boon companions, paying his ' schotte ' or contribution to the collective bill after the session, dicing, card-playing, or alternatively whiling his time away in conversation and scandalmongering in the town taverns.

The variety of consumer goods which the town shops were able to offer their customers showed the extraordinary rapidity with which internal trade was progressing and expanding. Whereas the medieval merchant in Wales had been forced to rely on locally produced wares, except in a few coastal or riparian towns supplied by sea, the Elizabethan merchant in Wales could take advantage of improved overland communications and more widespread business contacts to obtain a wider selection of commodities, particularly from London, Bristol, Chester and other English commercial centres. His role in encouraging and enabling all classes of people to cultivate a taste for quality and fashion was an important factor in their achievement of a higher standard of living. And it was from his shop that new clothing materials, exotic foodstuffs, improved household articles and furnishings, and even luxury goods began to flow, not only to the country mansion of the squire and the town mansion of the burgher, but to the farms and homes of the well-to-do yeoman and the less pretentious husbandman.

Among the dress materials sold over the counter there were silks and silk fabrics like taffeta, moccado and grosgrain, lace of many kinds, lockram and doulas—linen cloth manufactured in the Breton towns of Locronan and Daoulas—friezes and kersies, holland cloth and lawn, fustian and cotton, chamlet and worsted, and, of course, flannel and woollen cloth. Merchants specialised in the sale of pepper, cloves, saffron, ginger, raisins, sugar, comfits, soap, paper, pins, train oil—the boiled blubber of whales used as ointment—earpicks, pipes, ribbons and similar consumer goods, some of which were now regarded as everyday necessities. Cappers were making a good living, even in remote rural towns like Trecastle in Brecknock, out of velvet and worsted nightcaps and felt hats.[49] To these goods must be added numerous other items in footwear, domestic utensils, furniture, and personal ornaments, each producing incontestable evidence that the inhabitants of the Welsh town and countryside alike were benefiting from the growing prosperity of the times and realising an improvement in their standard of living.

The principal beneficiaries, of course, were the merchants themselves, some of whom made considerable fortunes and occasionally spent them on purchasing or leasing land. For although their profession was trade, they unreservedly accepted the criterion that it was the amount of property in a man's possession, not so much his money, that established his status and influence in society. And so it was that a Brecon merchant, with a fortune of £2,500, invested a substantial proportion of it in land so that, after his death, his family should enjoy some eminence as members of the propertied class.[50]

It is likely that the more far-sighted among the Welsh burgesses welcomed the extension of the parliamentary franchise to county towns conceded by the Act of Union. Their commercial prosperity was becoming so integrated with the nascent capitalist evolution of England, that any legislation affecting the industries and trade of that country was bound to have repercussions upon Welsh mercantile interests. To safeguard these, by supporting the economic measures proposed by people of the same class and opinions as themselves at Westminster, presented advantages which they were not slow to appreciate. Moreover, it offered one method of counteracting the influence of the gentry who had little regard for townsmen at home, but had to recognise the equality and immunity of their representatives in the House of Commons.

Not all the gentry were prepared to do this, and found it difficult to grasp the fact that burgesses could have a mind of their own, and adopt an attitude independent of the pressure of family ambitions and feuds which were so often the decisive factor in the election of the knights of the shire. A struggle ensued in which the reactionary section of the aristocracy attempted to force its will on the towns in the matter of selecting members for Parliament. In 1572, for example, the Earl of Leicester, who held the lordship of Denbigh, was infuriated that the burgesses of Denbigh should have ventured to choose one of their number without prior consultation with him. He ordered them immediately to invalidate the election and nominate a person approved by him.[51]

Where two principal towns within the same shire vied with one another in importance and pretensions, elections were apt to provoke ill-feeling and underhand intrigues. The same election that had precipitated the clash between the Salisbury and Trefor factions in Denbighshire, saw a neat piece of trickery in Cardiganshire. The burgesses of the town of Cardigan claimed that they alone were authorised to elect a burgess member, and accordingly returned a Mr. Delabarre. The sheriff of Cardiganshire, however, had other ideas and surreptitiously despatched the election writ to Aberystwyth, whose citizens, itching to administer a snub to their Teivyside rivals, elected a Dr. Aubrey. The sheriff sent an indenture to that effect post-haste to Westminster, mendaciously adding to it that Aubrey had been elected by both Aberystwyth and Cardigan. He was too late. Mr. Delabarre had already taken his seat, whereupon Dr. Aubrey complained to the Committee of Privileges. An enquiry was set on foot, but the whole matter was complicated by the fact that the Assizes were held alternately at both towns. Which of them therefore had the right to elect a burgess member? The Committee entered into an interminable discussion on this point, but Delabarre, a lawyer, said nothing and kept his seat until Parliament was dissolved.[52]

The Welsh burgess members were, on the whole, a quiescent bunch of backbenchers, and rarely intervened in the debates on the floor of the House of Commons. But William Maurice of Clenennau, Member of Parliament for Beaumaris, did create a commotion on one occasion in 1601. He rose to complain that on his way to London to attend the House, his servant had been arrested and imprisoned by the bailiff and sergeants of Shrewsbury, despite his plea that he enjoyed immunity as an employee of a Member of Parliament. The House fulminated against this disregard of its privileges and liberties. There were indignant cries of ' To the Tower with them.! Send for them ! ' The arrest of the offending officials was unanimously decided upon, but when tempers had cooled, it was discovered that Maurice's man had only accompanied his master as far as Shrewsbury, and had no intention of proceeding all the way to London. Besides he had been arrested for debt, which put a different complexion on the affair. When the aggrieved Member for Beaumaris raised the matter again, the House quietly passed on to other business.[53]

Parliamentary elections produced their periodic excitements, but the attention and energy of the citizens were reserved for the conflicts and complexities of town politics. Here, again, it was not a question of a difference of theory about town government. Its structure and functional offices had been strictly defined in the charter of incorporation, and the innate conservatism of the burgesses guaranteed their immutability. It was the authority invested in municipal administration that interested them, and the opportunity it afforded for exercising personal influence and promoting private affairs—in accordance, of course, with the highest traditions of the towns and mindful of their liberties and status. And, in fact, there were no more tenacious protagonists of these liberties than the people who wrangled, disputed and fought with one another for pre-eminence inside the dignified town and guild halls, which reflected the self-assurance and prosperity of their class.

They not infrequently jeopardised their lives by doing so, particularly when the neighbouring gentry conceived a dislike for them or tried to intervene in municipal politics by supporting one faction against the other or by imposing their own candidates for office.   Interference in town affairs became a fixation with some of the squirearchy, and the citizens were hard put to it to keep the aristocratic intruders at arm's length. When the burgesses of Newport, in Monmouthshire, assembled to elect a mayor for the year 1581, the proceedings were rudely interrupted by a number of local squires and their armed followers who attacked those present, overthrew the table upon which the town records had been placed, frightened the recorder into an undignified flight, and made it abundantly clear that they had a hearty objection to seeing Newport blessed with a mayor at all.[54]

The Newport burgesses seem to have been more alarmed than hurt.   Not so the citizens of Denbigh who had incurred the enmity of Sir John Salisbury. At one time, Sir John had been on terms of the closest amity with the town, and had vociferously championed its liberties ; in return, he had been allowed to control the appointment of aldermen and bailiffs.[55]   The feelings of the squire of Llewenni underwent a meteoric change, however, when Denbigh was made a free borough by Royal Charter, and the very aldermen he had nominated, elevated to the position of Justices of the Peace, with the exclusive right of exercising that jurisdictional office inside the town.

The eclipse of his influence in the dispensation of offices, and the realisation that these in the future would be allocated according to the choice of a lot of tradesmen owing him no gratitude, drove Sir John into a paroxysm of fury in 1600. The answer was at hand—his retainers. He sent a company of them into Denbigh with injunctions to harry the man whom he considered to be the prime mover behind the anti-Salisbury campaign, a local gentleman named Humphrey Lloyd. This order was expeditiously carried out, and Lloyd's skull broken. But the outrage roused the townspeople who seized its author and threw him into the town gaol. Regarding this as a sign of lack of respect for their old patron, Sir John hurled his men against the prison, but the door held despite the ' pushing and bouncinge at the said dore.' The town had won the first round, but Sir John awaited an opportunity for retaliation. It came when the people of Denbigh were holding one of their fairs, and were engrossed in their business. The unexpected onslaught of the Llewenni retainers swept them off their feet, and their stalls and holdings off their legs. There was utter confusion, citizens were bludgeoned right and left, and when the authorities appealed to Sir John to call off his men, the worthy knight replied curtly but with obvious satisfaction, ' Let them alone ! Let them knocke the knaves ! ' But it was his last attempt to regain a political influence that had been irretrievably lost.[56]

When they were left in peace by meddling squires, the townspeople found plenty of pretexts to break up the united front which they usually presented to outside interference. One thorny question that obtruded again and again into municipal politics was whether non-natives should be allowed to enjoy the same liberties as the indigenous citizen, and occupy posts of authority and trust in town administration.[57] There was open discussion on this point, since the traditional suspicion of strangers, except when they bought or sold goods in the town market, was taking a long time to evaporate, even in the liberalising atmosphere of the sixteenth century. Where it was firmly entrenched, especially in the old boroughs where the Welsh burgesses were as jealous of their privileges as their English predecessors had been, there was little infiltration of aliens into office. In some of the border towns, however, the position was different.

Whether it was due to the insidious effects of anglicisation or to the deep rooted instability of life and custom in the old Welsh Marches, there was more inclination to compromise on this question of the rights of ' foreigners.' For instance, in the borough of Blaenllyfni, in Brecknock, the seventy six burgesses had divided into two camps over the appointment of a bailiff. One had elected a native of the town to the office, the other a rank outsider. The result was that both bailiffs were engaged in the full-time work of preventing one another from holding courts and attending to their proper duties.[58] Much the same thing went on at New Radnor, where a dissident m'nority of the burgesses had flouted the decisions of the common council by electing 'foreigners' from Ludlow and Newtown, in Herefordshire, to fill the vacancies on that body caused by the death of members or their removal to other towns.[59] Economic and family reasons may have exerted a pressure here, for there was an increasing association between the Welsh countryside and the English market towns along the border, strengthened by marriage links between the gentry and by trading contacts between the farming and business communities.

There were occasions, of course, when town politics resolved themselves into a struggle between rival factions, intent on denying one another the fruits of office.[60] When David Rede was nominated by the burgesses of Carmarthen in 1573 to succeed Richard Phillips, the outgoing mayor, Phillips took to the idea so unkindly that he decided to engineer his re-appointment for a second term. On the day of the election, as soon as the burgesses had congregated in the guild hall, he showed his hand by refusing to lay the Corporation maces and sword on the table, as custom dictated. Despite this show of recalcitrance, Rede was chosen by a majority of voices. It was the signal for both parties to drop constitutional procedure. The recorder, one of Phillips's henchmen, leaped on to a bench, took out a book and began to administer the oath of office to the rejected mayor. Griffith ap Owen, one of the Rede faction, attempted to seize the book and, according to one report, to take hold of Phillips by the beard at the same time. He failed in both objectives and was thrown to the ground. During the fracas, Phillips kissed the book without troubling to repeat the oath of the Royal Supremacy, or indeed any other of the many oaths which the law demanded of him as coroner, Justice of the Peace, clerk of the market and other offices undertaken by him as mayor of Carmarthen. Finally, he assembled his partisans and marched out through the back door of the hall, still retaining the maces and sword. But two hundred burgesses remained behind to overstrain the political instability of an already distracted town by electing Rede as a rival mayor with a duplicate set of administrative officials.[61]

As if factional rivalries were not enough to disturb and disrupt the orderly conduct of town life, the ordinary citizens had sometimes to defend themselves against the dictatorial attitude of urban officialdom. The temptation to take decisions without consideration for other classes and opinions was an irresistible one to those in the highest ranks of the municipal hierarchy, who attended primarily to their own interests, and were inclined to act arbitrarily in matters relating to the general welfare of the community which they assumed to control.

The reaction they provoked was not always one of passive resistance. In Denbigh, it verged on an armed revolt in 1599. There the aldermen and bailiffs had promulgated a series of orders which were regarded as an affront by a minority of the burgesses. They had been compelled to pay fourpence to the borough gaoler for every burgess committed to his care for debt or misdemeanour. Moreover, any failure on their part to appear on juries was punishable by an amercement which— and this seems to have increased their resentment—was not paid into the Corporation fund for the benefit of the town, but allocated towards the repair of the parish church.

The discontented element rallied round a self-appointed leader, Jenkin Atkinson, whose pugnacity was well served by an uncontrollable tongue. Summoned before the town council to give an account of certain threats made by him publicly, he launched a violent attack on his accusers, and declared his intention of organising a ' mutany ' with the assistance of his friends unless their grievances were redressed. It was an ugly word to use, and a positively dangerous one in view of the well-known partiality of many Denbighshire men for the Catholic religion and the Queen's enemies. The case immediately assumed a political complexion, and despite Atkinson's protestations of loyalty to the Crown, he was charged with treasonable motives. Whether this was true or not, his confederates abandoned him, and there was no further dispute about the financial measures which had threatened to let loose a minor civil war on the streets of Denbigh.[62]

The entry of Welshmen into town life coincided with the gradual decline of the craft guilds which had played a conspicuous role in the economy of medieval towns. The confiscation of guild property by the Crown in the reign of Edward VI, the extension of State control over conditions of trade and employment, the new expansionist capitalism which demanded free competition and the removal of restrictions on movement and transactions, were all factors that eventually turned the guilds into anachronistic institutions. But they did not entirely lose their influence or usefulness in the towns of Wales, no more than they did in London, where seventy nine artisan and guild companies accounted for some eight thousand employees and employers during the reign of Elizabeth.[63]

In Wales, artisans were still expected to become members of the guilds representing their specialised crafts, although it became increasingly difficult to enforce this regulation outside the towns. There were few towns which did not have a substantial number of trade fraternities, with the usual hierarchy of masters, journeymen and apprentices. Although the control of wages and prices, and even the ordinances affecting the employment of apprentices and their conditions of work, were passing into the hands of the Justices of the Peace and other Crown officials, the guilds still enjoyed much respect. In Brecon, for instance, they were influential enough to arrange that the lower end of the parish church should be set aside for the burial of some of their members, and it was here that the tuckers of that town were laid to rest under tombstones upon which were carved the figures of a comb and shears, to designate their craft.[64]

They were also convinced that even the most menial trades were conformable with the enjoyment of social privileges. A member of the shoemakers' guild at Carmarthen went hunting and hawking regularly in the neighbourhood. And they would certainly tolerate no insult to the dignity of their calling. When the son of a Brecon shoemaker was elected a chamberlain of the town, and empowered to collect the money due to the Crown for incorporating it as a borough, his father's profession was thrown into his face by a servant of the redoubtable family of the Games, who could never refrain from being offensive to the citizens of Brecon. He was arrested on the spot and thrown into the town gaol.[65]

In some towns a serious effort was made to infuse new vigour into moribund guilds, and to liquidate abuses and irregularities which were undermining their reputation for good workmanship and honesty. Nowhere was the expurgation of malpractices and shoddy goods more thoroughly undertaken than at Carmarthen. The authorities systematically reorganised every craft fraternity within the town, and laid down express injunctions how they were to conduct their affairs and exercise their responsibilities. The corporation nominated their members, regularised the election of their officers, established the procedure for the eligibility and admittance of apprentices as masters, and explicitly stated what were the criteria for good craftsmanship. The shoemakers, for instance, were expected to sew footwear ' with good twisted Threade and waxe well rosened and the Stitches hard drawne with hand lethers.'

To protect the rejuvenated guilds against outside competition, the corporation of Carmarthen guaranteed that no one but members of the fraternities should sell their products, and introduced measures to guard against the illegal entry of both native burgesses and ' foreigners ' into their specialised markets. This protectionist policy had much in its favour. In the case of the tuckers, fullers and clothworkers of the town, it removed the fear of unemployment and impoverishment which had long oppressed them. For many years, some of the wealthier inhabitants had turned their homes into workshops, in which they employed unqualified men to process cloth. This intrusion into an industry which demanded a high degree of skill and efficiency was now stopped, and the manufacture of cloth entrusted to the skilled artificers who were capable of dealing with it. In the same way, the guild of leatherworkers was indebted to the corporation for its intervention. The encroachment of unqualified people on their trade and profession, and their offer of higher wages, had enticed so many apprentices away that they despaired of being able to carry on. Borough corporations could often be accused of a blind attachment to antiquated restrictive practices, but the solicitude of the mayor and council of Carmarthen for a high standard of work and the welfare of professional craftsmen could only redound to the benefit of the inhabitants and the economic life of the town.[66]

At Cardiff, too, the interests of the guilds were not neglected. In 1589, for instance, the privileges and special rights of the fraternity of cordwainers and glovers were reaffirmed and publicised for the benefit of its members and of those outsiders who may have judged the time propitious to enter into competition with the guild on its own ground. In addition to warning the latter that free enterprise in the manufacture and sale of footwear and gloves was not to be tolerated in Cardiff, this confirmation of their recognised trading privileges was intended to rouse a readier appreciation of their status and obligations among the members of the guild. There may very well have been some laxity in their observance of the rules of the fraternity, especially those bearing upon their attendance and behaviour at the meetings in the guild's hall, and upon the relationship between masters, journeymen and apprentices. There may also have been a distressing tendency among some members to indulge in a little clandestine free market activity by setting up shops and booths outside the town, in the church-yards and under the church porches of the neighbouring parishes.

But what was particularly interesting in this case was the renewed emphasis laid upon the democratic character of the discussions and deliberations whenever the fraternity met to consider its affairs. All decisions were to be taken by a majority vote, and those who refused to abide by them were to be fined for their recalcitrance. But so intent was the guild on securing the maximum individual participation in the discussions, and inculcating a sense of responsibility among its members when their interests were affected, that anyone who left the general meeting before the agenda was exhausted, laid himself open to a heavy fine.[67]

There was an influential shoemakers guild at Ruthin whose records show how the fraternity regulated the activities of its members, and sought to protect the monopoly of their craft and trade against encroachments by outsiders. In the reign of Henry VII, the guild had secured a valuable concession from the lord of Ruthin, the Earl of Kent. In return for a fine of twenty shillings and an annual rent of four shillings, it had been awarded the sole right to make and sell footwear in the town, and to impose a penalty of £5 on any person who dared to do so without its consent. The arrangement had worked well for some time, but a few decades later there was an invasion of 'forriners' on market and fair days, who sold stocks of shoes and boots and threatened to jeopardise the closed shop system of the guild. It was advised to offer a further fine to the lord of Ruthin for a reaffirmation of the old concession. This time the price was higher ; a lump sum of £5 and an annual rent of twenty five shillings. But it guaranteed the exclusion of the detested poachers.

The guild also drew the attention of its members to the obligation of observing certain basic regulations. Once a month they were to keep their ' quarterledge ' or general meeting in one of their wardens' homes, and a full attendance was expected. Anyone failing to appear without good reason was fined two shillings, half of which went to the guild box, and half towards repairing the parish church. Strict obedience to the wardens and stewards of the fraternity was exacted from all. If any member became refractory, these officials were authorised to enter his house or shop and distrain his footwear or raw materials until he had paid a fine of two shillings. For those who overtly challenged the authority of the guild or the validity of its rules, the punishment was more severe, for it amounted to immediate suspension. The dread sentence of expulsion was reserved for the master or journeyman who undertook the private manufacture of footwear for individual clients, and thereby transgressed the sacrosanct guild law that the conditions of work, in quality and quantity, were collectively binding on all members.

Half the fines inflicted for non-compliance with these rules went into the guild's box or funds which were used to defray all manner of expenses. These seem to have increased substantially, for in 1570, many of the richer members were requested to advance money to meet them. Only half the loans were repaid the following year, but the financial position was only one of the worries that disturbed the fraternity. Various abuses were creeping in, and their nature can be discerned from the two amended rules promulgated during these years. The first stipulated that no master was to allow shoes to be made by a journeyman in the latter's home. They were to be cut and sewn on the master's premises. The second concerned apprentices, and stated specifically that seven years was the minimum period of apprenticeship. Henceforth the date of the indenture or contract of apprenticeship was to be entered into a book kept by the guild's stewards, so that there would be written evidence that the apprentice had served his term, was eligible for the ' freedom ' of the guild, and could set up as a qualified shoemaker in Ruthin. Evidently some masters had falsified dates and committed other serious breaches of the guild's regulations. It was this treachery within the ranks that weakened the resistance of this and other craft guilds against the pressure of aggressive State and private capitalism.[68]

The trading fraternity of the Welsh towns was probably as hard-headed and perspicacious as any other business community within the realm, but in general its members were content to profit through the recognised channels from the unprecedented commercial activity that filled their lives. To some, however, the possibility of acquiring easy money by dangerous experiments in fraud and financial irregularities was a constant temptation. To tamper with these was a risk which could lead to personal disaster, as Roger Symonds of Ruthin was to experience.

Symonds was a respectable feltmaker who had served his apprenticeship in London and had established a flourishing shop of his own in Ruthin. He was able to employ a journeyman who disposed of his hats in the fairs and markets of North Wales, and to maintain a wife, a serving-man and a maid to attend to his domestic comforts. It was around Whitsun, in

1586, that the orderly progress of his affairs took a calamitous turn, when he chanced to meet with one of the most Mephistophelian characters who had ever crossed Offa's Dyke to inveigle Welshmen into the path of metallurgical perdition.

This person, Launcelot Browne, was to show that he possessed singularly few of the reputed virtues of his illustrious Arthurian predecessor. His antecedents were extremely doubtful. A native of Yorkshire, he claimed to have enjoyed six years of schooling before being apprenticed to a Welsh haberdasher in Cornhill, London. From there he had entered the service of a Lincolnshire squire, and had mastered the craft of fowling with gun and net. There was strong circumstantial evidence that he had become a specialist in other arts as well, notably that of counterfeiting the Royal currency, for his master's brother had found himself in serious trouble for coining false money. Browne's subsequent peregrinations had taken him to Ireland, where he confessed later to having filled the pockets of an impecunious Irish knight with money which had certainly not issued from any Royal mint. Eventually he had crossed the sea to Wales, and had managed to attach himself to the household of Edward Lloyd, the squire of Llysfasi. He had worn his livery as a servant for some time when he called one day at Symonds's shop to discuss the innocuous subject of trimming one of his employer's hats.

A friendship struck up between the two, which Browne fostered sedulously with gifts of wild fowl from his periodic shooting excursions in the woods around Ruthin. He was cordially invited to eat the pies, which appear to have been the invariable recipe for such birds, and it was during a particularly successful meal that he put forward a proposition which he had been meditating for some time. He offered to provide the means which would make Symonds the richer by fifty pounds a year, and produced tangible evidence of his ability to do so by taking out a counterfeit coin and challenging his host to distinguish between it and a genuine piece of the same value. Symonds's immediate reaction was to make the sign of the cross, which Browne countered with a more effective theological argument. Counterfeiting the realm's money might be a heinous crime in the eyes of man-made laws as expressed in Acts of Parliament, but it was in no way prohibited by God's law. He requested Symonds to test the validity of this assertion by repeating the Lord's Prayer and the Ten Commandments. His host was able to do so and realised, probably for the first time, that neither placed an interdiction on the unauthorised transformation of metal into coin. There was no further discussion. Symonds agreed to convert all his stock into gold and silver, and Browne undertook to produce three pounds in money for every twenty shillings' worth of silver entrusted to him.

During the days that followed, Symonds's household arrangements were violently disrupted. To ensure secrecy, he was prevailed upon to dismiss his journeyman, and to find accommodation elsewhere for his servants. Doors were secured with a variety of bolts, bars and locks. A special room in the courtyard was converted into a workshop, and Symonds's wife found herself in the humiliating position of being denied entry to that part of the house. In the meantime her husband had been despatched on various errands to procure the requisite moulds from a local joiner, and to buy tin, copper and chalk in Chester, as well as a pair of bellows. When these materials had been assembled, Browne installed himself in the house, and the confederates began to apply themselves exclusively to the operations in hand.

The atmosphere grew oppressive, and the relations between Symonds and his wife more and more strained, for it became his habit to dismiss her summarily to bed and to work into the early hours of the morning. When she ventured on one occasion to remonstrate and to suggest that Browne should be sent packing before he involved them in ruin by his nefarious schemes, she was completely cowed by the threat, ' I will sell all I have and goe with him into Ireland and leave thee behynde, for thou wilt not be contented with any that doeth me good.' She was persuaded to turn a more kindly eye on Browne, when he appeared triumphantly one morning and exhibited a number of counterfeit sixpenny pieces. Symonds was profuse with his compliments, but his colleague met them with the modest remark, ' worse stuffe might serve the country.' The number of false coins accumulated as the days went by until some twenty shillings' worth had been produced. The next step was to put them into circulation, and it was arranged that Symonds and his wife should visit individually a number of fairs in North Wales for that purpose, while Browne remained at home to entertain importunate callers and safeguard the instruments of forgery. But the plan miscarried in its initial stages, and one can only conclude that Browne's dexterity was no match for the discerning eye of the ordinary Welshman, whom circumstances had taught to turn over every piece of money carefully in more senses than one.

Symonds proceeded towards the fair at Llannerch-y-medd, in Anglesey, but on the way he called for refreshment in an alehouse at Porthaethwy. He paid for it with one of his counterfeit coins, which was returned to him immediately with a peremptory request for unadulterated money. The suspicion which fastened on him there accompanied him all the way to Llannerch-y-medd, and when he foolishly tried to get rid of the same coin the second time he was arrested and imprisoned in Caernarvon castle. His wife fared no better at Nefyn fair, in Caernarvonshire, where she had bought a cheese with false money. Within a short time she found herself in the hands of the local constables, who rummaged among her clothes with scant respect for her sex, discovered a purse full of counterfeit silver coin, and clapped her into Beaumaris castle.

The news of their arrest soon reached Ruthin. Symonds's house was straightway invaded by agitated aldermen and bailiffs, every object that could be associated with the crime was conveyed away, and Browne himself, who had lost his head and tried to hide in Symonds's stables, was routed out and committed to custody. He vociferously protested at first that he knew nothing of what had been going on in the house, then elaborated a plausible tale that he had merely used the iron ladle found there to make iron pellets for his fowling piece, and finally relapsed into a whine that if he was going to be hanged, then he knew of others in the valley of the Clwyd who were more worthy of public execution than he—for their religion.

The hint that he might produce evidence of Catholic recusancy in the neighbourhood was not lost on the local authorities, who had strict injunctions to ferret out those who remained
faithful to the old Religion. It was conjectured that Symonds,
in his turn, might have valuable information about other
counterfeiters in North Wales, and although he was tried and
condemned to death, both he and Browne were transferred to
Ludlow to be further interrogated by the Council of the Welsh
Marches. There were rumours that, properly handled, the
case might implicate people of more consequence, and that the
Crown might benefit to the tune of a thousand pounds in
amercements. This was sufficient to earn for the two culprits a
temporary respite from the horrible penalties of the law.[69]

COMMERCE AND INDUSTRY

THE sea carried the first Henry Tudor safely to the shore of
Pembrokeshire, to the relief of the expectant Welsh who
welcomed him as their leader and liberator. But they were
slow to realise that it could promote their fortunes in a more
material fashion. The picture of the North Wales littoral
towards the middle of the century is one of relative stagnation,
and even as late as 1578, the Justices of the Peace of Denbighshire were obliged to inform the Privy Council that there were
no landing places or port facilities in that shire.[1] In Flintshire,
there was only one haven capable of accommodating ships of
one hundred tons or more at full tide. There were a few creeks
which could handle barges and boats, but these were un-
inhabited except Y Foryd, near Rhuddlan, where there were
some forty houses.[2]

Neither could the other seaboard shires of Wales claim to be
very active in seafaring operations during the early years of
Elizabeth's reign. Merioneth, for instance, had only five
creeks which between them could muster seven houses and two
boats, the latter being used exclusively to ferry people across
the Mawddach estuary.[3] Cardiganshire, it is true, could boast
of two ports, Cardigan and Aberystwyth, in addition to some
five or six creeks. But when a survey of these was made in 1578,
none possessed a ship, and the existence of sand bars and other
marine obstacles prevented any vessel above ten tons from
entering most of them.[4] Pembrokeshire presented an imposing
list of thirty two ports and creeks, but only Tenby and St.
Brides had ships of sufficient tonnage to be of practical use in
overseas or coasting trade. The port of Fishguard was reduced
to such a state of impoverishment that when the harbour quay
fell into ruin in 1567, the inhabitants requested the Crown to
grant them permission to solicit money from well-wishers
towards the expenses of repairing it.[5] And despite its extensive
coastline, the merchants of Carmarthenshire had to rely upon

one sizeable ship and a handful of barks at Carmarthen, Laugharne and Burry to operate their commercial ventures.[6]

Apart from its restrictive effect upon trade, the paucity of ships resulted in a shortage of experienced mariners, and precluded any appreciable contribution to the naval defence of the realm in the early days of Elizabeth. It may have come as a shock to the Government to realise that the western seaboard of Wales, prior to 1570, could not be relied upon to provide more than some three ships and four hundred master mariners and seamen.[7] The situation did not materially improve in North Wales even during the years of counter-attack and vigilance after the destruction of the Armada. When the Privy Council ordered a muster of all able-bodied sailors between the ages of 16 and 65 in Caernarvonshire, to meet the constant threat of Spanish invasion, it was estimated that there were only fifty two men and youths who could qualify for the review. In any case the inspection proved a fiasco. The men of Nefyn refused to put in an appearance, a number of Justices of the Peace, nominated to supervise the muster at Conway, stayed away on the pretext of ill-health, and the whole affair, designed to impress the shire with the danger of Spanish aggressiveness, was carried out with intemperate speed.[8]

Deep-sea fishing, which the Government was at pains to foster as a nursery for experienced seamen, was confined to a few scattered communities. Pembrokeshire boats, for instance, of between eight and twelve tons and carrying a crew of four, made regular visits to the Severn estuary and the coasts of North Wales and Ireland. The merchants of Tenby occasionally ventured further afield, and invested their money in fishing expeditions to Newfoundland. But they were not always concerned whether their ship actually cast its nets along the famous Banks or despoiled other ships of their fish. The ship *Thesus*, which set out for the Banks in 1563, appeared instead at Orkney, where it intercepted an unsuspecting Flemish boat and forced its crew to surrender a hundred barrels of herrings. Further north, at Fair Isle, a Hamburg bark was rifled of stockfish and dry cod, and a third ship lost its haul of ling and wet cod before the crew of the *Thesus* decided that they had made a fair profit without over-exerting themselves. And, in fact, the fish sold well at Tenby with the exception of the herrings which were 'unpacked, ungyld, very yellow to behold and withowte any pickle.'[9]

Herring fishing predominated along the wide sweep of Cardigan Bay, where crews of six or seven in five-ton boats pursued the shoals during the weeks that followed on Michaelmas. A most interesting institution was associated with this season of intense activity between St. David's Head and Bardsey Island. All the vessels engaged in it, and they came from all parts of the kingdom, anchored in the creek of Dyfi, in Merioneth. There the crews elected their 'Admiral' who, in accordance with custom, was entrusted with the duties of deciding disputes between crews and imposing fines for the violation of regulations agreed to by the assembled fishermen. In return, he received a sum of money from each ship according to its size and equipment. This improvised system of discipline and mutual co-operation worked smoothly enough until a clash occurred between the fishermen and the Vice-Admiral of Merioneth over the question of jurisdiction. The crews offered open resistance to the Crown's officer, whereupon the latter had fourteen of them arrested and bound over to appear on charges of insubordination.[10]

Interest in seafaring activities quickened appreciably in the seventies and following decades, particularly in South Wales. Many Welshmen began to acquire a positive taste for seamanship, and took a prominent part in the naval expeditions and voyages of discovery which exasperated the Spaniards and finally goaded them into the disaster of the Armada. When Sir Humphrey Gilbert sailed on his voyage to seek for the elusive North-west Passage in 1578, one of his fleet's vessels was commanded by Miles Morgan, of the eminent Tredegar family, and the crew included a number of Monmouthshire gentlemen.[11] Sir Humphrey was on terms of warm friendship with Sir Edward Stradling, whose wife had nursed him during a bout of illness,[12] and it is possible that Sir Edward was instrumental in publicising his schemes in South Wales and encouraging volunteers to join him. Then there was John Morgan, a gentleman of Carmarthen, who was instructed by the Government in 1571 to proceed with two ships to discover whether the Spaniards were sending soldiers and emissaries to Ireland to foment insurrection against the English administration throughout that country. Morgan made for the port of Vigo, in north-west Spain, but there is no indication that he returned with military information, whatever else of Spanish origin he may have picked up and brought back with him.[13]

Another Welshman, who showed exemplary courage and initiative, was David Gwyn, a boatswain on a merchant ship to Spain. Arriving in that country sometime in 1580, he considered it his duty to obtain as much information as was possible on the dispositions and strength of the Spanish fleet. He journeyed across the country to the Groyne, better known as the port of Corunna, where the Spanish ships lay, and spent some time there noting everything of interest, completely unaware that he, in turn, was being spied on by Englishmen in the pay of the Spanish King.   He completed his investigations and inadvisedly entrusted his confidential report to a Harwich captain, who must have been in sympathy with, or had been intimidated by, the traitors, for Gwyn was arrested before he could leave Corunna. Nothing is known of his fate, but it can well be imagined, for he was sent to the House of the Inquisition at St. James in Galicia, ' where the Lorde knoweth his Ende,' as one report dolefully recorded.[14]

Concurrently with such activities there was an increasing expansion in the overseas trade of South Wales, which tended to gravitate more and more towards the ports of Glamorgan. The explanation lay in the tremendous impetus given to commercial operations on both sides of the Bristol Channel by the emergence of Bristol as the emporium of Western England.   Other important factors were the opening up of the sea lanes to the markets of Western Europe and the Mediterranean, the illimitable prospects of self-enrichment by exploration and exploitation in the New World, and also by the development of industries and exportable commodities in the Welsh shires bordering on the sea.

With these geographical and economic factors in their favour the ports of South Wales forged ahead rapidly in the expansion of their coastal and overseas trade. Those in Pembrokeshire were fortunate in being at the converging point of many trade routes—from Ireland, south-west England and the Continent. In addition to coal from the local mines, they exported Newfoundland fish to France, friezes to Portugal, wool and lamb, goat, martin and polecat skins to Bristol, cereals to North Wales and oysters to Barnstaple and Ilfracombe.[15]

Oysters were a delicacy much in demand, and Milford had an abundance of them. The choicest were obtained from the beds in Pennar creek, on the shelf known as the Crow, where they were collected by dredgers. The dredging was done,

' with a kinde of Iron made with barres, havinge a peece of horse or bullocke skynne sowed to yt like a bagge in such sort as that it being fastened to a ropes end is cast into the bottom of Milford at VIII or X fathome deepe, and is dragged at a bootes end by two rowers which rowe up and downe the channell, and so the bagge of leather, being made apte to scrape up all manner of thinges lyeing in the bottome, gathereth up the oysters that breede there over certaine knowne bedds, which bagge being filled they drawe up and emptie their oysters into their boate, applyeing their labour so all daye, and when they have done they rowe to some appointed place neare the shoare at full sea, and there cast out the oysters in a great heape which they call beds, where everye tide overfloweth them, and so are kepte for ladinge of boates to Bristol and other places.'[16]

Oysters were an important ingredient in the diet of the poorer classes, but most of them found their way to south-west England. There were other beds near Angle Bay, and a large one estimated to be a mile in length between Caldey Island and the mainland.[17]

In return, the Pembrokeshire ports received salt from France and Portugal, haberdashery from Bristol, cloth from Brittany and livestock from Ireland, more especially horses.[18] This trade grew appreciably from year to year, supplemented with consignments of horseshoes and spurs, and was valued more

E

than any other. Wales was not a country that bred horses of quality, although some shires like Montgomeryshire had formerly been famed for their horses.[19] By the end of the century, so many Pembrokeshire people were engaged in trade that it was accounted one of the principal means of livelihood. George Owen, the squire of Henllys, wrote of his own shire,

> ' The Countrey, especiallye of late years, is fallen much to trade to sea, and a great parte of the Countrye people are seamen and maryners . . . many of them contynuallye abroade at sea.'[20]

It is a profession that has ever since engaged the affection of the inhabitants of Pembrokeshire.

Carmarthen was a serious competitor with Milford in coal exports, but discreetly chose to avoid challenging the Pembrokeshire monopoly of the Irish market, and found a receptive clientele in the French port of La Rochelle, the Channel Islands and Brittany. At home, its strongest links were with Gloucester, which imported regular supplies of Welsh friezes, feathers, wool and skins, and reciprocated with domestic furniture, haberdashery, glassware, dryware and wines. The port of Barnstaple sent calico and cloth, Bristol despatched brass and pewter, and from the Continent there came salt, Gascon wines and Cognac.

The Glamorgan and Monmouthshire ports sent their ships far and wide, but their cargoes were less variegated than those of the western havens. Coal was the exclusive commodity shipped from Swansea and Neath, while Cardiff exported Welsh iron and coal, ordnance and munitions, wheat, butter and flitches of bacon, besides agricultural by-products like raw hides and tallow. Imports were more diverse, though hardly more valuable. Wines, of course—the demand for these among the Welsh gentry and burgesses was insatiable—cloth and canvas, prunes, peaches and more exotic fruits, sugar and confectionery, and occasional bales of paper.[21]

One cardinal factor in the growth of these south-eastern ports was their relationship with commercial circles on the English side of the Bristol Channel. Cardiff citizens entered into partnership with Devon business people ; Glamorgan merchants settled in Bristol, where they dealt in tropical goods and went abroad in the interests of trade ; Bristol ships called at Cardiff and elsewhere to recruit mariners for long distance voyages. Chepstow grew to be an important distributing centre for English cities and towns on the Severn, and was extensively used by English merchants who wished to avoid paying dues and taxes at Bristol. These commercial relations were intensified by industrial developments in South Wales, which attracted a number of south-western English business men across the Channel, and stimulated trade between the two regions. The importance attached to it can be partly measured by the fact that one particular part of Bristol haven was known as the Welsh Road.[22]

Deprived of such favourable economic and geographical conditions, the few ports of North Wales gradually decayed, although their facilities were not entirely overlooked by gentlemen adventurers and pirates. Beaumaris, the most important of them all, had long enjoyed the favour of position and influence in matters of foreign trade. Breton, French, Scottish, Portuguese and Spanish ships had frequented the port in considerable numbers ; cereals, iron, salt, cloth and wool had figured amongst the high quality goods discharged on its quays, but priority seems to have been accorded to wines. This was quite understandable, since the Constable of Beaumaris was entitled to levy a prizage of two tons of wine on every vessel that carried twenty tons or more of that estimable produce of French and Spanish vineyards, and, moreover, his chaplain could within reason also request a gift of a hogshead. But although the roadstead of the port extended as far as the island of Priestholme, and was—as one proud resident claimed —big enough to accommodate the ' greatest navie ' ; and although the trade of Beaumaris was at one time lucrative enough for the Crown's Customer there to sell his patent of office for £100, yet the port could not avoid a serious decline in its fortunes. By 1595, a Royal commission extracted the doleful confession from a witness that no foreign ship had unloaded its cargo at Beaumaris for twenty years. His memory may have been at fault, but the admission was evidence of the condition of decay in which the old port found itself at the end of the sixteenth century.[23]

Its decline may have been hastened by the action of the sea, which kept up a steady onslaught on the port and inundated the high street of the town on many occasions. The quay was reputed, as early as 1561, to be much too short in length to keep the waves back.[24] The towns of Anglesey, in fact, suffered from their proximity to the sea. Newborough, although not a port, was threatened with ruin because of the sand which was constantly being blown over it by the wind. Many inhabitants had been forced to evacuate their homes, and to avoid further destruction the civic authorities issued instructions for the cultivation of rushes between the town and the sea, and for the prosecution of those guilty of digging them up by the roots.[25]

It would have been too sanguine a hope to expect the mercantile communities in Wales to submit unconditionally even to the modified state regulation of overseas trade introduced by the Government. The incentive to acquire wealth through foreign transactions, stimulated by the demand of willing buyers abroad and the plentiful supply of negotiable commodities at home, was too strong to be circumscribed by official decrees from London. Besides, the executors of the policy of the Government for controlling exports and imports in accordance with national interests were the Customs officials— the searchers and customers established in the various ports and havens. These were, not unnaturally, susceptible to local influences and pressure, and felt that they too should have their share in the increasing prosperity of the country. The sentiment of rightful heritage was probably sharpened by the more practical consideration that the office of customer and searcher was generally leased by the Government, and that the holder was expected to make a living—and more—by the exercise of his authority. In these circumstances, it was inevitable that smuggling should enjoy the benefits of co-existence with the authorised transport of goods abroad, and that a steady stream of commodities should by-pass the custom houses along the coast of Wales.

Wheat, barley and malt were shipped to Spain, the uncompromising enemy of Protestant England, from the havens of Pembrokeshire, and the merchants of Tenby and Milford made it no secret that they would counter any interference by Crown officials with force of arms if necessary. The Government had good reason to be perturbed, for, apart from the incorrigibility of the merchants, this clandestine traffic to Spain depleted the wheat resources of the shire causing the price of corn to rise—to the distress of the poorer classes, always a sore point with the Elizabethan authorities.[26]

But Pembrokeshire must have been a constant source of irritation to the Government, and one reason was not far to seek. The searcher at Pembroke in 1572, George Clerk, was a rogue of the deepest hue, if all the accusations levelled against him were true. He had accepted bribes right and left, from the mayor of Tenby, who, with others, had sent a shipload of leather to Spain, from George Devereux, gentleman, who had despatched a cargo of wheat to the same hostile country, and from other interested quarters which had not forgotten to add the gallant gesture of presenting his wife with a valuable mantle. Any attempt to put an end to his pernicious practices had been decisively crushed. His under-searcher had presumed to interfere and had been assaulted and wounded, once at the hands of the mayor of Tenby himself. His superior, the Customs officer at Carmarthen, had undergone a series of tribulations when he had tried to interfere. They began with a spate of ' evil words ' showered upon him by the inhabitants of Tenby, the words soon being replaced by blows, and ended with his being marooned on the island of Caldey by the crew of a French ship, whose unlicensed cargo of leather, wax and beans he had rather hastily tried to confiscate single-handed. Clerk's conduct, brutality and machinations were not surprising, for everyone in Pembrokeshire knew—although London could not be expected to share the knowledge—that he owned a tavern in Angle openly patronised by Callice and other notorious pirates.[27]

The Glamorgan ports, especially Cardiff, Barry and Aberthaw, specialised in the illicit export of agricultural produce, mostly to Bristol and Barnstaple. The traffic was well organised, and the supply lines between Cowbridge, Cadoxton and other localities in the Vale of Glamorgan and the clearing depots along the coast operated uninterruptedly. Butter, cheese, tallow, wheat and skins were conveyed by night and temporarily deposited in the cellars of well disposed persons near the quayside to await loading—also by night. When additional accommodation was needed, as happened at Cardiff, no one had any objection to using the town slaughterhouse for that purpose.[28] Further east, at Newport, the law was circumvented by the gentry in the neighbourhood, who had a partiality for Spanish and French wines unflavoured by custom duties. One of the most prominent among them, George Herbert, owned a bark, the *Green Dragon* by name, which transgressed the Queen's regulations every time it left port, since its cargo was usually one of wheat carried down the Severn in trowes or barges from Gloucestershire and Herefordshire. This blatant evasion of customs tolls was common knowledge to Her Majesty's subjects in those parts, but not—by some inexplicable omission—to Her Majesty's Customs officials in Cardiff and Newport.[29]

Although the smuggling of wheat, cheese and butter was in flagrant contravention of established law, those involved might have argued in their own defence that a substantial proportion of these commodities entered into their countrymen's stomachs, and could therefore hardly be considered an offence against their interests. But there were other categories of non-edible goods whose export constituted a potential danger to the security of the realm, and showed that commercial practices did not always take kindly to the sentiment of nationalism, which was beginning to evoke a ready response in the hearts and minds of many people.

The discovery of gun-running at Cardiff, for instance, brought to light one aspect of this indifference to the stringent defence regulations imposed by the Government to meet the perennial threat of Spanish invasion. For many years some tons of armament—in the shape of guns and iron shot—had been surreptitiously shipped to Danzig, Amsterdam and Denmark.[30] These were Protestant countries, yet there was no guarantee that the minions, sakers and semi-culivers sent to them would not, at some future date, be turned against this island or fall, inadvertently, into French or Spanish hands. This was enough to justify the strict prohibition of ordnance exports, apart from the fact that every gun manufactured at home was needed to fortify the coast and equip the fleet.[31]

But no ingenious Welsh smuggler succeeded more in hood-winking the Government than John Vaughan, Her Majesty's Customer at the port of Carmarthen. He was the same person who had been mauled by the infuriated folk of Tenby, when he interposed his physical authority between them and their argosy of unlicensed cargo bound for Spain. Returning to Carmarthen, the shackles of dutiful remonstrations in the name of the Queen's port dues fell from him with surprising ease, and he proceeded to conduct himself on the quay at Carmarthen as if he had been inspired rather than frustrated by his experiences on the quay at Tenby.

Vaughan was a Carmarthenshire squire with a voracious appetite for office and a keen sense of selectivity in his choice of useful connections. He was a Justice of the Peace and a former mayor of Carmarthen, and, in addition, he served as Bailiff, Escheator and Coroner of Kidwelly. He numbered among his friends the influential families of Gwyn and Stepneth, as well as some of the prosperous burgesses and merchants of Carmarthen. As his brother in law was also the controller of the port, his fortunes may legitimately be said to have been bound up with its commercial activities.

He was a most accommodating customs officer. He graciously allowed his friends to transport wheat abroad without the formality of a licence, and was not averse to waiving customs dues in return for gifts or services rendered to him. Even the unexpected arrival of a French vessel from Guinea, laden with elephant tusks nine feet long, failed to induce him to impose the tolls to which the Frenchman was liable. As the ship was leaking, a Carmarthen merchant opportunistically offered to provide a bark to convey the precious freight to France for a fair reward, and Vaughan once again showed his capacity for mutual understanding between friends by leaving a blank space in the customs book.

As it was, entries were few and far between. One explanation was that Vaughan, who owned a number of coalpits near the Burry river, neglected to collect the dues levied on each vessel that carried coal out of the country. But there was another and more potent reason. He himself was engaged in the smuggling of leather, a commodity marked out for special prohibition from the days of the early Tudor monarchs.

Suspicion was first roused in 1571 by the erection of a tan-house near Vaughan's country residence, and by his diligence in purchasing hides in the adjacent parishes. Gradually it leaked out that the leather was being despatched to France in the ship of a Breton named Peter du Parrie. Evidence accumulated until it was possible to piece together the details of a deliberate conspiracy to defraud the Crown of its rightful dues. Du Parrie, it appeared, was an importer of French wines and a constant visitor to Carmarthen, where he either lodged in the same house as Vaughan, or was invited to the latter's country mansion. But he took the precaution of leaving his ship in the estuary of the river Towy, and it was there that the un-licensed loads of leather were taken, either by barge from the town quay or from a storehouse near Llanstephan. The building was Crown property, but Vaughan, who had leased it, had no inhibitions about using it to secrete his leather. It was a profitable trade, for each dicker or piece of leather fetched £4 in foreign parts, whereas the maximum price in Carmarthen-shire was under £3.

From stealthy loading by night the smuggling grew into an exhibition of flamboyant contempt for the law, and this proved its undoing. Du Parrie went about soliciting the local shoe-makers to buy leather for him, and aggravated an already uneasy situation by threatening to throw inquisitive searchers, who boarded his ship unknown to Vaughan, into the whirlpools of the Towy. Finally, the Carmarthen shoemakers revolted at the exorbitant price of leather, and invaded du Parrie's ship to prevent their means of subsistence from sailing out into the ocean. There was a violent skirmish before they were ejected,

many with broken heads, by Vaughan's son who was guarding
the load. The clamour and protests reached the ears of the
Privy Council, and another of the interminable Royal commissions succeeded eventually in unravelling one of the inter-
twisted fibres of clandestine trade in South Wales.[32]

The sparsely populated coastline of Wales, the absence of
communications which often constrained the inhabitants to
supplement their own limited resources with extraneous
supplies wherever possible, and the general passive resistance to
Government control and supervision, made ideal conditions for
the practice of piracy. And in the course of time it became
increasingly difficult to distinguish between an honest merchant
vessel and a buccaneer's ship along the sea lanes between
Wales and Ireland, south-west England and the Continent. It
would hardly be an exaggeration to say that any pirate who
chose to call along the Welsh coast for provisions, or to arrange
the sale of goods which had not originally been his, could
expect as courteous a welcome and as business-like an attitude
as circumstances permitted. Whether he put in at Cardiff or
Milford Haven, Bardsey or Beaumaris, he could rest assured
that there would be a temporary suspension of any Government
decree or edict directed against him personally or condemning
his fraternity in general. Haynes, Cole, Ffetiplace, Fortescue,
Woolfall—to mention only some of the pre-eminent English
pirates of the day—could have testified to the immunity which
they enjoyed from the arm of the law that was strangely
paralysed as soon as it stretched this side of the Severn river.
The indefatigable Privy Council might despatch an unending
stream of orders, alternately admonishing, threatening and
appealing, to its official representatives in Wales, but these
gentlemen, although sincere in their loyalty to the Crown,
could never resist a desire to feather their nests whatever the
circumstances—with the help of stolen plumes, if necessary.[33]
And so Haynes could sail with his prizes into Beaumaris, and
his men could pick and choose their accommodation and walk
about the town with impunity. Sir Richard Bulkeley might
inform the authorities in London with commendable indig-

E*

nation that this 'was contrary to his will,' but he displayed a greater alacrity in requisitioning the prizes after Haynes had left the port, and selling them for his own profit. One of them, it is true, he equipped for a fishing voyage to Newfoundland. This might have indicated that Sir Richard was an enthusiastic supporter of the national policy of encouraging fishing in order to produce experienced mariners, if it had not been revealed later that the fish delivered by this same vessel had been pirated off the coast of Scotland. The Vice-Admiral of Anglesey, for Sir Richard also occupied that post, possessed the happy faculty of knowing where to place his goods. It was disclosed to the Court of the Admiralty that his brother, a respectable counsellor of Lincoln's Inn, had at one time invited a London grocer[34] to Sir Richard's house in the capital, to view a number of chests and barrels of powdered sugar which had been brought there from Beaumaris.[35] The resultant sale realised the handsome sum of £122 for the prosperous knight of Anglesey,[36] but the Court might have pertinently asked where the sugar had come from, or recalled to mind that the pirate Ffetiplace had been known to land 'dusky' sugar, together with wines, molasses and Castile soap, on Beaumaris quay.[37]

Such delicacies were no less appreciated by the representatives of law and civic administration in South Wales, particularly at Tenby and Cardiff, where the respective mayors and corporations could hardly conceal their gratification at the unfailing variety and richness of the goods which they were invited to share. There was a positive profusion of ginger, pepper, cloves, boxes of marmalade, raisins, lemons, oranges, prunes and figs, in addition to a choice assortment of silks and wines, and a special category of exotic wares like elephants' teeth and ostrich feathers for those who owned to more expensive and unconventional tastes. And there was that amusing incident at Swansea, when the local gentry were introduced to a species of undomesticated creatures which made their first appearance in Wales.

It began with the arrival of the *Primrose* of London at the Mumbles in 1581, and the request of her master, Phillip Smith, that he should be permitted to purchase a cargo of coal from the pits at Neath. There was a persistent rumour that he had transacted some business with the notorious pirate Haynes during his voyage, and a court of enquiry, composed of local squires, was set up to investigate the charge. Smith was exculpated and expressed his thanks by presenting the members of the court with unusual gifts. Sir William Herbert found himself handling a monkey, Sir Edward Mansell had to divide his attention between a monkey and a parrot ; even Her Majesty's searchers at Swansea had one of these birds thrust upon them. Smith sailed away with his coal, but, unlike him, few of the parrots survived the visit to Swansea.[38]

The popularity of Bardsey Island with many English gentlemen of fortune could hardly be attributed to the tradition that some ten thousand saints had been buried there. What attracted them, apart from its inaccessibility except by sea, was the periodic shortage of grain on the neighbouring mainland, which often reduced the inhabitants to a near state of famine, and encouraged a promiscuous traffic in corn with complete disregard for the official tariff of prices. No one excelled in appraising the difficulties of these unfortunate people more than the Lancashire pirate, Thomas Woolfall, who, on one occasion in 1563, arrived at Bardsey with a foreign bark loaded with wheat and rye and captured by him in the English Channel. The food situation was so desperate that the poorer classes in the countryside sold their cattle to obtain the necessary money to buy grain from him. There was a precipitate rush to Bardsey with local landowners and parish priests in the van, and it was inevitable that their social status and greater wealth should have procured for them the lion's share of the cereals.

Woolfall, however, had sensed that not all his customers were imbued with a sentiment of gratitude, and his suspicions were justified when he was accosted by a group led by John Griffith, who accused him point blank of piracy. He replied that he had been given a letter of marque by the Earl of Warwick to relieve certain foreign ships of their cargoes. Griffith requested him to produce it. Woolfall retorted that it had been written in French, and—with the assurance of one who thought that he was dealing with a batch of untutored yokels—offered to produce it if somebody there could read that language. He was informed that a squire in the neighbourhood was conversant with French, whereupon he excused himself on the grounds that he had mislaid the document.

His accusers left the ship, but Griffith was determined to bring about his arrest. He sent a personal message to Sir Richard Bulkeley, notifying him of Woolfall's presence and demanding his assistance. Sir Richard, regrettably, of course, could not see his way clear to intervene at that moment, and appeals to the sheriff of Caernarvonshire and the Queen's Armourer in Caernarvon Castle found those two officials similarly incapacitated. Griffith, therefore, improvised a hasty plan. He approached John Thorne, a Bristol merchant who happened to be staying in his house, and offered him £30 in return for his co-operation. Thorne automatically pocketed the money, and agreed to buy a quantity of corn from Woolfall, to convey it to Caernarvon under pretence of selling it there, procure men and arms, and return to make an assault on the pirate. The merchant, however, revealed the scheme to Woolfall, was rewarded with a gift of corn, and, with Griffith's money untouched in his pocket, retired from the scene.

Suspecting nothing, the Welshman went on board the pirate's ship, and was invited to join the company whom Woolfall was entertaining in his cabin. Suddenly the pirate spoke out, and a few minutes later Griffith was seen to dash from the cabin and leap into a boat, which he rowed for his life to the shore. With understandable caution, Woolfall decided to hoist his sails and make for the open sea. It was all the consolation that Griffith got for his pains and the loss of £30. Those who had come to terms with the pirate had no reason to complain of their lot. They proceeded to market their newly acquired supplies of corn at exorbitant prices, particularly the parson of Llanbedrog parish, who had bought his at 2/6 a bushel and sold it to the famished countryfolk at thirty shillings.[39]

As the century advanced the excitement and dangers of piracy, coupled with its gratifying perquisites, began ot exercise an ever increasing fascination for Welshmen in the maritime shires. And as in the case of some English pirates, not a few of those who hazarded their lives in this perilous calling were the sons of small squires. In many cases it was, no doubt, the lack of money or employment to lead a life commensurate with their status and ambitions, that persuaded these young men to engage in buccaneering, but there must have been an innate disposition amongst others to throw themselves without restraint into that life of adventure, reckless initiative and self-assertion that was characteristic of the Elizabethan age in many respects. The annals of sixteenth century piracy would certainly have been the poorer if they had sought to express their individuality in any other way, or had contented themselves with a more humdrum existence.

In March, 1597, a London merchant, Thomas Hewett, freighted a ship of the indisputably Welsh name, *Pendragon*, to convey certain goods abroad. The cargo was ostensibly one of iron, lead and tin, but Hewett made secret arrangements for the vessel to call in Plymouth on the way out, and to pick up surreptitiously a consignment of guns—two minions, a sacre, a falcon of brass and a demi-culverin—in addition to several hundredweights of iron shot. Trading in armaments with foreign states was, of course, strictly prohibited by law and attended by severe penalties. But the profits of gun-running were tantalisingly high, customs officials notoriously lax, and the risk of detection could be circumvented by ingenuity or bribery. In any case, Hewett—like many of his business friends—did not suffer from an over-indulgence in respect for Government decrees. What was indispensable to the success of this kind of transaction was a fast and seaworthy vessel and a ruthless, reliable captain. He already had the ship, and he eventually found the captain in the person of Hugh Griffith.

Griffith was one of the three sons of the squire of Cefnamlwch, in the extreme south-west corner of Caernarvonshire. His father, Griffith ap John, was of sufficient account to enjoy the friendship of the redoubtable Sir Richard Bulkeley, and to marry his daughter to a Welsh lawyer of Lincoln's Inn. Hugh seems to have persuaded his father that his nature was as restless as the sea that pounded the exposed coast of the Llŷn Peninsula, for the squire furnished him with money and packed him off to seek his fortune. What strange vicissitudes he experienced have not come to light, but when the *Pendragon* sailed into Plymouth it was Griffith who commanded her, with Hewett's instructions constantly in mind.

The illicit armament was hoisted aboard, and Griffith set his course for the Italian and French ports of the Mediterranean. Off the coast of Spain he proceeded to operate another confidential directive, which he had received from Hewett. One of the merchant's servants accompanied the expedition, but he had been ill-advised enough to quarrel with Hewett prior to joining the ship. Whatever the reason, he was to pay heavily for his contumacy. As the *Pendragon* drew near to Majorca, Griffith ordered that he should be seized and taken in a boat to the island. There he was deliberately marooned— an act of callous brutality, for Griffith must have known that the island was Spanish, and that Englishmen captured by the subjects of Philip of Spain were treated as heretics, or in the best of cases, as galley slaves. He continued his journey, calling at Toulon and Leghorn where he disposed of the guns to ready buyers. He then—temporarily, at least—eliminated all traces of his clandestine dealings by taking advantage of a maritime custom that permitted a captain to sell his ship in certain circumstances, and turned the *Pendragon* over to a Toulon merchant.

The success of the venture convinced Griffith that his future was unmistakably bound up with the sea and with the ships that passed over it—irrespective of the national flags that flew at their masts. Returning to England, he went to Gosport and was invited by a merchant there to take over the captaincy of his ship, the *Phoenix*. Whether the owner had any suspicion of the Welshman's motives or not (he was later arrested for complicity), Griffith soon made his objectives known to the crew. He obviously could have expected little opposition, and the fact that one of them had formerly been in the service of the King of Spain and had actually piloted a Spanish galleon in the attack on Penzance in 1595, must have reassured him that the *Phoenix* was a floating nest of unregenerate lawbreakers.

The year 1599 was a particularly remunerative one for the pirates. The *Phoenix* harried and stormed many vessels which crossed her path between the Breton coast and the Rock of Gibraltar, and her hold began to fill with a colourful collection of captured goods. The English Government was not left in ignorance of these piracies, and the bill of indictment against Griffith grew ominously as the months went by.

It was sometime during the same year that Hugh decided to re-visit his home, and to invite his relatives and friends to a public exhibition of the choicest of his piratical pickings. These he transferred to a French vessel which had fallen into his hands, and after despatching the *Phoenix* home, he sailed for Wales and eventually anchored off St. Tudwal's within comfortable reach of his father's house. A wave of excitement and curiosity swept through the countryside. The ship was inundated by visitors of all degrees and ranks, and there was one moment of high-pitched expectancy when a chest belonging to the captain was taken ashore, and required two strong horses to drag it on a sledge to the home of one of his brothers, John Griffith. Speculation as to the value of its contents grew rife, especially after one of the crew was heard to mutter that he would willingly offer £500 for them. Meanwhile Hugh, revelling in a blaze of publicity and admiration, borrowed a horse and rode off to Beaumaris to pay his respects to Sir Richard Bulkeley. Something more than the usual formalities of courtesy passed between them, for within a day or two a trusted servant of Sir Richard's appeared at St. Tudwal's, hoisted the ship's anchor and set course for Beaumaris.

It was not a minute too soon. Shortly after his departure, Captain Morgan of the Queen's Navy bore down on St. Tudwal's in a warship, and, stepping ashore, harangued the inhabitants on the many iniquities committed by their local hero on the high seas. No time was lost in informing John Griffith, who galloped post haste to Beaumaris. Hugh was equally responsive to the situation. When his ship arrived there, he quietly sold the cargo, ordered his company to disperse, and himself faded into temporary obscurity. To complete a hastily improvised transaction, Sir Richard Bulkeley bought the ship from the original French crew, who had been held on board as lugubrious but passive prisoners all this while.

It was then that the Government found itself confronted once more by a personality, who was less susceptible to its authority than even the elusive Hugh. It transpired that one Rhydderch ap Richard had kept a watchful eye on the movements of the pirate and his ship, and had communicated them to the Court of the Admiralty. To reward him—or, perhaps, to put his law-abiding proclivities to a more practical test—the Court entrusted him with a commission to stay the sale of the French vessel. Rhydderch hurried off to Beaumaris, but when he attempted to board the ship he received a rough welcome, ' a skurvy roge was like to have brayned him with a clubbe.'

Summoning his courage, Rhydderch ventured to beard Sir Richard Bulkeley himself and to demand the restitution of the ship. As anyone acquainted with the choleric temperament of that gentleman could have expected, ' Sir Richard spake very prowde words and little esteemed the commission.' Any hope of recovering the pirated goods was soon dashed when it was found that they had been bought by Sir Richard's brother, Edward Bulkeley, by the Recorder of Beaumaris and other eminent burgesses. The task was too formidable, and Rhydderch ap Richard wisely abandoned it. The Government, for its part, consoled itself by issuing a proclamation for Hugh Griffith's arrest and annoying his family with protracted interrogations.

By this time, Hugh had resumed his freebooting activities. With a crew of forty-five tough mariners, including a barber, and with two Welshmen from Swansea as his Master and Lieutenant, he returned to his old haunts off the Breton coast. He had baptised his ship the *Pendragon*, possibly as a nostalgic reminder of his first voyage, but some of the ferocity implicit in that name began to characterise his actions as a pirate. His treatment of the Breton ship, the *Peteryn* of Le Conquet, was particularly brutal. Having boarded her, he and his men thrashed the captain and the crew unmercifully before stripping the vessel of every moveable object, from the main sail and anchor to the kitchen utensils in the cook's quarters. The discovery of a sum of French and Spanish money suggested to Hugh that there might well be other concealed hoards of coin on board the *Peteryn*. He took her captain to the *Pendragon*, put a rope round his neck and hoisted him up and down a few times to encourage him to talk. The torture produced no tangible result, since it was only too apparent that his men had ransacked the *Peteryn* thoroughly.[40]

For two more years, Hugh continued the hardy and dangerous life of a sea-rover, and eventually transferred his operations to the coast of Barbary. He established amicable relations with the Moors, and when, in 1602, he fell ill—a victim, possibly, of the recurrent plagues there—he had taken up his quarters in a Turk's house in Tunis. Here he was found by a former shipmate, Richard Lamb, who agreed to arrange for his removal to Algiers. But the illness proved fatal, and within a short time Griffith was dead. His death released something more than his own adventurous spirit. Immediately upon his decease, the Turkish authorities seized the house and imprisoned a number of Englishmen living there, on the suspicion that they had stolen his money. In fact it was Lamb, who, with the dying man's connivance, had conveyed it away, and it was with the help of this money that he eventually obtained the release of his countrymen.[41]

It would be interesting to learn whether Hugh ever met, or ever collaborated with, an acquaintance of his on the pirate-infested coast of Barbary. What induced Edward, the brother of Sir Richard Bulkeley, to exchange the urban amenities of Beaumaris for the rigours of a seafaring life, is open to conjecture. Possibly the exhilarating tales that Hugh Griffith may very well have poured into his ears at the time of his visit to Sir Richard ; or, what was common to many Welsh gentlemen in the Elizabethan age, a desire to improve his fortunes by a judicious combination of retaliation on Spain, the national enemy, and a readiness to take risks.

Setting out in a ship, aptly called the *Bravado*, he followed

Hugh's path through the Bay of Biscay, snapping up Spanish and other ships where he could, and selling a variety of plundered cargoes in the Turkish ports of the Mediterranean. It was rumoured that at one time he had amassed the extraordinary fortune of £10,000 at the expense of the unfortunate Spaniards, who were forced to run the gauntlet of pirates on their way home from the New World. But his success came to an abrupt end. He put in at Algiers at an unlucky moment, when the Bey was beside himself with rage at the news that some English captives had escaped in a boat under the nose of his officials. His sense of propriety had been outraged, and scapegoats had to be found. Before he could realise what was happening, Bulkeley found himself, together with his ship's company, in the Bey's dungeons, and the *Bravado* with all its treasures was confiscated. Some time later, the ship was redeemed by an English merchant, but the ultimate fate of Sir Richard Bulkeley's brother has yet to be investigated.[42]

Those of the inhabitants of South Wales (and they were many) who were inclined to regard the spoliation of other people's goods on the high seas with equanimity, must have found much to admire in the recklessness and good fortune of a Monmouthshire gentleman named John Callice. Born at Tintern, he left home at the early age of eleven, and had been placed in the care of a London alderman, who discovered a natural aptitude for seamanship in the boy and encouraged it by sending him on trading voyages to various continental countries. There came a day in 1573 when Callice did not return to London. He appeared instead at Penarth on board a Portuguese vessel which he had captured near the Azores, and in the happy possession of a valuable cargo of sugar. It was evident that he had decided to abandon legitimate commerce for piracy, and both the Government and the receivers of those goods, which evaded the Queen's customs houses along the South Wales coast, made their respective arrangements to deal with him.

Callice sold his sugar, and with the proceeds he purchased a stout ship, the *Olyphant*, in which he began to chase every category of merchant vessel from Dover to the Azores, and from Ireland to France. Not even the alarming experience of being blown as far west as Newfoundland convinced him of the errors of his course, and, in fact, he took advantage of his un-announced visit to raid the French fishing fleet and to ballast the *Olyphant* with their catches of cod. It was about this time that he entered the service of the Huguenot port of La Roch-elle, and obtained letters of marque to prey upon the ships of Catholic France—and of every other Catholic country for that matter. It was a shrewd move designed to disarm the highly critical attitude of his own Government towards him, for even the Queen had little objection to her subjects engaging in the struggles of the Protestant communities abroad, as long as their intervention did not overstrain the uneasy relations between this country and its neighbours.

Within a year or so, Callice found that he could not continue to observe these limitations imposed for reasons of State, and he reverted to the freedom of action which was more consonant with his profession. He acquired such a reputation for intrep-idity and success that even the notorious English pirate, Robert Hicks, became one of his admirers and entered into correspondence with him, offering Callice his wholehearted collaboration. His offer was accepted, the two pooled their resources in ships and crews, and their depredations between 1575 and 1577 became a nation-wide scandal and a painful reminder of their impotence to the members of the Queen's Privy Council. There was hardly a Vice-admiral or Crown official in South Wales who did not receive at some time or other an urgent order for the arrest of Callice, but the pro-position was wholly impracticable. The ' mainetayners and aiders ' of the pirate were to be found everywhere and belonged to all classes.

Then came the news that he had brazenly landed in Milford, had lodged comfortably in Haverfordwest, and then returned to his ship without the slightest attempt being made to appre-hend him. Shocked by the indifference of the local Justices of the Peace to their express demands, the irate Council wrote to Sir John Perrot, the Vice-admiral of Pembrokeshire, that,

' they do not a letill mervell at the negligence of suche as are Justices in those parts that, knowing the said Callice to be so notable and [*sic*] offendour and spoiler of suche her Majesties neighbors as are in good league and amytie with her, a matter greatelye touching her Highnes in honor, woulde suffer him to departe in that order and not apprehend him.'[43]

Sir John, the Council directed, should investigate this dereliction of duty and take immediate steps to arrest Callice. Sir John obeyed to the extent of making some routine enquiries in Haverfordwest, but when the mayor of that town protested that he had not even been aware of Callice's presence there, it was plainly a waste of time to pursue the matter any further.

Meanwhile Callice had excelled his previous exploits by a daring attack on a Danish ship with a rich cargo of raisins, almonds, olives and wines, which had anchored off the coast of Sussex. The crew had resisted, and some of them had been killed by his men. Whether Callice knew it or not, these commodities were destined for the King of Denmark and members of the Danish aristocracy, and the enormity of the crime was only too keenly appreciated by the distracted Privy Council, who dreaded the repercussions on the policy of mutual understanding with the Protestant Court of Copenhagen. It was in the midst of their misgivings that the news arrived that the pestilential pirate had at last been caught by the Governor of the Isle of Wight. Orders were despatched that he should be securely guarded, and inordinate precautions were taken when he and his men were conveyed to London and Callice himself placed in the Tower.

No person in the land would have doubted that a miracle was needed to save Callice from the hangman, but the miracle happened. For some incomprehensible reason he was allowed to walk about in London accompanied by his keeper. Then came the astounding news that he had been granted a pardon by the Queen on the condition that he found sureties for his future good behaviour. He found them without much difficulty, and for the incredibly low sum of £50 one of the most skilful and notorious pirates of the age walked out of the Tower a free man. Those who had trafficked in the goods stolen from the Danish ship were forced to compensate the owners to the tune of £500, while Callice had sufficient common sense—and, perhaps, adequate reserves of concealed money—to abide by the terms of the Queen's clemency and retire from public life.[44]

In many respects Wales was a poor country, but in the flocks of sheep that pastured on the mountains and in the valleys, the Principality possessed a source of wealth which multiplied with the greater demand for wool and woollen cloth. Whatever the attractions of foreign textiles for society—and the purveyors of silks and satins, velvet and damask, found ready purchasers in Wales as in England—woollen cloth still enjoyed an undisputed supremacy in the home market, and was much sought after abroad. And although Welsh cloth could not compete with that of England in the finer and more variegated processes of manufacture, its hardwearing qualities were appreciated in the commercial world, not least as excellent wrapping material for the shipment of English commodities overseas.[45]

Welsh friezes and cottons were particularly popular. They were woven in great numbers up and down the countryside either by local weavers or by the wives and daughters of the farming community, who contributed in this way to the family income. So popular did they become, in fact, that a spirited dispute broke out between Chester and Shrewsbury as to which city should have the staple for Welsh cloth from North Wales. The staple had long been monopolised by Shrewsbury, but in 1582, it had been removed to Chester on the grounds that it would benefit the economy of a port which was indispensable to the defence of the realm.[46]

Prior to the transfer of the staple, most of the Welsh friezes and cottons in North Wales had been concentrated in Oswestry, famous for its cloth market. It was the custom for the owners of the material to attend the market accompanied by their weavers and fullers, and for the three parties to divide the money between them immediately after the sale of the cloth. Some twenty packs were brought weekly—usually on men's backs—to Oswestry market, and an average of one hundred tons of cloth a year were conveyed thence to London by Cockney carriers. A substantial proportion of the cloth was, in turn, shipped from London or Rye to Dieppe, but more particularly to Rouen, where there was a ready market for it, since it sold at a cheaper price than a similar material manufactured locally.[47] Other cargoes of Welsh cloth went further afield—to the Low Countries, Italy and Spain.[48]

In 1601, there was a distinct deterioration in the quality of the exported cloth. The French merchants, to their chagrin, failed to perceive the defects in it until after its distribution amongst their customers, owing to the dishonest practice of camouflaging them by straining the cloth upon tenters. But tests by water revealed that the cloth was capable of shrinking to an unheard-of degree. Whereupon the French authorities confiscated the defective cloth, and the English Government was obliged to prohibit the use of tenters or any other methods for straining Welsh cloth.[49]

West Wales also produced adequate supplies of friezes and cottons to maintain a busy export trade with the major ports of Western England, and with Ireland, France and Portugal, although the Pembrokeshire sheep farmers preferred, in the main, to sell their wool directly to merchants from Somerset and North Wales buyers.[50] Another kind of cloth that found its way into the English market was Welsh flannel and wadmal. This was generally woven by the poorer section of the community, according, as one description has it, ' to their poore habilitie.' The cloth was not accorded a high marketable value, since it was made from raw woollen stuff and rarely weighed more than ten pounds a piece.[51]

The rich coal deposits of Wales were still a secret of the future, but from medieval days there had been a haphazard quarrying of outcrops along the fringes of what eventually became the principal coalfields of the Principality. The demand for coal had, of course, been insignificant, since the fuel requirements of the population could be satisfactorily met from the abundant woodlands and the equally exploitable moorlands in all parts of the country. There was also a sufficiency of timber for the few industries and crafts, which were leading a sheltered life behind the protection of town walls.

During the Elizabethan age, however, the Welsh people were forced to revise their opinions drastically as to the serviceability and value of coal. The steady increase in population with its concomitant demand for housing materials and household goods, chiefly of wood ; the clearance of forest land in the interests of arable and pastoral farming ; the wholesale destruction of trees to provide fuel for the incipient iron, lead and copper works ; and the realisation that coal was a profitable item of export—all these considerations combined, as in England, to enhance its usefulness. Its smell might be offensive to Welsh nostrils, but that unaesthetic quality was outweighed by its relative cheapness. Moreover, its extraction promised greater opportunities of employment, which no member of the lower classes in that age of restricted occupations could afford to ignore. The result was that coalmining became an operation of some magnitude, which brought in its train both wealth and tragedy for many Welsh people.

Apart from the pressure of industrial and domestic needs, one factor in the expansion of coal exploitation was the interest which the wealthier members of society were prepared to take in it, and the extent of their personal investments. Some of the shrewder gentry did not hesitate to take a lease of Crown property, where there were already mines in existence or where there was evidence of coal deposits, and to shoulder the responsibility of extending the scope of operations and disposing of the output. This was the case in the lordship of Kidwelly, where the mines at Llangennech, Llwynhendy and Llanelly were taken over by neighbouring gentlemen, who paid an annual rent to the Crown.[52] Sir George Herbert of Swansea had a personal interest in developing the mines around Neath, for he drew a good income from the coal which he supplied to ships engaged in the exchange of that commodity for salt at La Rochelle. The coal mines in the parish of Llansamlet near Swansea were likewise owned by a local squire.[53]

In North Wales, the lessees of Crown property exercised careful supervision over the surface workings under their control, and issued licences to private individuals who wished to dig—or employ others to dig—for coal.[54] It was a Crown lease granted to Sir Nicholas Bagnall in 1565, with full liberty to dig and sell coal at Esgyfiog, in Anglesey, that enabled his son thirty years later to come to an agreement with Owen Holland of Berw, within the same township, whereby the two squires divided the waste and common land between them for the purpose of exploiting the coal seams presumed to lie there.[55]

Another factor was the intervention and encouragement of the Government, which never failed in its paternal solicitude to see its citizens engaged in some useful occupation. When, in 1588, a report was circulated that coal could be mined on the Royal manor of Dinas, in Brecknock, a commission of enquiry was set on foot to explore the possibilities. In due course its members declared themselves in favour of mining operations, which, so they maintained, would not only provide acceptable fuel to the tenants of the manor, but actually improve the quality of their land by mitigating the chilliness of the soil, which the commission attributed to the presence of coal. However, in view of the heavy initial cost of excavation, it was suggested that a sum of no more than ten shillings should be the maximum rent imposed on future prospectors.[56]

The main coalfields during the Elizabethan age were three, situated respectively in Flintshire and Denbighshire, Pembrokeshire, east Carmarthenshire and Glamorgan. The North Wales mines, perhaps, enjoyed seniority, but they were soon to be outstripped in expansion and productivity. The principal workings in Denbighshire were centred around Brymbo and Broughton, which were so identified with the industry that it became the fashion to refer to persons hailing from those parts as people from the ' mynes.'[57] In Flintshire, there was substantial quarrying of coal at Ewloe, Bagillt, Mostyn, Holywell and Whitford. Many of these mines, as in Denbighshire, were levels driven into the side of the outcrops, and necessitated little more than physical strength for their exploitation. But with the

steady increase in the consumption of coal and the imperative
need for greater output, the traditional and now antiquated
methods of extraction were gradually replaced by the enlarge-
ment of the mines and the sinking of shafts capable of penetrat-
ing to deeper and richer seams. The depth of the new mines
varied considerably, but in one recorded case it attained as
much as ninety feet.[58]

The miners who sank and worked the pits continued to use
their customary implements—hammers, wedges, spades and
' tweybills ' or pickaxes, but the dangers to which they were
constantly exposed made their calling a particularly precarious
one. A basket or barrel called variously ' Picke ' or ' Hoke '
was used to haul up the coal to the pit head, and to convey the
men to and from their work. There were many fatal accidents
when the rope drawing the basket broke and precipitated men
and coal to the bottom of the mine. Falls of earth often
smothered workers ; others were killed by dislodged stones and
boulders ; not a few were asphyxiated by what was known as
' dampne ' ; and there was an unending struggle against the
water that seeped into the mines and threatened to submerge
the workings.[59]

Life for most miners was a monotonous round of subterranean
excavation with very little opportunity for leisure or recreation.
One form of relaxation, however, was to drink and dice in
taverns, and it would appear that some of the gentlemen
owners of the coal pits were not averse to joining in these
convivialities.[60]   In fact, relations between employers and
workers seem to have been fairly harmonious, and there is
little evidence of industrial or any other dispute.

The Pembrokeshire coalfield extended from St. Bride's Bay
to the western side of Carmarthen Bay, and there were many
mines in operation at Saundersfoot, Jeffreston, Begelly, Picton,
Freystrop and Johnston. The coal extracted was anthracite,
and it was extremely popular in town and countryside since it
gave out neither smell nor smoke,[61] provided a steady fire for
roasting and boiling meats, and dried fine materials like lawn
and cambric without staining them. It was found indispensable
to the domestic comforts of Pembrokeshire householders, who

were perturbed by the possibility of shortages and a consequent rise in prices.[62]

There seemed on the face of it to be little cause for anxiety. New mines were being opened, especially in the eastern half of the coalfield. For instance, in the parish of Begelly in 1581, so many pits were dug near the highway from Haverfordwest to Tenby that it threatened to subside, and no one dared to pass over it in a carriage or cart without risking a serious accident.[63] The industry had also benefited from technical improvements and innovations. The system of sloping entrances or levels had been abandoned, and shafts were being sunk to a depth of a hundred feet or more. And, as in North Wales, windlasses and barrels were being extensively used to draw up the coal to the pit face—a method that was popularly known in Pembrokeshire as the ' downe right door.'

Every mine had its category of workers with their well-defined tasks. There were the diggers, each with his hole underground, where he laboured at the coal face by candle light with his pickaxe, wedges and ' fledges ' with which he battered the rocks that obtruded in his way. Then came the bearers, boys for the most part,[64] who carried the coal in baskets on their backs, proceeding from level to level and constantly stooping because of the lowness of the passages, until they reached the main shaft. Here a filler emptied the basket into the barrel which was drawn up by the winders, and the coal transferred to the attention of the riddlers, whose speciality it was to separate small coal and culm or dust from the larger lumps. With a twelve-hour shift—from six in the morning to six in the evening, except for an hour's break at noon to eat the allowance of $1\frac{1}{2}$d. worth of bread and a farthing worth of drink provided by the mine proprietor—an ordinary pit was expected to produce about a hundred barrels of coal a day.

There were dangers here too ; sudden falls of stone, inundations which blocked exits, asphyxiation by gases, and the collapse of headings that entombed workers without hope of extrication. It is not surprising that the Pembrokeshire miners were noted for their superstitious beliefs, and that they insisted upon observing all ancient religious holidays long after they had been abolished by the Protestant Government of England.[65]

As early as 1566 a brisk trade in coal and culm had grown between the ports of Pembrokeshire and Spain, France and Ireland. Political and religious differences soon interrupted and finally killed all exports to Spain, but the loss was more than retrieved by those to Wexford, Dublin and Drogheda, which eventually accounted for 90% of overseas deliveries. Culm or coal dust was much favoured by the Irish customers as a cheap and economical fuel.[66] By the end of the century exports had intensified to such an extent that the people of Pembrokeshire became alarmed by the danger of shortages and excessive prices. The Government, however, did not share their apprehension, and recognising another exploitable source of taxation, clapped on a new imposition in 1603.[67]

The South Wales mines appear to have been concentrated at the western extremity of the coalfield which has since become one of the most notable and productive in the world. In Carmarthenshire, they tended to group within the limits of the Gwendraeth valley, where prospecting for coal and its exploitation had already been carried on for more than a century. The Glamorgan mines, for the most part, lay in the hinterland behind Swansea and Neath,[68] although there were a few operating in the eastern part of the shire, as well as in Monmouthshire. But the beautiful wooded valleys of mid-Glamorgan had not yet been invaded by the capitalists of the period with their train of miners. There, the inhabitants still specialised in the rearing of cattle, horses and sheep.[69]

Some of the mines in the vicinity of Swansea are described as lying in ' claie and slymie ' ground, and necessitating much outlay in equipment, especially in timber for supporting shafts and levels.[70] Little information is available about the conditions in these mines, but there can be no doubt that they were the scene of the most feverish activity and striking development in the history of the Welsh coal industry during the Elizabethan period. For apart from supplying fuel to the general public and to certain industrial enterprises, such as the copper smelting works at Neath, the bulk of the coal sent abroad and to other parts of the kingdom from Wales was raised in this coalfield. Swansea alone quintupled its exports between 1580 and 1595, and its total traffic in coal to London, Brittany, the Channel Islands and the principal ports of Cornwall and Devon, according to the customs entries recorded for the years 1580, 1595, 1599, 1600 and 1601, amounted to over 360,000 bushels valued at about £700 in Elizabethan currency.

These figures would seem indicative of the potentialities of the South Wales coalfield, but, curiously enough, the economic experts of the Government were not impressed by them. On the contrary, one of them argued that the coal deposits of Wales barely sufficed to meet the needs of industry and domestic consumption, which were bound to increase as the area of woodland became gradually deforested and converted into pasture and corn land. In the view of this expert, the threefold increase in the use of coal and the sharp rise in its price likewise portended a crisis in coal productivity which, so he maintained, could only be countered by a substantial curtailment of exports or, alternatively, a heavier if not prohibitive customs duty on coal shipped abroad. It was a jaundiced point of view which was not allowed to prevail and impede the growth of the industry.[71]

It was the abundance of cheap and suitable coal around Neath that induced a London company to establish a smelting works there in 1584 to treat copper ores.[72] The company had invested considerable money in the Cornish copper mines, but exasperated by the technical difficulties of extracting the ore, the alleged lethargy of the miners and the paucity of smelting fuel, they despatched one of their ablest managers—a German named Ulrich Frose—to superintend the equipment of the new smelting works at Neath with water weirs and furnaces, and to attend to the processes of refining the crude ore. Arrangements were also made to transfer a master coppermaker from the well-known mines at Keswick to Neath, together with a qualified under-smelter and a German carpenter. Two furnaces were erected, and it was estimated that 560 tons of ore could be melted in forty weeks at an average consumption of nine sacks of charcoal and three horseloads of coal for each 24 hundredweights of ore. The scheme was to be expedited by an exchange of Welsh timber for Cornish ore, but the prevalence of foul weather at sea and the low production of ore at the Cornish mines threatened the success of the entire venture, and actually led to the suspension of smelting operations during the first winter of its existence.[73]

A certain amount of prospecting had also been conducted into the copper deposits of Parys Mountain in Anglesey. No less a distinguished personage than Sir Henry Sidney, Lord President of the Council of the Welsh Marches, had shown a personal interest in the operations, and his example had been emulated by a number of Welsh gentlemen. An experiment had been conducted in their presence to determine whether it would be a practical proposition to spend money on the exploitation of the copper. A great quantity of iron was reduced to a powdery form and placed in half a dozen great boilers of lead, each having flat bottoms, which were filled with mineral water drawn from Parys Mountain. The boilers were heated with fires of turf to a very high temperature, and then allowed to cool. When examined they were found to contain an upper stratum of green copper, an intermediary layer of white alum, and a substratum of a yellow substance which could be smelted like lead when laid upon charcoal in a brick furnace. Despite the satisfactory quality of both copper and alum, it had been decided not to proceed with the working of the copper deposits, which were not fully appreciated and exploited until the eighteenth century.[74]

Lead was another valuable ore which opened up a further avenue of profit. The mines at Cwmystwyth, Llanafan and other localities in Cardiganshire were in full production by the end of the sixteenth century. This was due to the adoption of more progressive and systematic methods of extraction and treatment by Charles Evans, who took over the management of the mines during the early years of Elizabeth's reign. When he arrived in Cardiganshire, many of the mines had been abandoned owing to the lack of timber to melt the lead ore. Those that were still operating were so wet and dangerous that few miners were prepared to work in them more than three hours a day because of the water that percolated into the headings, dislodging stones and exposing the men to sudden falls of rock. Evans was fortunate enough to enlist the services of an experienced German engineer, who in time succeeded in eliminating many of the risks and discomforts that had reduced the productivity of the mines. Water was diverted from the shafts, sudden gusts of wind that extinguished the candles of the miners were checked, the roofing was shored up with timber, and a new system of ventilation introduced.

At the same time some imperative economies were effected. Where one or more loads of wood had formerly been used to roast a ton of ore, a similar amount was found to be sufficient to treat five tons. Less wood was also required for the two furnaces which melted and refined the ore. The saving in fuel costs permitted a substantial reduction in wages and the employment of more miners, and it was estimated that there was enough work to employ forty men upon the extraction of the ore throughout the year. Their output was expected to reach eight tons a week, which would produce about three and a half tons of lead valued at £70.

The activity in the mines gathered momentum from 1586 onwards. New headings or ' heights ' were made, new levels dug to follow the veins of lead, and a main shaft bored to the unusual distance of 600 feet. A modern smith's shop was built at Cwmsymlog, and houses repaired or improvised to accommodate a new intake of miners. Another mine was opened in the same locality, which was found to be particularly rich in silver content. Such were its potentialities that it was generally reckoned that twenty men could mine four tons of ore each week, from which 1¾ tons of lead worth £35 could be extracted. With the discovery of these rich deposits, the lead mines of Cardiganshire entered upon the most prosperous period in their history, which continued into the following century.[75]

Not less notable was the lead refining industry in Flintshire, at Colehill, Rhuddlan and, particularly, near Holywell.[76] The erection of the first smelting mill at this place in 1589 occasioned a dispute, which may be fairly described as an upsurge of rural resentment towards the predatory claims of Elizabethan capitalism.

When Lord Burleigh and the Privy Council decided to authorise Samuel Fleet and William Radclyffe, two London merchants and speculators, to construct the mill on Holywell stream, they forwarded a request to a prominent squire in the neighbourhood, Piers Mostyn, that he should assist the Londoners in their enterprise. The idea of having an evil-smelling plant within a short distance of his mansion house did not appeal to Mostyn, and when at last it was built without his aid, his son declared publicly that it ' stode to neare his fathers nose.' Flouting the Council's authority, Mostyn gathered his kinsmen and friends together, and made many raids on the mill, finally destroying it. There ensued violent recriminations between the two factions, who resorted to all manner of tactics in order to discredit one another. The London merchants tried to persuade some of the inhabitants to commit perjury under the threat of being taken to London, whipped at the cart's tail and having their ears cropped. Mostyn's partisans attempted to stir up ugly feelings by an appeal to the latent hostility against the English.[77] There is little doubt that the concensus of public opinion at Holywell favoured Mostyn's cause. The yeomen and smallholders in the neighbourhood had good reason to complain about the mill, for the pollution of the air and the infection of Holywell stream had ruined harvests and hedges, and killed cattle and poultry to the value of £100.[78] The Flintshire lead mines seem to have lost some of their attraction for the speculator by the end of the century. At least, no one was found willing to take a lease of them in 1599, and the Crown had to forego the sixth part of the profits which it was accustomed to draw every year from the productive and extensive lead workings at Holywell, Englefield and Faenol.[79]

The north-west corner of Wales was rich in quarries of stone and slate. The latter were, for the most part, to be found a-Penrhyn and Cochwillan in Caernarvonshire, where the inthabitants produced thousands of slates annually to supply the neighbouring towns and to export to Ireland. For instance, they were used to roof houses in Wrexham, as well as the mill and town court house. They were cheap in price, six thousand of them, together with their transport, costing only forty shillings.[80]

Anglesey could boast of having stone quarries in almost every parish, where millstones were made in considerable quantities and in various colours—white, red, blue and green. The most productive were four originally owned by the Priors of Penmon, and which had been worked since the days of the independent Welsh Princes. The Priors had utilised the stone to repair their house or to sell to their neighbours, and had not been averse from granting a licence to dig stone in return for the gift of an Irish mantle.[81] After the dissolution of the Priory the quarries passed into the possession of the Crown, and were exploited more thoroughly to increase the Royal revenue, so much so that by the end of Elizabeth's reign one quarry alone was estimated to have one thousand pounds' worth of millstones. At least thirty workmen were permanently employed at this quarry, and the millstones were regularly despatched to mills in North and South Wales, and in western England, besides being sent abroad.[82]

So remunerative became this trade that new quarries were opened at Llangefni and elsewhere in Anglesey,[83] mostly by individual freeholders, who had an eye to the lucrative possibilities of developing a local industry. The Crown, claiming a disputable monopoly, declared that it alone had the right to dispose of millstones, and followed this up by encouraging the lessee of the Royal quarries in North Wales to prosecute those who disregarded the prohibition. The freeholders resisted what they regarded as an arbitrary negation of their immemorial rights, and, in 1601, a test case was fought out at the Exchequer Court in London. The freeholders of Cilcoed, summoned for digging millstones on the local common, sent two of their number to argue their grievances and justify their action. According to their report,

> ' they should have gotten the upper hand in the suite if they had had money with them to ffollowe the said case.'

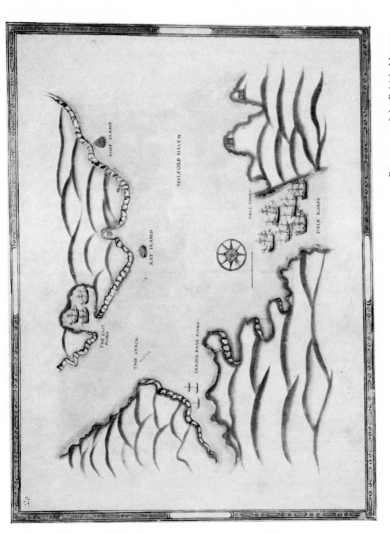

A MAP OF MILFORD HAVEN TEMP. ELIZABETH

By courtesy of the British Museum.

SIR JOHN PERROT

Eventually the verdict—or so it was averred—went to the freeholders, although the Crown lessee insisted that it had been declared in his favour.[84]

The gradual depletion of the forests of Kent and Sussex, which had fed the iron furnaces of south-east England with charcoal for hundreds of years, forced Government and private capitalists to look elsewhere for reserves of iron ore and the timber with which to work them. The urgency to act was made more acute by the demands of the navy for bigger and better ordnance, for it was evident that supremacy at sea was going to be gained and held by the fleet that combined experienced seamanship with superior gunmanship. In common with other parts of the kingdom, Wales was surveyed for what it could offer in iron, and the deposits discovered in Monmouthshire and Glamorgan were put to immediate use.

The development of the iron industry depended, as in the case of other industries, upon the readiness of private individuals to invest their money in it, but the profitability of iron manufacture was too good a bait to be ignored or refused anywhere. There was a rush of Welsh gentlemen and London merchants to erect furnaces, recruit local labour, and acquire a constant supply of fuel from the woods which were a feature of the Gwentian landscape at that time. One of the most lucrative investments was the Crown's iron ore mines at Cwm, which were reckoned to be worth £300 a year.[85] Some speculators, who distrusted the ability of the Welsh miners to handle the ore properly, brought experts from the English iron industry to work in the Welsh mines. One of them, a Sussex man, agreed with his employer to be paid at the rate of sixteen shillings for each sow of iron which he produced, but he died of fever or physical exhaustion in 1574, after four years of exile in the Glamorgan hills.[86]

Lewis Price, a Glamorgan gentleman, borrowed money from Bristol tradesmen to establish an iron works, and paid off his liabilities with weekly deliveries of iron.[87] Two speculators[88] from Aber-carn set up a furnace at Pont-y-moel, in Monmouthshire, and then contracted with a Bristol merchant to

F

despatch 50 tons of iron at £10 a ton ; but they wisely stipulated that there should be no fixed date for the delivery. Bearing in mind the difficulties of transport, and the thirst that afflicts carriers in all ages, the iron was promised ' as wine and wether would permit the transporting of the same.'[89]   But William Mathews of Radyr and Thomas Menyve of Aberdare, who had erected furnaces at the latter place, were foolish enough to discount the vagaries of Welsh weather, and agreed to send iron to yet another Bristol merchant by a date acceptable to both parties. The consignment was successfully carried across the Taf and Cynon rivers, but when it reached Cardiff a gale blew up and prevented the final passage across the Bristol Channel. As the English merchant had only paid a little more than $7\frac{1}{2}$ guineas a ton, and contemplated making a handsome profit by re-selling the iron at 10 guineas a ton in the Bristol market, his annoyance at the delay led him, unfairly perhaps, to bring an action for non-delivery against the helpless Welshmen[90].

As in other industries, unwise speculation and too liberal investment could result in disaster. A notable victim was Anthony Morley, a rich landowner, who had erected forges and furnaces at Merthyr Tydfil and Llanwonno.   Borrowing recklessly to improve the efficiency of his workers and their implements, he soon found himself owing £600 to various creditors in the neighbourhood, and a succession of bad debts forced him, in 1585, after seven years of unremitting activity, to admit failure. The Statute of Bankruptcy was applied mercilessly, all his property and the iron works—the latter alone were valued at a thousand pounds—were sequestrated, and he died penniless.[91]

The most successful and enterprising industrialist in South Wales was Richard Hanbury, a London goldsmith and associate member of the Mineral and Battery Company established by Royal charter, in 1565, to exploit the iron resources of the realm. He arrived in Monmouthshire in that year, and dovetailing his own interests into those of the company which he officially represented, he set up forges and hammer mills at Pontypool and Monkswood, acquired older but indifferently organised works such as those at Pont-y-moel and Aber-carn, and galvanised them into greater productivity. He discovered that the best iron ore was to be found at Blaen-avon, and monopolised it for his forges to turn out superior iron.[92] Within a few years, he was employing between 160 and 200 men daily—miners, woodcutters and colliers or charcoal makers. Production increased, but so did his problems. Not the least of these was the fraudulent dealings of his manager.

Hanbury, aware of the endemic dishonesty of that age to which he contributed not a little himself, had tried to protect the interests of his employees and his own by conceding to them the right to examine the ledger in which their wages were entered, and so nip possible defalcations in the bud. His manager, however, did not lack stratagem. He kept two ledgers, one for correct, and the other for false, entries. In this way he was able to charge more for the transport of coal and lime than had actually been paid, and to manipulate the wages due to the workers. Moreover the latter, who generally bought their food, clothing and tools at the stores attached to the iron works, found themselves paying excessive prices for them and contracting debts. Their dissatisfaction turned into indignation when they were not only faced with deductions from their wages, but saddled with fictitious debts. Many took the sole course open to them—absenteeism or migration to other parts of the country.[93]

The dismissal of the manager led to some improvement, but almost immediately Hanbury found his hands full with opposition from another quarter. The rapid development of his iron works had been possible because of the uninterrupted supply of fuel from the woods near his forges. But the destruct-ion of trees had been dreadful. Within three years, some six thousand beech trees had been felled for charcoal in the woods of Glascoed, Gwentwood and Glyntrosnant.[94] The resultant scarcity of timber had brought about a 100 per cent. increase in the price of wood, and the inhabitants of Monmouthshire were becoming restive. In the opinion of one observer, this was disastrous for the domestic economy of the shire, ' because ther ar neyther turfes nor coles to be had for money in this countrey.'[95]

The warning was reinforced by the demonstration organised by the tenants of the lordship of Usk, who, led by a priest, attacked Hanbury's charcoal makers at Glascoed.   Matters came to a head when a common informer—John Leeke, a London mercer—denounced Hanbury for having violated a law of 1558, prohibiting the felling of certain kinds of oak, beech and ash for fuel.   Leeke claimed to be acting on behalf of the inhabitants of the parishes stripped of their timber, and there began a keen litigation between him and Hanbury. Eventually they reached a compromise.   Leeke agreed to accept £200 and to surrender to his opponent, in exchange, all incriminating evidence.   But by a piece of fraudulence, worthy of his dismissed manager, Hanbury only paid him a quarter of that sum.[96]

Having circumvented these obstacles, Hanbury went on to make a large fortune from his iron works.   Yet, although he was typical of the ruthless industrial tycoon of the Elizabethan age, his will shows him to have also been of a charitable disposition, for he left money to release debtors from London prisons and to assist deserving workers.[97]   But before he was able to give this proof of his beneficence, he was to wage a prolonged and embittered struggle with the Mineral and Battery Company over his obligations to them and to the Tintern wireworks.

In the same year that the Mineral and Battery Company was incorporated by the Queen's charter, its members—who included the Duke of Norfolk, Sir William Cecil, later Lord Burleigh, and other state ministers and public personalities— decided to embark upon the ambitious project of establishing a wireworks at Tintern, in Monmouthshire.   It is probable that they were guided by two main considerations.   Much of the iron wire needed for the manufacture of essential goods, both consumer and industrial, had formerly been imported from abroad, but was now prohibited from entering the country by Act of Parliament.   The Company felt that this was an opportune moment to step in and relieve the market with home produced and cheaper wire. But more important than this was the arrival in England of Christopher Schutz, a German engineer and inventor, who claimed to possess the secret to the modernisation and enhanced efficiency of the wire industry which the times demanded.

Schutz had conducted experiments in the extraction and utilisation of iron ore in Saxony, and had discovered a revolutionary technique in the use of calamine for mixing metals, and in rendering iron more malleable for industrial purposes. The Government was quick to appreciate the invaluable contribution that he could bring to the incipient metallurgical industry of the kingdom. When he and William Humfrey, an official of the Royal Mint, entered into close amity and collaboration, initiated the idea of a privileged company to conduct investigations and experiments, and asked for assistance, the Queen's advisors immediately acquiesced in the formation of what became known as the Mineral and Battery Company, and encouraged Schutz to proceed with his plans for revitalising the iron wire industry under its aegis.

It was decided to set up a new enterprise in the vicinity of Bristol, but when Schutz and Humfrey went down personally to examine possible sites, they found that one indispensable factor was lacking. The rivers which were to supply the motive power were too slow and sluggish, and were, moreover, monopolised by the local corn and fulling mills. The two pioneers crossed the Severn, and after a preliminary exploration of the Usk and Wye valleys, they selected Tintern as the site which best met their requirements. And it was here, in September 1566, that the foundations of the new wireworks were laid.[98]

An agglomeration of houses, buildings and engines quickly sprang up where some thirty years previously the monks of Tintern Abbey had enjoyed undisturbed tranquillity. An innovation that roused great interest was the introduction of water wheels to drive the strange assortment of hammers devised by Schutz to beat iron bars into various lengths and thickness of wire. They often, not surprisingly, broke down, and had to be altered or renewed from time to time.[99] Labour was recruited in the neighbourhood, and Schutz sent for a master craftsman, an experienced iron wire drawer from Germany, to instruct the unskilled Welsh workers in the most advanced processes of wire-drawing.[100]   With a reformer's uncontrollable enthusiasm, he altered all the engines in the building where the wire was drawn, and for the next 2½ years subjected the workers to intensive training in their use.   It had little practical result. The Welsh wire drawers were inordinately slow in mastering even the first principles of the new technique, and their lack of skill reflected itself in the adverse balance sheets of the company.   The workers, one report complained,

> ' were soe dulle learners that in that tyme they made no good wyer. But in that tyme, by the naughtie yron, evill drawinge, and marringe and spoilinge both tooles and wyer, and their wages, the companie lost £800.'[101]

The situation was aggravated by the fact that,

> ' One Crumpe, a Clarke to the company, ymbeseled from them above £300.'

and, in fact, the maintenance charges of the wireworks cost the company over £3,500 during the first five years of its activity, with little or no compensatory profits.

There followed a series of dubious manoeuvres in which the works were successively leased out to members of the company, who tried to pay as little rent as possible and extract the greatest profit. At the same time, the Tintern enterprise made substantial progress. Although it had not been possible to obtain the right kind of iron, the resourceful Schutz had set up a refinery for the experimental preparation of iron for wire, and the products of Tintern were being eagerly sought after by the wire merchants of Bristol, Gloucester and London.[102]

The years that followed witnessed a gradual expansion of the wireworks, and by 1587 the various categories of wire manufactured there were bringing in a satisfactory profit to the company, who had felt themselves justified in raising the rent from £200 to about £600 in less than ten years. One distinguished member of the company was particularly elated by the enhanced value of the shares that she held, for the Queen had acquired those formerly held by the Duke of Norfolk whom she had executed for his share in the Ridolfi plot in 1572.[103] Between 120 and 160 persons were now employed daily at Tintern, and it was estimated that some five thousand people in England and Wales were dependent for their livelihood upon the wire which they received regularly from Tintern, and which they made into cages, rings for curtains, hooks, woolcards and other consumer goods.[104] But this same year of 1587 saw the first of three crises which, in rapid succession, threatened to destroy the prosperity which had been so assiduously built up by Schutz and the legatees of his innovations.

The first, like the second, was precipitated by Richard Hanbury, whose relations with the company had lately grown perceptibly cold. In addition to the fact that he had, on two occasions, been arbitrarily deprived of a lease of the wireworks, there had existed for some time an understanding that he was to supply Tintern with Osmond iron—considered to be the only category of iron suitable for the making of wire—from his iron works at Pontypool and elsewhere. But in common with other Monmouthshire iron-masters, Hanbury had chosen recently to concentrate upon the production of Merchant iron, which fetched higher prices on the home market. Rumours of these activities reached the authorities in London, together with the more specific information that while Monmouthshire woods were being devastated to feed the iron forges, Tintern was suffering from an attrition of Osmond iron which might at any moment force the wireworks to suspend its operations indefinitely. A commission was hastily despatched by the Privy Council to Monmouthshire, and the situation was judged sufficiently serious for a decree to be issued prohibiting the manufacture of Merchant iron, and reserving the woods for those iron works which had undertaken to furnish Tintern with adequate supplies of Osmond iron.[105]

Hanbury may have accepted the decree with a shrug of his shoulders. If so, it was a gesture of defiance rather than of compliance, for he set about to nullify the Council's injunctions by a scheme which did justice to his consummate subtlety.

The regular consignment of iron from Pontypool to Tintern was indeed resumed, but its quality began to deteriorate so rapidly that it became almost unworkable. Complaints flowed in from buyers, retailers and wireworkers about the shoddy and unserviceable wire that was being distributed to them. Criticisms were levelled at the performance of the hammermen, nailers, rippers, strainers and wiredrawers who formed the core of the specialist workers at Tintern, and they, in turn, defended themselves by casting aspersions on one another's skill. Their relations became embittered, and the situation was aggravated by the loss in wages, since most of the employees were paid for good wire and received nothing for waste and rejects. Finally, there came the ominous news that the price of wire was being arbitrarily forced up because of these circumstances, and that the standard of living of the wireworkers, especially in London, had been adversely affected.[106]

The Government could no longer ignore the growing disaffection at Tintern. It authorised a number of Monmouthshire gentlemen to investigate whether there was any truth in the allegations of some workers that the fault lay primarily in the defective iron supplied by Hanbury. Experiments were carried out, and they proved conclusively that better Osmond iron could be produced than was permitted by him at Pontypool. He was ordered to amend his ways and the quality of his iron, and to observe the conditions of the contract for the provisioning of Tintern with suitable iron, which he had signed with the company a few years before. Hanbury, however, ignored the order. The terms of the contract remained unfulfilled, the Tintern wireworks closed down for three months, and the unemployed workers began to wear as pinched a look as the iron which they had been accused of maltreating with their tongs. Eventually Hanbury's obduracy incensed the Privy Council. He was summoned before it, committed to the Fleet prison for insubordination, and all his Monmouthshire iron works were seized and their operations entrusted to the care of the sheriff of the shire and a committee of gentlemen. But before they had time to meddle with them, Hanbury had been released in return for a suitable apology and a promise to abide by his contract.

The third crisis, which occurred towards the end of Elizabeth's reign, was due to the treachery of some of the master workmen themselves. A certain Thomas Steere had conceived the idea of establishing a rival wireworks at Chilworth, in Surrey, and had flouted all industrial conventions by enticing a number of Tintern men to enter his service, and to place their experience and skill at his disposal. A few had succumbed to his liberal offers of money, including the son of the German engineer whom Schutz had invited to teach the first Tintern workers. It was he who actually drew up the plans—' a plott in writing,' as he called it—for the erection of the Chilworth works. All the water wheels, engines, tools and instruments set up at that place were exact reproductions of those used at Tintern, and there was a justifiable anxiety that the Surrey enterprise would prove prejudicial to the interests of the community in Monmouthshire. But the danger passed away. Steere failed to keep to his bargain with the Welsh engineers and specialists, and they returned to Tintern where they were reinstated without the slightest hesitation.[107]

The last year of the Queen's reign found the wireworks in a most flourishing condition. Its employees had increased to at least six hundred, and so much wire was being produced that there was an actual surplus of a thousand stones of it, valued at £800, available for sale. Appreciable quantities were being exported to France, Turkey and the Barbary States, and there is little doubt that the extraordinary variety of sizes—there were twelve of them, one thinner than the other—and the improved quality of the wire had earned an enviable reputation for the Tintern craftsmen. In addition, about ten thousand wireworkers in the kingdom were by now incessantly turning the wire into knitting needles, fishing hooks, lattices for windows, girdles, buckles, keychains, mousetraps, ferret and dog chains and a host of other consumer goods.

Harmonious relations existed between the workers and the speculators who leased the wireworks from the company, and they resulted in the institution of a welfare scheme which had

F*

few parallels in those days. A part of the profits was set aside to provide a stipend of £8 for a preacher to instruct the employees in Holy Scripture, and another £2 was allocated to a schoolmaster for teaching their children. Aged and impotent workmen were paid pensions for past services, widows received financial compensation, and in the event of plague, money was made available to assist those afflicted by it and to maintain their families. It was a contented community with little apprehension of the future, except for those percipient few who were disturbed by the rising costs of raw materials, and the gargantuan consumption of the timber resources of Monmouthshire.

IV

LAW AND LOCAL GOVERNMENT

THE legal and administrative union of Wales and England
in 1536 had established the supremacy of English law and
judicial system within the Principality, and by the time
Elizabeth came to the throne the English common law courts
and the Crown's prerogative courts—the Great Sessions on the
one hand, and the Courts of Star Chamber and Requests as
well as the Council of the Welsh Marches on the other—were
dealing with an ever increasing number of Welsh litigants. It
was one thing, however, to encourage the Welsh to bring their
cases to these courts ; in fact, little persuasion was necessary
since ' they will wrangle and contend one with another so
longe as they are worthe a groate.'[1] But it was another matter
to get them to accept their verdicts and to submit to them with
a good grace. One defendant, who had lost his case, positively
refused to quit the tenement in variance. On the contrary, he
cut down all the trees on the property, and filled the farm
house with a company of friends armed to the teeth and ready
to resist eviction. His comments on the court, which had
returned a verdict against him, were hardly more temperate
than his actions ; it was, he declared,

> ' the basest in this realme of England, and none came to sue to
> the same but beggars, poore people, saylors and sea faringers.'[2]

Part of the difficulty lay in the problem of how to enforce the
rulings of the courts. Honest and impartial verdicts might be
recorded in them, but within the Principality they were often
not worth the parchment they were written on. The officials,
whose duty it was to execute the findings of the courts, were
more amenable to the claims of kinship, corruption, influence
and intimidation than to the authority of the law. Even when
they were prepared to perform their duty, it happened too
often that the litigant who had the weaker legal case had the
stronger physical argument in the shape of friends and weapons.

The Government rightly believed that only the power of the

Crown could enforce respect for the law of the land, but the prerogative court established in Wales to impose it—the Council of the Welsh Marches—suffered from serious disabilities. The merciless regime of Bishop Rowland Lee, in the reign of Henry VIII, had inculcated some fear of it among the Welsh, but succeeding presidents had failed to turn the Council into an effective tribunal of justice. Its delays in trying cases were exasperating, and it proved again and again that it was incapable of commanding obedience from the gentry whom it was intended to discipline. Above all, there was more than a hint of corrupt practices in the proceedings of the Council. An indignant plaintiff complained in London that his property had been unlawfully detained by a certain Ieuan Lloyd whom he described as a ' clerk towards the Law ' and as one who,

> ' followeth your Mats Counsell established in the Marches of Wales and your Highnes Justices in ther Circuite in the Countys of Fflynt and Denbigh, thereby he may maintayne any suite or action before your Mats said Counsell and Justices not payinge any ffees and without any Charge other than his ordinary expenses.'

The complainant doubted whether he would have ' an indifferent Tryall ' in these circumstances, and it is significant that he opted for the Court of Requests as the only court where he could be certain that his case would be tried on its merits.[3] There is a suggestion here of a feeling that true justice was more likely to be obtained by the ordinary citizen in a common law court rather than in a prerogative court backed by the authority of the Crown. It was a feeling destined to grow, to swell and eventually to explode and bring down all the independent Royal courts in the following century.

One feature of the old Welsh laws which shocked the ethical susceptibilities of the English jurists and administrators in Wales, was their complaisance towards homicide. It had been the custom for the party guilty of murder or manslaughter to compound for the crime, and pay the family of the victim a sum of money which was intended to assuage their sense of grievance and turn aside their desire for revenge. It did not always do so, of course, but it had attempted to curb passions

and limit the danger to limb and property which an uncontroll-
ed vendetta would have perpetrated. To the orderly and
legalistic English mind, this financial composition for murder
was intolerable. It was the kind of primitive, accommodating
attitude towards crime which undermined the whole principle
of justice, little tempered by mercy, which they regarded as the
only possible basis of a well-ordered society.

The application of English equity put an end to this custom
in its crudest form. Murder was made punishable by death,
and the Welsh grew to appreciate the impartiality of a judicial
system which hanged both peasant and gentry for the crime.
But, like so many other Welsh customs, it reappeared in
another form, which perhaps could be commended in that it
saved the ordinary Welshman a deal of money. It often
happened that when a theft had been committed and the
thief identified, he would offer money as compensation to the
aggrieved owner through the good offices of a third party. If
the owner was prevented by a sense of personal dignity from
accepting the money from the hand of the thief, it would be
placed on a platter or dish and presented to him. He could
then take it and satisfy his conscience at the same time that he
had not dealt directly with the person who had wronged him.
If he objected to the financial composition, gifts of sheep or
cattle would be offered instead. It was a rough and ready form
of justice which obviated the heavy expenses of litigation and
saved much human misery.[4]

If the Council of the Welsh Marches was powerless at times
to enforce the law, the ordinary courts of the land were even
more pervious to the malevolent influences of those who had
little regard for the forms of justice, except when they could be
manipulated in their favour. The Justices of the Great Sessions
regularly held their circuits, and showed exemplary patience
and impartiality in their handling of Welsh transgressors and
witnesses. But even their presence and authority could not
restrain outbursts of hooliganism. At Brecon, a juryman was
assaulted in court by one of the public who shouted at him,
' Thou art a butcher ' and pummelled him cruelly.[5] It was in

the same town that two gentlemen attacked another juryman with drawn swords and wounded him severely within a few yards of the Chief Justice and other legal dignitaries.[6]

It was also too often the case that the verdicts of the Justices were ignored as soon as they had turned their backs. Bailiffs refused to levy fines if they had been awarded against their friends.[7] Companies of squires and yeomen banded together to rescue felons from the prisons where they had been committed after trial.[8] Murderers who could pull strings in high circles escaped their due punishment. Ieuan ap Thomas, who had knocked William ap Hugh on the head with a stone and fatally injured him, hoped to cheat the gibbet in this way. He had been aided and abetted by the constable of his parish who was his cousin ; he had been a faithful servant of the Salisbury family, like his father before him ; the sheriff of Denbighshire was the father-in-law of Sir John Salisbury. With such a galaxy of officials and gentry behind him, it would have been an act of blind faith to expect the Law to get the better of him, especially as he insisted that the fatal blow, given in self-defence, was ' but a flye bitinge ' and that William ap Hugh had died from his own negligence.[9]

Again, there was the problem of laying hands on felons and bringing them to the courts. After committing murders and other outrages, quite a number of them fled the country—the gentlemen sometimes to sea, where they soon became at home as rovers and buccaneers, and the common people to the woods and mountains. As many as thirty criminals left Brecknock hurriedly in 1592, and swelled the ranks of vagrants elsewhere.[10] The hills behind Tregaron, in Cardiganshire, were infested by people who had been declared outlaws for failing to appear at the Great Sessions of the shire. But whether all outlaws were genuine felons is debatable. An interesting case was that of Harry Richard of Northhope, in Flintshire, who disappeared in 1577 after presumably killing a certain Bellington. Twenty years later he returned to his native parish, was arrested and, when interrogated, declared that he had been offered forty shillings by Bellington's son to assume responsibility for the murder, as well as an annual pension of forty shillings.[11]

Outlaws seem to have been the bane of the authorities everywhere, and it was found that the only method to reduce their number was by issuing a general pardon from time to time. Those included in the pardon made a formal submission to the local Justices of the Peace, and showed that they were once again on the right side of the law by appearing publicly in their parish churches and in neighbouring market places. A general pardon was sometimes imperative to save some parts of rural Wales from a complete dislocation of economic life.

Then there were the Welsh juries whose unpredictable behaviour disturbed even the imperturbability of English Justices. When David ap Howel was acquitted in the Great Sessions of Brecknock, in 1583, of stealing two heifers, Chief Justice Sir Edward Walter became so infuriated and disgusted that he threatened to cite the jurymen before the Council of the Welsh Marches. He later changed his mind, and decided to make an example of them at the next Great Sessions.[12]

Sentiment or perversity may often have dictated the verdicts of Welsh juries, but a more powerful motive was the fear of, or respect for, the gentry of the neighbourhood. An independent judgment was a hazardous experiment in individual liberties at a time when even Members of Parliament risked imprisonment for exercising their critical faculties too openly. Welsh jurymen found it more expedient to allow their judgments to be formed for them by those whom they regarded as their intellectual and social superiors. When a commission was set up in Denbighshire to examine the Crown's claims to concealed lands, both the Recorder and Justice of Chester were delegated to address the jury and persuade them to pass a verdict in favour of the Crown. All their weighty legal arguments fell on deaf ears, for there were two gentlemen on the jury whose opinions were sufficient to prevent a recognition of certain royal claims.[13]

Oliver St. John, an English gentleman who owned some property in Glamorgan and who was anxious to establish his title to the parsonage of Penmark, had no illusions about the rough handling that he would receive from a servile jury. In a

letter to his friend, Sir Edward Stradling, he declared his
intention of appearing personally to fight his opponents, the
influential Mansell family. He added :

> ' And for that I am but a stranger in your countrey and allso the
> sheriff is my neere kinsman, as you knowe, so as I am sure the
> jurie must be empanelled by the coroners of your shire, to whom
> I am a meere stranger, and therefore I am most ernestlye to
> desyre yow to helpe your cosen (meaning himself) att the pynche,
> and to deale with the coroners for their lawfull favor to have an
> indifferente (impartial) jurye retorned, when the tyme shall
> come : and also in the meane tyme to labor such frendes for me as
> you maye, for, yf I were sure of indifferencye, I would not care.
> I pray you, good cosen, when my bailiefs shall come over hither
> to me, that you will send me the names in writtinge of XXIIII
> substanciall and honest men, suche as you are assured will be
> indifferent, that we may trust to, as then I may peruse them
> and seeke to get them retorned with your good helpe and others
> of my frendes.'

But even reliable juries were not enough, for the intimidation of
witnesses and the falsification of their depositions were only too
common. As St. John pointed out :

> ' Special regarde is chiefly to be had in the choyse of a clerk which
> will not be corrupted for affectyon to the contrary party, or by
> other meanes, but deale plainely and truly in settinge downe the
> deposicions of the witnesses examined.'[14]

There were, however, some brave men who were prepared to
face the whole brunt of physical coercion and the aftermath of
revenge rather than compromise with their consciences in
returning verdicts based on an honest appraisal of evidence.
When a case of murder was examined by the Justices of the
Great Sessions for Merioneth at Bala, in 1601, the jurymen
were directed to return a verdict of guilt against the two
prisoners charged with the crime. Among them there were a
number of squires who were interested in securing the acquittal
of the two murderers, but meeting with the adamant opposition
of some yeomen serving on the jury, they decided to negative
their arguments by less creditable methods than verbal
persuasion :

> 'Having secreatlie provided for themselves some kinde of
> victualls, preserves or some other drugges for there sustenance,

did by menacinge and threateninge wordes and termes, declare and confidentlie affirme to the rest of the said Jurye that yf they, the rest of the said Jurie, would not yeald to acquite the said prisoners, that it would be better and lesse losse than the rest of the said Jurie should be famished rather than the said prisoners, beinge gents of bloud, should be condemned to so ignominous a death, and accordinge to which there threates and menacies, they themselves beinge provided of sustenaunce as aforesaid, did att lengthe compell the rest of the said Jury bothe by threats and diverse strookes, and allso they the rest of the said Jury beinge through Could and Hunger allmost starved and famished aftere two daies and two nightes resistaunce, to yeald for safgarde of theire life to agree for the acquitinge of the said prisoners directlie against theire wills and consciences.'

Here force had overcome conviction but only after forty-eight hours of relentless pressure, which itself was an unsolicited testimony to the integrity of independent-minded Welsh yeomen.[15]

The Act of Union had expressly decreed that all legal procedure in Wales was to be carried on exclusively in the English language. The prohibition of the use of Welsh in legal matters, however, was an unrealistic and impracticable piece of parliamentary legislation if the true ends of justice were to be served. To expect a monoglot nation to respond to the niceties and tortuosities of a foreign system of law codified in an unintelligible language could only lead to a welter of abuses and injustices. Common sense prevailed, and a compromise was reached on the prohibition of Welsh in law courts. Although English continued to be the official medium of most forms of judicial procedure, oral evidence, interrogations and statements could be given in Welsh without restriction. Not only in Wales, it should be added, but also in the supreme courts in London, where there was no lack of interpreters among the numerous colony of Welsh gentlemen and merchants.

But even the collaboration of interpreters did not always satisfy the exacting requirements of impartiality and non-perversion of evidence. Some thirty years after the enactment of the Act of Union, their reliability was discussed in conjunction with proposed legal reforms affecting the Assizes of

Carmarthenshire, Cardiganshire and Pembrokeshire. The objection was put forward that testimony given in Welsh was too often translated according to the personal disposition of interpreters, and misled judges into giving unfair verdicts. To avoid future miscarriage of justice, it was suggested that one of the Justices of Assize for these three shires should be thoroughly conversant with the Welsh language.[16] This enlightened opinion stood out in welcome contrast with the disparagement of the language openly evinced in the Act of Union, and accorded to it a degree of dignity of which it was to stand in dire need in later centuries.

Although the Privy Council in London was the real governing body of the realm, it could not hope to preserve law and order in Wales without the support of the Justices of the Peace whom it selected from among the gentry, and to whom it looked for the implementation of its policy in all domestic fields. The Justices of the Peace have rightly been called the ' maids of all work ' of the Government,[17] for there was little in the way of local administration that they were not asked to do. The enforcement of statutes against recusancy, the suppression of witchcraft and sorcery, the provision of relief and maintenance in accordance with the Poor Laws, the strict observance of the Gaming Laws and the preservation of game, the prosecution of offences against a multitude of prohibitions, the distribution and control of grain in times of scarcity—these were only some of the duties which the Justices had to undertake.[18] Neither did the Crown and officialdom in London show any particular appreciation or gratitude when these onerous tasks were conscientiously carried out. They demanded an unswerving obedience to their instructions, and any perfunctoriness or procrastination were sharply criticised. The gentry who fulfilled the duties of Justices of the Peace were expected to regard themselves as servants of the central authority, and to subordinate their personal interests to the execution of laws conceived in terms of national and not class or sectional legislation.

Naturally the reaction of the Welsh Justices of the Peace to the burdens laid upon them varied according to their readiness to shoulder them, and to their interpretation of what was practical and what was not in the stream of directives that reached them from London. Like all specialised organisations, insulated from the every day lives of ordinary people, the Privy Council could sometimes commit errors of judgment in its regulations, and fail to allow for local difficulties and problems. Its prohibition of, or permission for, the export of corn, for example, might inflict misery on the very people whom it wished to protect, and it was the Justices of the Peace, knowing the local conditions, who mitigated the harshness of the regulation and often ignored it in the public interest. When a ship engaged in transporting corn from Conway and Rhuddlan to Scotland was attacked and invaded by a number of Conway men led by a priest, an appeal was sent to the local Justices of the Peace to remove them. The licence to export the cereal had been given by the Bishop of St. Asaph and Sir Thomas Mostyn, probably with the knowledge of the Privy Council ; but the Justices had the courage to ignore the authority of these two persons, and to bear in mind the need of the people for corn. They sent word that :

> ' they wolde not meddle with them [ie, the intruders], sayenge they were unruly fellowes and such as were not to be dealt with for that they have out that who soever offered to come on boarde them should come on the swordes pointe.'[19]

Pusillanimity was definitely not a characteristic of the Welsh gentry, even as Justices of the Peace, and the feeble excuse hoodwinked no one.

The Justices of the Peace often showed a humanity that would have been incomprehensible and even deplorable to officialdom in London. On two occasions, the Justices of Denbighshire allowed a notorious recusant, Richard Vaughan, to be temporarily set at liberty in order that he might arrange his private affairs, apprentice some of his seven children to various crafts, and protect his wife from being disturbed in her property by dishonest elements.[20]

There were, inevitably, vicious types among them who abused their authority and took a sadistic delight in venting their spleen on defenceless people. Edward Herbert of Mont-gomèryshire, for example, who intervened in a dispute about land and mendaciously informed one of the disputants, John Richard, that he had received an order for his eviction from the Council of the Welsh Marches. When Richard asked to see the order, Herbert arrested him. During his imprisonment, and despite a writ of Habeas Corpus from the Court of Requests to take the prisoner to London, Herbert deliberately ordered his men to destroy Richard's crops, incarcerate his wife and leave his children to starve. One of them, in fact, died from lack of food and care and was left unburied for a fortnight.

It was this kind of inhuman action, no doubt, that caused a certain Giles Owen of Wrexham to lose his head completely and to address the local Justice of the Peace, John Lloyd, as an ' errant knave, an easing dropper, a hooremonger and a rascal.' When reminded that Lloyd was, after all, a Justice of the Peace, his reply was short and snappy—' He a J.P. ! There is no justice within him ! '[21] It was the expostulation of a much harassed individual, and it inevitably led to his indictment for slander.

But what Giles Owen and many others felt and sometimes expressed in blunt language, was only too often experienced by the Privy Council and the Council of the Welsh Marches. The discreditable behaviour of the Merioneth Justices of the Peace on one occasion, provoked their wholesale con-demnation by the Lord President of the Council. They had proved themselves to be utterly incapable of dealing with the crimes that proliferated in that shire, so much so that the organisation for the detection and prevention of felonies had to be completely revised. They were ordered to divide the shire into ' allotments,' each with a resident Justice of the Peace, and to appoint a number of overseers responsible for the good behaviour of every township and parish. The overseers were given extraordinary powers of interrogation and control, and, in fact, were delegated to do much of the work that normally fell to the Justices of the Peace. The latter were strictly en-joined to meet often to discuss the new arrangements, to publicise them in every Quarter Sessions, and to have them read in Welsh up and down the shire.[22]

There were no busier courts in the land than the Quarter Sessions, where the Justices of the Peace administered petty justice and enforced the multifarious laws and statutes that were slowly transforming the Welsh people into a modern and progressive nation. The Quarter Sessions were excellent training schools for the indoctrination of all who took part in their proceedings with a sense of responsibility, duty and equity. What was almost as important, they showed up the advantages of local government, and how it could be conducted in collaboration, not in conflict, with local interests.

But these benefits only came to be appreciated after a long period of legal and administrative apprenticeship. For the greater part of Elizabeth's reign, the Quarter Sessions had their hands full with the intractable problem of adjusting the common people to their new conditions of life. That the Welsh were unruly would be an understatement of fact. They themselves did not deny it, nor did they hypocritically try to camouflage it. The Pembrokeshire squire and historian, George Owen, weighing up the qualities of his countrymen in some North and South Wales shires, described the inhabitants of Carmarthenshire as ' unruly and quarulous ' ; those of Montgomeryshire as being afflicted with ' troubles amonge themselves,' and the folk of Denbighshire as being ' much geeven to quarrellinge and Suites in Lawe,'[23] Only the people of Flintshire seem to have escaped his indictment ; they were ' verie civile.'

It was this contentious people that the Quarter Sessions had to handle and induce to acquire a less belligerent frame of mind. The process of self-control was fitful, to say the least, and what the explosive Welsh temperament was capable of doing produced a somewhat nightmarish atmosphere in the courts. Murders were common, but some were ferociously cold-blooded. A labourer, who had failed to break into a house at Llangynwyd, in Brecknock, deliberately set the building on fire and burnt a whole family to death.[24] The seduction of a wife or daughter, or an offensive remark at their expense, was rarely regarded as a case to be fought in court. The outraged relatives simply sought an opportunity to meet the offender and dispatch him. And it was in Flintshire, commended by George Owen for the civility of its inhabitants, that Thomas Cockeram, whose son had been bitten by a dog owned by Henry Thomas, assaulted and killed the latter with little compunction. The crime was made the more odious by the fact that it was committed immediately after the two men had been reconciled in the parish church of Dyserth, and were returning home together from evening prayers.[25]

The coroner was elected by the freeholders of the shires, and his primary duty was to arrange inquests on the unfortunate victims of fatal accidents, murders and sudden decease, and to establish the cause of, or responsibility for, death. Wherever circumstances permitted, the inquest was held at the place where the corpse was found, and a jury empanelled by the coroner from among those who happened to congregate there or who had witnessed the tragedy. The object was to obtain as impartial an opinion as possible on the question as to what extent the fatality could be attributed to human agency, to ' an act of God ' or to sheer misfortune. Where this was not possible, the coroner summoned a jury to a convenient place to weigh up evidence, and to arrive at a verdict in accordance with their views, or, in many cases, in compliance with his own.

The task of the coroner was not always an easy one, although in the majority of cases, inquests presented no difficulties. Accidents were too common in those days to excite much discussion or necessitate more than a cursory view of the victim's body. But there were often occasions when circumstantial evidence of foul play was too strong to be dismissed, and it brought into play the forces of suspicion, fear, prejudice—and superstition. The suggestion that death was not due to natural or accidental causes was sometimes sufficient to dissuade people from acting as jurors or giving evidence, although they were liable to be fined for default. And even when they obeyed the summons to attend an inquest, the coroner was occasionally

forced by them to base the verdict on the exercise of superstitious custom rather than on trustworthy evidence.

This appeal to superstitious belief was put to the test in
Flintshire in 1574, where an old woman had been found dead
in a field after a severe rainstorm. There was a persistent
rumour that she had been murdered by her nephew, a youth
who had been in her company on the day of her death. At the
inquest, one of the jury demanded that the boy should stand by
the corpse and touch it,

> ' for that some dyd holde opinion that if the person hadd byn
> thoccason of her deathe, the same person handeling the bodye, it
> would appere by bledinge or some outward aperaunce.'

The nephew did as he was commanded, and, probably to his
great relief, there was no effusion of blood. To confirm his
innocence, a brother of the dead woman then took hold of her
foot in one hand and declared to the jury,

> ' I take it upon my soul and dampnacon that this woman cam to
> her deathe by reason that she was lame of one hand and foote and
> the extreme coldness of the stormye weather and not otherwise.,

The jury accepted this primitive oath without reserve, but the
English law had misgivings, and a further inquiry was ordered.[26]

Another difficulty with which some coroners had to contend
was the truculence of juries, even the threat of violence at their
hands. It presented a Montgomeryshire coroner with a few
minutes of real danger on one occasion in 1594. At an inquest
summoned by him to view the body of a youth drowned in the
river Wye, a refractory member of the jury tried to create
trouble and confusion amongst his fellow jurors by suggesting,
against all evidence, that the young man had been murdered.
There followed a violent altercation between him and the
coroner, in which he used ' very evill and indecent speeches '
and threatened to attack him with a hedge-bill. According to
an eye-witness he then intemperately informed the coroner,

> ' if he were not a young man and the said Coroner an ould man,
> he wolde further displeasure him and surely abuse him, using
> other unseemly woords and speeches at his pleasure, and in that
> fury departed and cam no more to his said felowes,'

Emboldened by this display of churlishness, another juror, although he was prepared to agree to a generally accepted verdict of accidental drowning, refused to deliver it in writing, that is of signing the written verdict drawn up by the coroner, and unceremoniously withdrew from the proceedings. The unfortunate coroner was left in the predicament of having to submit an incomplete form of inquisition and findings to the Chief Justice of Assize at the next Great Sessions of Montgomeryshire.[27]

The preservation of law and order in the parishes was entrusted to a high and a petty constable. The former was usually a gentleman of means whose duties were nominal and supervisory, and who generally left his subordinate to cope as best he could with the exigencies of his office. On the other hand, the person invested with the authority of a petty constable could legitimately look forward to his tenure of office with mixed feelings. Although one of the elected representatives of the law in the parish, he was only too conscious that devotion to duty might be construed as interference and arouse the hostility of those to whom the law was a nuisance and its local officials a menace to liberty of action.

The principal concern of most constables was the prevention of petty larceny and the detection of those implicated in it. It was certainly one aspect of their duties that kept them on the alert night and day. The law allowed them wide powers of investigation. They had the right to visit any house in the locality without a warrant, and to subject its occupants and furnishings to the most thorough search. Moreover, they could request any parishioner they wished to accompany them in their tour of investigation, and qualify any refusal as contempt of law. It was seldom that they were not afforded the wholehearted co-operation of the parishioners, since it was the one occasion when the latter felt that the law was protecting and not meddling with their interests. It was for this reason that htey also readily accepted the authority of the constable to conscript them regularly to keep watch at night, particularly in the more remote and mountainous parishes where cattle and sheep pasturing on large stretches of common land were liable to be stolen if left unguarded.

In the fulfilment of some other duties, however, the constable could be prepared for opposition and not amicable collaboration. Few interfered with him as long as he was occupied with arresting vagrants or impounding stray cattle, or conducting captured felons safely across his parish to deliver them into the hands of the constable of the neighbouring parish. Difficulties and tempers arose when he was obliged to execute a commission which involved persons within his own sphere of operations. Winkling out pressed men from their homes, attaching people for minor offences and indiscreet behaviour, such as listening to private conversations behind hedges or under open windows and originating scurrilous rumours and tales, laying recusants by the heels, and carrying out other unpleasant orders from the Justices of the Peace to whom he was responsible for their prompt execution—all these activities could bring upon him every kind of indignity. The picture of the constable being ambushed, covered with abuse, attacked with weapons, mauled and sometimes seriously wounded, is a common one. And what must have aggravated his resentment at such cavalier treatment was the fact that some of his attackers, upon closer acquaintance, proved to be themselves Justices of the Peace, his superior guardians of the sanctity of the law.

When the law, in the person of the constable, was infuriatingly slow to take action, the parishioners often took matters into their own hands, and showed a surprising initiative in the detection and pursuit of law breakers. Keen observation and quick thinking enabled some of them to undertake some useful detective work. The unsuspecting Sir David Morris, curate of Buttington parish in Montgomeryshire, who had broken into one of his parishioners' houses, was astounded by the alacrity with which he was followed by a group of people and arrested by them for larceny. But he had forgotten that his right shoe had a patch which left a visible mark in the muddy track leading away from the house. His parishioners, however, had possibly taken greater note of the dilapidated state of his shoes than of his prayers, and they were able to establish his guilt and see him safely in prison.²⁸ At Wickweir, in Denbighshire, where a hue and cry was raised after a vicious assault on a household, a careful survey of the ground disclosed the track of a horse shoe which had four nails on one side and two on the other. By singling out this track from a maze of others, the pursuers were able to follow the retreat of the attackers for a considerable distance and through many parishes, until it terminated in the yard of a house several miles from the scene of the assault.²⁹

Any consideration for the law, however, was prone to evaporate at the slightest dispute among the same people who could render it such estimable service. It was often only after a brawl in which someone was hurt, that the law was allowed to intervene and its local strong arm, the parish constable, able to do more than wave helplessly in the air.

Altercations between families were, perhaps, not more numerous than in any other age, nor the motives more complex, but actions certainly spoke louder than words. Dogs were favourite instruments for prosecuting these private quarrels. A yeoman of Llangolman, in Pembrokeshire, not only maltreated the sons of a neighbour of his, but incited a ' bludy hound ' to bite them.³⁰ A Denbighshire farmer, who had crossed the path of an irate gentleman, had good reason to regret his pugnacity when a mastiff, trained for such eventualities, fixed his teeth in his shanks.³¹ Where humans were considered unsatisfactory objects for retribution, the attack was switched to their moveable property. Maredudd ap Griffith of Carweddfynydd, in Denbighshire, turned his back on his enemy, Griffith Lloyd, and sent in his dogs to worry his sheep. Two of them were killed outright, and the rest of the flock reduced to utter exhaustion by the mad chase that ensued.³²

The dissolution of the monasteries and the secularisation of religious institutions and property had obliterated the familiar figures of monk, nun and roving friar from the social landscape of Wales. At the same time it had brought into undesirable prominence a class of people who had been attached to religious houses, but principally for the satisfaction of material rather than spiritual needs. Deprived of the alms and consolation so long extended to them, the beggars and other social outcasts of the age were forced to turn to less hospitable quarters for their relief, and began to invade town and countryside alike. They did so in such menacing numbers that soon after Elizabeth's accession, their containment became a serious preoccupation with the Government.

The heterogeneous elements found amongst them reflected the economic and other factors which aided and abetted the growth of mendicancy in Wales as in England. There were the agricultural labourers and small yeomen, who had been victimised by rack-renting or who had simply been evicted from their homes by legal chicanery and force of arms. There were the demobilised soldiers and sailors, who had been pressed into service for the Irish campaigns and the intermittent expeditions against metropolitan Spain and her colonies. For many, especially those incapacitated by wounds and sickness, release from the Crown's forces meant hardship and misery, for they received little or no compensation. And the prospect even of casual employment seemed sufficiently remote for them to become resigned to begging as the sole alternative. There were also the felons who had evaded the instruments of justice, the dismissed industrial workers who were the perennial victims of periods of fluctuation in the country's overseas trade, and the English vagrants whose wanderings brought them into the heart of Wales from as far as Dorset, Somerset and more distant shires.

There was also in Wales a distinctive and colourful class of vagabonds, who cultivated an art besides that of exciting compassion and extracting alms by a display of abject poverty. These were the strolling singers, dancers and minstrels who travelled in companies from parish to parish, sleeping in barns and under hedges, and sometimes putting up at the house of a more sympathetic or musically-minded alehouse keeper, who was prepared to allow them to sleep there during the day on the condition that they entertained his customers at night.[33]

They were particularly conspicuous in North Wales, where the parish constables of Denbighshire and Flintshire were constantly at their heels. It would appear that custom dictated that the profession of minstrel not only entitled a man to earn his living by vagabondage, but positively thrust this occupation upon him. When the local Justices of the Peace decided upon the expulsion of a colony of beggars near the church at Spytty, in Denbighshire, in 1578, one of the mendicants was interrogated as to why he frequented the church. He answered that he was a minstrel and came there to publicise his songs, and added as an extenuation of his lack of fixed domicile—' for that he is a Rymer, he wandereth abrode.'[34]

That many of the vagrants were helpless victims of adversity was eventually recognised by the authorities, but there were some also who affected an extreme distaste for any sort of orderly life. These were the professional beggars, some of whom had been on the road for forty years or more, and who supplemented their eleemosynary pickings with petty pilfering of shirts, shoes and oddments of clothing from the premises of unsuspecting householders. Quite a number were women, from the age of sixteen upwards, who in the fulness of years became oblivious of the distinction between mendicancy and harlotry. It was also inevitable that there should be the unscrupulous purveyor of physical deformities, like the ineffable Robert ap John of Denbigh. Himself a gentleman of the road, he retained in his service a number of impotent beggars without arms or legs, and despatched them in relays up and down the shire to solicit alms for which he paid them a regular commission.[35]

Stern measures were considered necessary to deal with these and the less culpable vagabonds. Not only was it strictly forbidden to relieve their wants, but flogging was enjoined as a salutary punishment and as a deterrent to this method of earning a living. Where it was practicable, vagrants were to be returned to their place of birth, and a book kept for the purpose of their identification. That the local government authorities meant business was made transparently clear by the announcement that any parish constable, who allowed a vagrant to go unpunished, was liable to a fine of ten shillings.[36] Those who applied the lash seemed to have been more conscious of their duties than the constables who found themselves often torn between the demands of common humanity and the threat of a substantial fine. At least twenty-three Radnorshire constables turned a blind eye to the movements of beggars through their respective townships in 1568.[37]

In this they were merely emulating the behaviour of many of their superiors, for despite proclamations to the contrary, the gentry and common folk continued to open their purses to those who were forced by misfortune to beg. Charity of this kind might be frowned on in London, but it undoubtedly saved some miserable creatures from dying on the roads and the snow covered hills of Wales. Others were redeemed from that fate by the issue of special licences by the Justices of the Peace, which permitted them to importunate their betters for help. They were the privileged few who could wander with impunity from parish to parish, for a licence was a legal document which demanded respect. But respect was not always extended to their persons. An Anglesey beggar, who chanced to enter an alehouse cap in hand, was manhandled by the company there, who denounced his licence as a forgery, rifled his pockets and threw him out of doors. They might have been led to believe that he was masquerading as a mendicant by the fact that he had in his possession over six shillings—a sum difficult to equate with the customary impecuniosity even of approved mendicancy.[38]

The badge of poverty was not worn only by the itinerant musician and the wandering beggar. Rural and urban communities alike were shackled by a depressed class of citizens which lay upon them like an incubus, neutralising a source of energy which might have been used to some purpose, and creating an atmosphere of discontent and frustration inimical to law and order. The high incidence of murder, theft and less violent illegalities, which was so much in evidence during the reign of Elizabeth, can be attributed in good measure to the desperate conditions in which many of the lower orders in Wales found themselves. Heads of families, who had no means of support, were too often faced with the invidious choice of either breaking the law or seeing their dependants starve. In North Wales, the custom of leaving sheep and cattle to pasture unattended was an irresistible temptation to these unhappy people. Yearlings and lambs were furtively stolen at night, quickly killed and their skins thrown into the local river or buried, the meat hurriedly cooked and eaten, and the remnants concealed under the straw which often served as a communal bed.[39] There inevitably followed a visit by the parish constable, for it was an unalterable discriminatory practice that suspicion should fall upon the poor whenever an animal was missing, and their hovels thoroughly searched before an alternative explanation of its absence would be considered. Sheep stealing, of course, was punishable with death, but some Justices of the Peace were humane enough to substitute the pillory and flogging for the extreme penalty.

Where fear of the law was more potent than the physical distress of malnutrition and misery, the innate resourcefulness of the poor was strained to the utmost to eke out an existence. Women and girls hired themselves out to spin in the neighbourhood ; some families managed to scrape enough money together to purchase whole sheepskins, which they plucked before selling to local glovers to be turned into leather goods ; and in times of harvests there was a concerted rush to assist with the reaping and garnering of corn. This was particularly welcome, for the voluntary services of the poor were repaid with sheaves of corn and permission to glean the fields after the harvest. In this way, a little but useful store of corn could be acquired as well as straw for thatching the roofs or for spreading over the earth floors of their homes.[40]

The poor of Anglesey had evolved a highly organised system of mendicancy. It was customary for husband and wife, during the year following upon their marriage, to go begging but not together. The husband generally made his way to other Welsh shires or across the border to solicit grain and seed during the harvest season, and to gather ' houkes ' and ' thraves ' of corn all over the country. The wife, usually accompanied by an old woman, wandered from place to place during the months of June, July and August, and begged for cheese, wool, hemp, flax and other materials. In Anglesey, these women were known by the name of *Gwragedd Cawsa* or cheese-gatherers.

Another category of female beggars in that shire were the milkwives, who lived alone or in groups, and toured the countryside asking for gifts of milk, cheese and butter. Having accumulated a stock of these, they disposed of them by private sale in their cottages and divided the profits between themselves. They were also notorious gossips and scandalmongers, who had long excelled in the art of breeding dissension between families and parishes by malicious tales and inventions.[41]

Perturbed by what seemed to be the ungovernable tendency of the times to pauperise large sections of the community, despite the external manifestations of wealth and prosperity, the Government initiated its Poor Law system which was to be accounted one of its greatest achievements. The object of this revolutionary experiment in Elizabethan social legislation was to inculcate the nation, by a series of progressive measures, with the sense of communal responsibility for the welfare of those economically disabled by age, ill health or circumstances. The decrees promulgated by the Privy Council ranged from the imposition of a compulsory Poor Rate to the establishment of Houses of Correction, where work was provided for the able-bodied poor, but the Justices of the Peace entrusted with their implementation were allowed considerable latitude in adapting them to local conditions.

It became the general practice to divide the poor into two classes. The first consisted of the old and the impotent, who were allocated sums of money for their maintenance. The requisite funds were provided by the compulsory Poor Rate and the Poor Boxes placed in parish churches to encourage voluntary contributions. There was no escape from the rate, although some parishes were remiss in appointing collectors, but there is evidence that the poor boxes often received as cold a reception as the law that prescribed them.[42]

The second category included the able-bodied men and women who were unemployed. Various measures were applied in their case. Some were placed in the care of the wealthier inhabitants, who undertook to employ them as servants or apprentices, or else to support them. This they did individually or by forming groups of householders to share the responsibility and financial obligations.[43] Where this plan was found to be impracticable, quantities of flax, hemp and wool were purchased by the parish authorities and distributed amongst the poor, who were set to work on them and received fixed payments for the finished products.[44] Any refractoriness or disinclination to work on their part was reported to the Justices of the Peace by the overseers appointed to supervise the operations of the Poor Law, and laid the culprit open to imprisonment or flogging.

Fortunately for the poor, they were not entirely dependent upon State organised charity and relief, nor wholly subordinate to the whims and discipline of Justices, overseers and constables. There were many compassionate and sensitive people horrified by the degrading conditions in which so many of their countrymen lived, and who bore them and their plight in mind when disposing of their wealth. It was a lady of means, Elizabeth Morgan, who founded a charity for poor matrons at Caerleon in 1593.[45] Welshmen who had amassed wealth in England remembered their less fortunate brethren at home. Phillip Gunter, a skinner by trade, who was on sufficiently friendly terms with Lord Burghley to bequeath him a cup of silver as a ' gentle remembrance,' was one of these benefactors. He set aside a sum of money to provide twenty five poor men in Monmouthshire with coats of cloth worth 13/4 each, and a further sum for twelve impoverished inhabitants of his native parish of St. Michael Dyffryn Usk.[46] Another was a native of Llanfrynach, in Brecknock, who was a London citizen and member of the noble company of salters, while William Evans of the same shire, a merchant tailor in the capital, bequeathed £100 towards the improvement of poor clothiers in Brecon town.[47]

One of the best known of all establishments founded for the relief of the poor was the hospital erected at Ruthin in 1590 by Gabriel Goodman, the eminent Dean of Westminster. The regulations governing the admission of destitute persons were inordinately strict, but the fervour of the good Dean for superlative Christian virtues and the moral indiscipline of the Welsh possibly justified or, in any case, explained their severity. Ten

PLAN OF HAVEN AT AMLWCH TEMP. ELIZABETH

HUGH PRICE

men and two women were to be admitted on the condition that
the former were chaste and unmarried, and that the women
possessed qualities which would have disarmed the misogynistic
doubts of St. Paul. They had to pass some form of intelligence
test, which amounted to a correct recital, in Welsh or in
English, of the Lord's Prayer and the Ten Commandments.
They were to attend divine service every day, and any irregularity in their behaviour in church was to be reported by one of
their number chosen to spy on them. They were, of course, to
refrain from drinking, gambling and associating with disreputable persons ; neither were they to make a penny on the sly by
undertaking work which had not been approved by the hospital
authorities, nor fall into the perils of seduction by keeping
lodgers. And they were, finally, to keep regular hours, a
regulation enforced by the extinguishing of all lights from
9 to 6 in summer, and from 8 to 7 in winter.[48]

The normal intercourse of trade had always been a negligible
factor in the economic life of Wales prior to the reign of
Elizabeth, and consequently the lack of an adequate system of
communications had not made itself felt. Outside the towns,
the inhabitants made use of the old Roman roads which had
survived the passage of time, and where these did not exist they
travelled on foot and horseback along paths and tracks, many of
which could boast a similar antiquity.

This method of travelling was not without its hazards. Apart
from the presence of fissures deep enough sometimes for an
unwary person to fall into and break his neck, or landslides
which could obliterate a road, there were other dangers to be
considered, particularly where rivers had to be crossed.
Bridges were few, and being mostly built of wood, were liable
to be suddenly undermined or swept away by floods or by the
jetsam carried down by the rivers. The bridges of some of the
wealthiest and most important towns were victims to the
constant destruction of incorrigible Welsh rivers.

Towns and the more populated districts could be expected to
build and repair bridges in their own interests, but in the
outlying rural areas travellers had no alternative but to ford

G

rivers at their own risk. The treacherous currents and the often unpredictable increase in the volume and force of water took a constant toll of life, which was not confined to men and horses. For where rivers were impassable, except by ferryboat, accidents were not infrequent. A river with an unenviable reputation for fatalities was the Dee, where the ancient and primitive coracle was used to transport people to the English side, and proved too often to be no match for whirlpools and currents.

There were a cluster of ferries along the Menai Straits— Tal-y-foel, Porthaethwy, Bon y Don, Abermenai, Porthesgob, y Garth and some four others, which made a profitable business of transporting people and wares between the mainland and Anglesey. Porthesgob was the property of the Bishop of Bangor, who farmed it out for the annual rent of forty shillings, reserving the exclusive right of being rowed to his palace in Anglesey whenever he desired. Three pence was the usual charge for conveying people and animals across the Straits, but there was one condition attached to the lease. Every Saturday, which was market day at Beaumaris, the boatman ferried people across to the town, but whenever a fair was held there, it was tacitly understood that the ferryboat should be immobilised that day.[49] This may have been a subtle manoeuvre to keep ' foreign ' tradesmen from competing with the native artisans and merchants on their own ground.

Gradually the need for the better maintenance of roads became a pressing necessity, and the many testamentary bequests of land to mend parish highways showed that some of the more progressive inhabitants were fully aware of the harmful effects of bad roads upon the life of the community.[50] The growth of domestic trade, the circulation of traffic in goods and livestock, the introduction of carriages and waggons for travel and transport, and the desirability of speedier contact between government departments in London and local officials in Wales, were all potent arguments in favour of remedial measures for the improvement of communications. Another serious consideration was the fact that Wales lay nearer to Ireland than did England, and could, with the provision of good roads, be turned into an efficient military base for dealing with that turbulent island.

It was the Government's view that a competent administrative organisation was all that was necessary to transform an inchoate labyrinth of paths into a framework of well-appointed highways. In 1555, an Act had been passed which decreed that each parish was to be responsible for the upkeep of all roads within its boundaries, arranged for the appointment of a surveyor of the highways, and laid upon him the onus of extracting six days of roadwork from every parishioner. It was this act that the Elizabethan Government now proceeded to apply with all vigour, with due penalties for neglect and omission, with the assistance of its local government officials.

In Merioneth, the overseers of the highway were appointed every Easter week, and were empowered to impose a fine of one shilling on defaulters or on those who failed to find a substitute to do their work for them, for the Act permitted parishioners to evade their obligations on this condition.[51] The negligence of the inhabitants of the hundred of Menai, in Anglesey, to repair the highway from Abermenai to Beaumaris, brought down a heavy fine upon all the residents there. The sheriff was authorised to punish any refraction of the decision imposing the fine with forcible distraint of personal goods.[52] Fiscal penalties of this sort appeared to the Government to be the only method of inculcating parishioners with a sense of responsibility which, it must be confessed, was certainly not sought by them.

The efficacy of the Act of 1555, of course, depended upon the resolution of the surveyors, since the quasi-feudal character of six days of forced labour on the highways would hardly commend itself to the ordinary folk of Wales. Many refused to consider themselves bound by the stipulations of the Act, and judging from the presentments of local juries up and down the Principality, the passive resistance of the inhabitants was fairly general. Very little improvement was effected on the roads up to the end of the century, and even in some towns there was a culpable neglect of thoroughfares which could only militate against their commercial interests. Such was the case at

Denbigh, where Henllan Street was described in 1587 as being so,

> 'ffowle and dangerous to be passyd and travelyd that the subjects coming and ryding weekly to the markett are in great daunger, and ther horses with bagges and loades are dayly there, by reason of the deepness of the myre and dirte, overthrowne.'[53]

The authorities were predisposed to commit people to gaol on the slightest pretext, but they seem to have given little thought to providing adequate accommodation for those who were awaiting trial or who had been sentenced by law. They merely incarcerated lawbreakers in whatever buildings were available and sufficiently commodious to receive them. Some towns were fortunate in having castles—or the dilapidated remains of castles—in which to house prisoners ; other towns, like Wrexham, were obliged to imprison them in private dwellings, with results that were not always conducive to a healthy respect for the sanctions of the law.

Prison life for the ordinary transgressor, who did not enjoy the patronage of an influential burgess or squire, and who lived by the labour of his hands or the exercise of his wits, was one of ineffable misery and degradation. In common with all other prisoners, irrespective of social class, he was expected to maintain himself at his own expense, for there was no obligation on the community to keep him alive. For the well-to-do prisoner, this was an easy matter, and even strangers, who had no local acquaintance to assist them, could mitigate the rigours of captivity if they had objects to pawn. Rings, cloaks, and also swords, were some of the things that could procure for them preferential treatment in the matter of victuals and lodgings, and were redeemable if they chose to return to claim them after they had served their turn or been freed.[54] But the prospect of slow starvation was no delusion to the prisoner who had no relations or friends to supply him with food and money, and his only hope for survival was to appeal to the charity of sympathetic souls, or to insinuate himself into the good graces of the keeper of the gaol.

Gaolers existed then, as now, to serve the law, but within the precincts of their prisons, they were an undisputed law unto themselves. This was unavoidable, for they were not paid for their services but allowed to extract what remuneration they could from the exploitation of their prisoners. The authority that they exercised over them was absolute, and their disciplinary regulations so many screws to be tightened or relaxed according to the obduracy or servility of the unfortunate inmates. Naturally, there would be little inclination to apply them to the more prosperous minority who could afford to pay for comfort and regular meals, and who were in a position to retaliate at a later date for any incivility and lack of consideration. It was the defenceless labourer, the homeless wanderer, the recalcitrant criminal and other social outcasts who had everything to fear from the tyranny of gaolers.

The case of Gilbert Humphreys, who had been granted the office of town gaoler at Welshpool for the term of his life, was typical of the lawlessness that existed as much within as outside the prisons of Elizabethan Wales. Not only had he developed a taste for pocketing the monies deposited with him by debtors to satisfy their creditors, but he had had the audacity, on one occasion at least, to ignore the instructions of certain Justices of the Peace to release a number of prisoners on bail, and had kept them in irons instead. It is not surprising that when further information came to light, he was found to be actively collaborating with thieves who had unaccountably escaped from Welshpool gaol and were busy in the countryside.[55]

Where money and influence were lacking, complete submission might have its compensations, and, in fact, it occasionally resulted in a temporary suspension of rules. One delinquent in Wrexham gaol, who regularly went to fetch meat and charcoal for the keeper, was often given a fortnight's leave of absence to work with his brother who was a sawyer.[56] The gaoler at Flint took quite a charitable view of the depressing effects of prison atmosphere, for he had no objection to some of his charges making a rendezvous in a friend's house in the town to spend a convivial evening in drinking and singing.[57] But these were exceptions to the iron rule of segregation from the outside world—a rule enforced by irons on one or both legs.

This was a legitimate precaution, for there were desperate characters among the prison population. One such in Denbigh gaol took a violent dislike to the keeper's friend, who happened to be visiting him, and although encumbered by irons, he snatched up a pair of heavy tongs and inflicted a fatal wound on him[58]. Another criminal in the same gaol, who had already been whipped for stealing, was reduced to such extremes of desperation that he deliberately slit his tongue rather than be forced to confess to a further charge of theft.[59]

Shackles, of course, could not always guarantee the immobilisation of prisoners. There was that case of unquenchable temerity at Denbigh, in 1589, where a woman prisoner walked out of the town gaol, visited the market place, and calmly helped herself to some linen, a pig and a brass pan before returning to her cell. It may have been inexcusable laxity on the part of the keeper, but the astounding thing is that none of the lynx-eyed vendors in the market seem to have noticed that she was wearing an iron on one of her legs. There could have been no more tangible evidence of her place of residence.[60]

The privations, squalor and gloom of gaols inevitably led to many personal tragedies. Suicides were frequent, and the very name of 'Black Chamber,' by which one of the cells in Wrexham gaol was known, is suggestive of the scenes of human despair enacted there. But one of the most demoralising of all fears affecting the emotional life of the prisoners was the anticipation of plagues and fevers that might come their way. When these did materialise, they transformed some gaols into veritable charnel houses. For instance, in Brecon gaol, three epidemics of flux, fever, black sickness, colic and the 'newe sickness' or hot fever, possibly influenza, killed eight prisoners in 1569, thirty nine in 1587, and twenty nine in 1598.[61]

In these circumstances, it would be natural for the boldest and most incorrigible elements to make a dash for liberty whenever they could, and not a few managed to effect their escape. There were unusual facilities for evasion at Caernarvon Castle, where the walls were in such a state of disrepair that the inhabitants of the town, more concerned with the solidity than with the romantic decrepitude of the ancient fortress, had protested about their condition to the Government. Those within took the opposite point of view, and it was enough to push a rope through a hole in one of the walls, reserved for passing victuals to the prisoners, to enable some of them to escape.[62] Another category of delinquents, however, conducted their breakaway with less physical effort, and probably left with the connivance of their keepers. Where the perquisites of office were insufficient, gaolers—like other and more distinguished functionaries of the Elizabethan State—had no difficulty in adjusting their responsibilities to the pressure of personal needs.

V

EDUCATION AND RELIGION

ONE of the consequences of the gradual identification of Welsh political, religious and commercial interests with those of England, which followed upon the Act of Union, had been the realisation of the need for a more progressive system of public instruction. It was only too apparent that without schools modelled upon the grammar schools of England, there would be little opportunity to take advantage of the new, liberal professions which co-citizenship and the abolition of discriminatory legal restrictions brought in their train to Wales.

The landed gentry, in particular, were quick to appreciate the benefits that would accrue to them and their families from the foundation and patronage of educational institutions. Now that their energies and natural turbulence were being canalised by the Government to more useful purposes, and the perquisites of office as well as influence and honours placed within their reach, something more than literacy was considered to be an indispensable condition for self-advancement and for the satisfactory performance of the many duties entrusted to them. A knowledge of the classical languages and the acquisition of useful general information would pave the way for their children, not only to enhance the importance of the family at home, but to carve out careers for themselves either in the Church or in the new spheres of activity, where few Welshmen had attained any distinction hitherto, more especially in the administrative and legal professions. The fact that the younger sons of the gentry had now been deprived by law of a share in the territorial patrimony of their fathers was a further powerful argument in favour of the more practical aspect of education.

The Welsh squirearchy, however, was not the only class to assess correctly the importance of education in an age which allowed full scope for personal initiative and ambitions. The prosperous trading fraternities in towns and ports, and the wealthier yeomen in the countryside, entertained similar notions and saw no reason why their sons should not derive equal advantages from daily tuition, and from the physical correction that went with it. This growing concern of an incipient middle class in Wales with the provision of educational facilities was the first tangible evidence of an aspiration that was later to develop into a national characteristic.

One of the principal pioneers in grammar school education had been Bishop Barlow of St. David's, who decided to suppress the old ecclesiastical college at Abergwili, in Carmarthenshire, and to re-establish it at Brecon under the new name of Christ College. Despite the ' much wailing and weeping ' of the disconsolate people of Abergwili, the resolute Bishop organised the transfer in 1541 with a keen eye for publicity and effect. The college staff, with a multitude of prebendaries, canons, choristers and the official organist, and accompanied by waggons loaded with books, organs, vestments and ornaments, were ostentatiously conveyed to Brecon where they were greeted by the bells of that town. After a solemn ceremony, the Bishop proceeded to incorporate the old staff in the new college, and exhorted them to continue with ' singing and organ music,' as they had done at Abergwili. Finally, to protect the dignity of the new establishment, he issued a proclamation to all the neighbouring parish churches that he would excommunicate on the spot any person who failed to refer respectfully to it as Christ College.

A further step taken by Bishop Barlow was the foundation of a free grammar school within the college itself for ' the glory of God, the edifying of the People and the good education of youth.' His original intention had been to establish the school at Carmarthen, and to provide for a daily lecturer in Holy Scripture, ' whereby Gods honour principally preferred, the Welsh rudeness decreasynge, Christian cyvilitye maye be introduced.' The scheme was conditional upon the transfer of the seat of the See of St. David's from the old cathedral in west Pembrokeshire to Carmarthen. When it fell through, the Bishop, still in the interests of ' Christian cyvilitye ' but mainly through the medium of the English language, conceived the plan of founding an alternative grammar school in Brecon.[1]

The staff consisted of a master, an usher and a lecturer in

Divinity, who was to receive £24 a year for his services. This scheme was revised some years later, and the money allocated towards providing exhibitions for twenty four scholars.[2] There was no discrimination in the selection of these fortunate recipients of bursaries, and it is interesting to note that they included a youth, who eventually took up the profession of a tucker, and a priest who entered the school at the advanced age of thirty. The organisation of the school reverted to its original form when the custom of appointing a lecturer in Divinity was revived by Richard Davies, Bishop of St. David's, who collaborated with Thomas Huet, himself a canon of Christ College, in the translation of the New Testament into Welsh.[3]

The school received special commendation from the Commission set up by the Government of Edward VI to enquire into educational foundations and to recommend grants. By this time twenty scholars were in receipt of annual bursaries of £1. But, like other institutions, this school had its financial worries, aggravated, no doubt, by the cost of maintenance which tended to increase with the general rise in prices. Passing through Brecon, the English poet Thomas Churchyard described the condition of the school in the following lines :

> ' A free house once, where many a rotten beame
> Hath bene of late, through age and brackt of tyme,
> Which bishops now refourmes with stone and lyme,
> Had it not bene with charge repayred in haste
> That house and seate had surely gone to waste.'[4]

There were similar foundations at Carmarthen, Abergavenny, Bangor, Ruthin and Beaumaris, and less notable establishments in smaller towns, so that by the end of Elizabeth's reign, Wales possessed a well organised system of secondary education. The grammar schools differed little from each other in their internal administration and methods of teaching. They were placed under the supervision of a board of trustees, who managed the finances, selected the master and usher or under-master, received their reports, and expedited the application of the regulations drawn up for the guidance of staff and scholars.

One of the most commendable features of these schools was

the facilities that they offered for the free education of the sons of less well-to-do people. Wherever it was possible, a number of free places were reserved for ' poor ' scholars, who were to be taught gratuitously on the condition that their parents supplied the minimum necessities of schooling—pen, paper and the boys' clothing. At Bangor there were ten of them, and it was arranged that they should be accommodated in the Master's house. At Ruthin, a kind of means test was devised for all classes of applicants, with the exception of the local youth who were privileged to be educated without costing their parents more than the entry fee of fourpence. At the head of the list, the eldest son of a gentleman worth £30 a year was to pay 2/6 to the Master in addition to a quarterly sum of two shillings. At the bottom came the son of the squire worth £2, who only paid sixpence and fourpence respectively.

To be accepted into a Welsh grammar school in Elizabeth's days was no sinecure for the indolent and the introspective. Work began at six o'clock in the morning, and continued with a break for breakfast and lunch until five in the afternoon. Discipline was severe, and concerned itself as much with clean face and hands, tidy clothes and good manners as with attention in the classroom. Ruthin senior boys were appointed monitors to exact a strict observance of these rules, and it was, no doubt, in order to restrain their disciplinary enthusiasm that an admonitory injunction was placed on the School Statute Book that, ' Boys shall not be struck on the Ears, Noses, Eyes or Faces.' Any indulgence in games was frowned upon. Some intermittent playing of ball was allowed at Ruthin, but fairs and markets, the natural ground for juvenile pranks, were strictly put out of bounds. There appears to have been a predilection amongst the Bangor boys for dice and cards, for these were expressly prohibited by name. Instead, a kind of base ball game was organised on Thursday afternoons. Whenever the opportunity presented itself, the scholars were encouraged to shoot at the butts. To master the long bow was still considered to be an essential part of a youth's education, whether inside or outside a school, and the parents of the

Bangor pupils were indeed required to provide, amongst other things, a bow and shafts for shooting practice.

The curriculum adopted in the grammar schools was based upon the intensive, sometimes the exclusive, teaching of Latin, since familiarity with that language was considered indispensable to any professional career. Although English was coming into greater general use, especially in the daily administration of the country, it was still inconceivable that any aspirant for an ecclesiastical, diplomatic or legal post should not be conversant with Latin, and be able to speak and write it with some degree of fluency. Greek, too, was introduced into some schools, but never enjoyed the privileged position accorded to Latin.

Every effort was made to discipline Welsh boys to steep themselves in Latin. From their first day in school, they were made to understand that their capacity for learning it was a prerequisite, not only of a successful career, but of their continuance at school, for if they showed no aptitude for study they were often expelled at the end of the first year. Not that they were expected to perform linguistic miracles at first. The usher at Bangor school, who taught the rudiments of Latin to the lower forms, was reminded that :

> ' in all things and at all times he shall use such mildness of countenance and such Gentleness in speech that he may influence the Dullards (if any such there be) to study.'[5]

But as they progressed from form to form, the more were the scholars enveloped in the folds of latinity. They wrote Latin verse and prose compositions, were taught to declaim in that tongue, and finally were prohibited from speaking any other language but Latin on the school premises. At Ruthin Grammar School the boys of the senior forms were permitted the choice of Latin or Greek as their normal medium of conversation, and anyone caught breaking this rule was given an ' imposition.'

In this way, the grammar schools of Elizabethan Wales produced proficient latinists, who not only qualified themselves for future employment in academic and professional posts, but also cultivated a knowledge and appreciation of the classical writers of antiquity. Cicero, Vergil, Caesar, Terence, Plautus,

Horace, Seneca, Isocrates and Xenophon were some of the authors whom they read assiduously, and whose uninhibited reflections on human conduct helped them to evaluate much that motivated the actions of men in this age, when the liberalising tendencies of the Renaissance and the Reformation were releasing society from the bonds of medieval ethics and feudal customs.

But there was always a lurking fear among the patrons and founders of these schools that an oversurfeit of pagan literature might very well prejudice the more spiritual side of education, which aimed at indoctrinating the young scholars with a genuine feeling of piety and a taste for good morals. For this reason, the works of Christian authors like Erasmus were used as appropriate text books for study, and stringent orders were given to masters and ushers to omit any passages in pagan writing which might tempt the boys to indulge in adolescent thoughts, neither proper nor conducive to undivided attention to their work.

The prudish editing and expurgation of the pagan poets, however, did not satisfy the more vocal section of the pedagogic community, who were distressed by the preponderance of classical over religious instruction and feared its effects upon the character and morals of the scholars. It appeared indefensible to them, for instance, that so much attention should be paid to Latin verse and Greek prosody at Ruthin Grammar School, and so little to the precepts of Holy Scripture. For had not the founder of the school, Gabriel Goodman, the eminent Dean of Westminster, intimated to Queen Elizabeth that the primary purpose of the institution was ' the virtuous and godly education of children in their duties to God and her Majesty whereby they may be able to serve in God's church and the commonwealth.'[6] Surely that admirable purpose required as practical a knowledge of Christian ethics as of Latin hexameters ! Or so Richard Parry thought.

A scholar of a most Puritanical disposition, he had left Wales for England, possibly to take up various private teaching posts ; but his irrepressible affection for his native land found an outlet in the purchase of religious books, which he forwarded to his friend and relation, an Anglesey squire, to be translated into Welsh. It was in a letter, referring to the despatch of six such books, that he ventilated his criticism of the secular nature of grammar school education. Two of the books—*A Reformed Catholick* and *A Catichisme*, he recommended for immediate translation into the vernacular ' for the benifite of my loving contrymen.' The other four were in Latin, and had not yet been turned into English, but which, he wrote :

> ' I do wishe might be commonly taught in all yowr sckools in stead of Cato, Ovid and other prophane bookes, for in my opinion a skoler shall Reape more perfecte knowledge concerninge the fower principall or Cardinall vertues, as Wisdome, Justice etc out of the later parte of one of their bookes, which parte is caled Specalum de Moribuz & contains not fully tenn leaves, in on yeare than he shall learne owt of Vergill or Ovid in XIti yeares.'[7]

So much concentration on Latin and Greek left little time for any other studies. There was no provision made for the teaching of mathematics and foreign languages, and only two schools— Abergavenny and Montgomery—ventured to allocate some hours every week for singing, a national cultural pastime in Wales but one which found itself ostracised in most schools. As was the Welsh language itself. The Ruthin school rules made it a punishable offence for any boy to be caught speaking his mother tongue in the junior forms, and although there is no evidence as to its status in other grammar schools, the probability is that the use of the language was rigorously debarred everywhere. This prohibition did not necessarily reflect a contempt for the Welsh tongue, for the same treatment was meted out to English in many English schools at that time. Both languages had to be held at arm's length within the schools so that the boys should be compelled to express themselves in Latin or in Greek. That the grammar school could be used to divorce Welsh boys from their native tongue, and thus progressively wean the educated classes in Wales from their own culture, may have appealed to some philistine minds. But it was, on the whole, a futile attempt at denationalisation and renegation. The attachment of the majority of Welsh youth to their maternal language remained strong.

The opportunities offered by the grammar schools were quickly grasped by ambitious parents, not least by those who lived in the countryside. So eager were they to have their sons educated, even at some personal sacrifice, that one contemporary writer felt himself compelled to record their attitude of wholesome respect for the seats of learning :

' There is no man so poore amongst them but for a while will set his sonnes to schole to learne to write and read, and those whom they find to be apt, they send to the Universities & cause them for the most part to give their minds to the study of the civill law.'[8]

This idealised generalisation hardly corresponded to the actual attendance of Welsh children at school, but it contained a modicum of truth in that the appreciation of institutionalised learning was widespread among the Welsh people of all classes.

The expense of maintaining the young scholars was met in a variety of ways. Some parents took the precaution of stipulating in their wills that sums of money should be set aside for that purpose until their sons or young kinsmen had reached an age when they could be apprenticed to a trade,[9] or proceed by patronage to a university. For instance, John Mathews, a London merchant and native of Llangollen left the residue of his estate to purchase property near his birthplace, and instructed his executors that the revenue derived from it should be employed to keep four young relations of his at school or at a university. Sufficient land was bought to provide the boys with £4 a year, and the selection of the four was entrusted to the vicar of Llangollen and Chirk.[10]

In some grammar schools the generosity of the gentry made it possible for poor but promising youths to continue with their studies, without fear of being withdrawn because of a financial crisis at home. At Bangor Grammar School, for instance, the Wynn family of Gwydir had founded a scholarship for a scholar from Beddgelert, whom they nominated after consultation with the vicar and churchwardens of the parish church there.[11] Noble patrons could be useful in another way too. A young scholar at Beaumaris Grammar School, and cousin to

Sir Richard Bulkeley, was able to curtail his food bills without impairing his healthy adolescent appetite, by resorting to Sir Richard's table in his town house on every possible occasion.[12]

Not all the gentry supported the grammar schools to the extent of sending their own sons to them. Either the curriculum and the pedagogic attainments of the masters seemed insufficient or, what is more probable, they wished their heirs to be taught in an atmosphere completely divorced from the influence of a Welsh environment. The Gwydir family were, undoubtedly, warmly attached to Bangor Grammar School, but Sir John Wynn saw to it that his son attended the school at Bedford, in England, furnished with his own bedding and a silver spoon, and where a year's board and lodging cost his father a little over £13. It may have been the wider range of subjects taught there that persuaded Sir John of the advisability of sending young John to Bedford, for in addition to Latin Grammar, Greek and Hebrew, the boy was instructed in two modern languages, French and Italian, and in instrumental and vocal music.[13]

Another and more famous English school that attracted scholars from Wales was Winchester College. Its register contained the names of the sons of notable families in Caernarvonshire, Denbighshire and Glamorgan, some of whom later became scholars and public men of repute.[14] Christ Hospital or Greyfriars School, in London, also drew a steady stream of Welsh boys, principally from Monmouthshire, for the schoolmaster's wife was a native of Chepstow, and could be relied upon to show solicitude for her young countrymen. The school was conducted along strictly Protestant lines, and apart from their lessons in Greek and Latin, the boys were taught to read the Bible in English, attended prayers regularly, listened to sermons preached by eminent divines and lapsed Catholic recusants, and took notes of their edifying exhortations and confessions.[15]

Entry to the grammar schools was inevitably restricted by considerations of money and distance, and the generality of the

Welsh country people had to rely upon more local institutions for the education of their sons. The responsibility fell upon those parish priests who had enjoyed some measure of higher education, and were prepared to impart their knowledge to the more intelligent and aspiring of their youthful parishioners. Many of them, although transferred to isolated rural communities, kept librarie of books in theology and philosophy. It was these humble but enlightened vicars and curates who gathered their ' scolers ' around them at their homes or even in the parish churchyard,[16] illumined their understanding of Christian principles and taught them how to read and write.

Where such progressive members of the clergy were not at hand, or were exclusively employed as private tutors to the children of the local gentry, resort was had to less distinguished dispensers of learning amongst the laity. As at Denbigh, where Alice Carter, late of London, tried to make both ends meet in 1574 by turning her small shop, where she made stockings, into an improvised classroom for needy children.[17] It was to a similar school, in all probability, that a pedlar woman sent her young on to improve his mind. She had come to the neighbourhood of Bangor on Dee, in Flintshire, to seek work at harvest time, and out of the meagre wage that she received after a long day's arduous activity in the cornfield, she paid threepence for his elementary tuition at the town school.[18] The boon of literacy was something to which even the members of this humble and despised class aspired in Elizabethan Wales.

The grammar schools were fortunate in enjoying the patronage and liberality of both Church and squirearchy, but the advancement of learning was not the exclusive domain of ecclesiastics and gentry. One of the most creditable features of the Elizabethan age was the enthusiasm shown by people in the ordinary walks of life for the foundation of schools, and their solicitude for the well-being of teachers. William Jones of Usk, for instance, bequeathed £10 towards the maintenance of a school in that town on the condition that it should be established within two years. Unfortunately it was not.[19] The same ill-success attended the disinterested efforts of William Lloyd of

Willington, in Flintshire, to found a free grammar school in the town of Hanmer. He left some property to that end, but his will was bitterly contested, and Hanmer remained accordingly without a school.[20]

Presteigne was more fortunate. John Beddows, a clothier in the town, who founded a free school there in 1565, appointed trustees to look after the property and set the finances of the school on a firm footing. Where educational enthusiasts did not have the means to establish schools, they showed their good will by leaving sums of money to schoolmasters, most of whom were definitely in the lower income group in Elizabethan Wales. The master at Llandinam was as grateful for the legacy of ten shillings given him by a yeoman of that place, as was the master at Montgomery for the revenue from the property reserved for his maintenance by Edward Herbert, a Montgomeryshire gentleman.[21]

The grammar schools were an inestimable boon to the advancement of education in Wales, but the progress of native scholarship was prejudiced by the absence of a university within the Principality. Ambitious and successful products of Carmarthen, Ruthin and other grammar schools, who wished to attain some academic distinction or improve their chances for more remunerative employment, had no alternative but to enter the ancient universities of Oxford and Cambridge, as so many Welshmen had done during the preceding two centuries.

It was not difficult for the sons of the relatively wealthy gentry to do so—for the purpose of study or diversion, and many Welsh squires, who had not had the advantages of university education, insisted that their sons, or at least one of them, should proceed to either Oxford or Cambridge. They were, like the parents of later ages, apprehensive lest these young men should fail to identify the university as an institution where study was a normal part of a student's life, and waste their time and their parents' money in idleness and dissipation.

One detects a familiar note of anxiety, enveloped in much parental advice, in a letter written by William Wynn, the squire of Glyn, in Merioneth, to his son Cadwaladr at Oxford :

' Therefore prayse God that thou hast carfull parents to place thee in Oxenford, a famous University, the fountayne and well head of all learning. Keepe company with Honest students who aphore evill courses as drinking and taking toebacko to their own losse and discredit of ther frends and parents, who sent them to the University for better purposes.'

The squire urges his son to be present at debates on worthy subjects, to be attentive to good sermons and to cultivate the habit of taking down brief synopses of their principal points. There follows a direct reference to the importance of economy in money matters, a hint that constant vigilance is required to avoid being cheated by university servants, and a plea that he, Cadwaladr, should do his utmost to acquire a good English accent :

' I will allow you noe servitor. You may serve yourself and spare 6d a weeke. Take heed least you be gulde by the buttler that he sett downe in his booke more for bread and beere than you call for. Specke no Welsh to any that can specke English, noe not to your bed-fellows, and therby you may . . . freely specke Englishe tongue perfectly. I hadd rather that you shuld keepe company with studious honest Englishmen than with many of your own countrymen, who are more prone to be idle and riotous than the English.'[22]

The poorer student was faced with the perennial problem of his kind—how to subsist on the knife-edge margin of necessity in order to complete his course. Not a few resorted to the established expedient of filling some minor office or performing some domestic work within the colleges. But it was the generosity of the Church and the lay patrons of the universities who assisted the majority of them, with exhibitions and scholarships, to spend fruitful years digesting the ponderous erudition of those days. The Welsh element at Oxford increased in number and volubility after the foundation of Jesus College by Hugh Price in 1571, and it is estimated that about 230 or more students from North and South Wales were entered in its registers between that year and 1622. Many preferred to enter the other constituent colleges, but the aim of the greater part of them was to equip themselves for a successful career in scholarship, government service and ecclesiastical preferment.[23]

A glimpse or two of the life led by Welsh students at Oxford can be obtained from the surviving letters of what was probably an erratic rather than a well-conducted correspondence with their families. They had to provide their own bed linen, usually one or two pairs of sheets, and table ware—a drinking pot, spoon and trencher. They were also responsible for paying their tutors, as well as their living expenses and college fees and dues, including ' battels.' They were expected to buy their own books for study, and paper materials for taking notes at lectures, and it is obvious that a fairly brisk trade in second-hand books flourished at Oxford. William Brynkir, writing to his godfather, William Maurice of Clenennau, informs him gleefully that he had bought Caesar's Commentaries and a number of other textbooks at considerably reduced prices, and had only paid eighteen pence for a paper book which had originally been worth 3/3. He seems to have found some excellent bargains, for he wrote :

'I have allso bought sum at the seconde hande for which I would not take 3 times as much as I payde for them.'[24]

Where books were unobtainable, it was necessary to procure them from London booksellers, but the prices were naturally much higher.

Family servants bringing money and letters from home were eagerly awaited. Without their periodic visits and their bags of coin, life was apt to become grim while debts accumulated. Clothes, shoes, laundry, rent for lodgings—the colleges had not yet become resident—and tuition, all produced a plethora of bills which had to be met. Sometimes it was the unfortunate tutors who had to bear the brunt of the financial perplexities of their charges, and their desperate appeals to parents two hundred miles away in Wales were not always heard. Griffith Roberts, who had agreed to supervise the studies and defray the expenses of a Welsh student at St. Mary's Hall in Oxford, found himself out of pocket to the extent of £5 at the end of term, and was sadly disillusioned to discover that he was expected to resign himself to the loss.[25]

The majority of the Welsh students at Oxford worked hard, no doubt, but any fluctuation in their financial resources was liable, however, to threaten many of them with a drastic cessation of their studies and a precipitate return to their country. This was the fate of four young Welshmen in 1563, when the money allocated towards their exhibitions and deposited for safety in the treasury of Rochester Cathedral, was stolen by the servants of the Dean of Rochester.[26] The sum concerned amounted to £54, which, when divided among the four, would account for the austerity to which the ordinary Welsh student was condemned during his sojourn at Oxford.

At Cambridge it would appear that Welsh students were sometimes the helpless victims of a chauvinistic prejudice against their nation. That, at least, was the impression conveyed by a doleful remonstrance addressed to Lord Burghley in 1578, and signed by three fellows of Magdalen College— Buckley, Jones and Vane. They averred that the Master of the College, Diggory Nichols, had declared upon his elevation to the principalship, that he would not tolerate the presence of a single Welshman, and had proceeded to winkle them out of their livings and rooms in the college. Jones, an indefatigable lecturer in Greek, had found himself replaced by a shoddy individual, who was incapable of delivering more than ' thirteen lectures in three quarters.' The Butler of the college, a Welshman desperately trying to pay for his studies by acting in that capacity, had been summarily dismissed and sent to earn his living ' by adventures.' Buckley, a Senior Fellow and spokesman of the dispossessed Welsh minority, had lost the presidentship of Magdalen to which he was entitled, as well as his pupils who had been deprived of their exhibitions. The indictment of the Master of Magdalen ended in an inflammatory denunciation of his insensibility to smell and sound. His cows had conceived the habit of congregating in the court of the college to be milked before the hall door ; that operation finished, they were permitted to wander nonchantly into the chapel, or to peer inquisitively through the hall door at meal times. Moreover, the Master's wife was an ungovernable scold, whose voice penetrated into every corner of the building. In fact, the venerable college of Magdalen was rapidly becoming a farmhouse dominated by an unscrupulous Master and his bellowing wife.

The Master's reply to these charges was a model of verbal strategy. Ignoring the references to his bucolic interests and repudiating any anti-Welsh sentiments, he made it perfectly explicit that he had denied Buckley certain collegiate honours because of serious defects in his character, person and pedagogic attainments. He possessed neither learning nor discretion ; he neglected divine service and positively disliked sermons ; he was continually in debt ; he absented himself from lectures in the most irregular manner. What was equally reprehensible was his sartorial taste, which clashed vividly with the sombre dignity of his calling, for he wore ' blewe nethersockes, chamlet venecyens, sutt satten dublet, gret ruffes, a hatt and band, following the fashione.'[27] Such foppishness was contrary to the statutes of the college, but the Master had even a stronger card to play. He wrote that Buckley had arrested and imprisoned a Fellow of Magdalen for having declared that he was either a Papist or an Atheist in view of his non-attendance in chapel and his aversion to sermons. It was not necessary for the Master to elaborate on this subject. As he was fully aware, the merest hint of Papist affiliation was sufficient to turn the scales against any man. There was no further correspondence from Buckley.[28]

With the completion of their studies, the Welsh students at the two English universities had to cast around for a livelihood, and it was here that personal contacts, influence and patronage were often more important than academic distinctions. The sons of the gentry could be fairly certain that there would be no lack of openings for them in the service of Church and State. There was a plenitude of administrative and legal work reserved for their class, and in the case of those who took orders, the Church regarded good birth and breeding as desirable qualifications for its highest offices, although it did occasionally show a real appreciation of learning and character by promoting poor but erudite scholars to the topmost ranks of the ecclesiastical hierarchy. Neither did the sons of the richer yeomen and burgesses have to worry unduly about their future.

Trade and the law were the obvious professions for them, and there were opportunities for advancement in both fields in England and at home, where the perquisites of commerce and town government were being drawn more and more into the hands of the wealthy and privileged class of citizens.

There were, inevitably, a number of students who enjoyed none of these advantages, and who had to make their way in the world as best they could. The majority had to be contented with a form of existence which was hardly conducive to intellectual vigour—the post of parish curates living on a miserable income, and attempting to grapple single-handed with the problem of ministering to the spiritual needs of a generally indifferent, irreverent and turbulent peasantry. Some were more fortunate in gaining the good will of influential gentlemen, who employed them as their private chaplains and as tutors to their sons, in England and Wales. Not that they all professed a liking for this kind of occupation. With the passage of time, the dull routine of daily lessons, the poor remuneration, and the petty tyranny of small-minded patrons could drive even the most conscientious and enthusiastic tutor to revise his opinion on the usefulness of private teaching.

For instance, when the squire of Bodwyryd, in Anglesey, solicited the services of John Price, a former Cambridge scholar, as tutor to his children, he received a courteous but firm refusal, and a rather sour explanation why one graduate had abandoned private teaching for the ministry. Price wrote to him :

' Tyme was when I myself had wondrous great delight in trainning up of youth. But now . . . I have taken my Ultimum Vale of that toilsome & cumbersom kinde of life, for (in good sadness) of all other vocations in the world, I have found both by wofull experience (the Mistres of fooles and Dottrels) and by some readings (the compendiary & ready way to profounde learninge) that the Paedenticall profession is, and ay hath beene, most thankless according to that threadbare versicle—"Scire volunt omnes, mercedem pendere nemo".'[29]

But without patronage or employment of this kind, a university graduate was face to face with a depressing prospect, for his classical or theological scholarship was not of the kind to fit him for practical vocations. A note of bitter frustration, which was their common experience, is evident in a letter addressed by one of them to Sir Edward Stradling of St. Donats :

> ' The world hath showen yt selfe soe ungratefull towards me and soe backwards in requitinge the greate charge which I have byn att for the attayninge of lerninge that never yet was I in any possibilitye of having anye resonable staye.'

A friend of his, however, had managed to secure for him the post of chaplain to the Warden and Fellows of New College at Oxford, but, unfortunately, it would cost him £10. There follows an appeal to the benevolent squire to provide this key money—the ' ten pound silver key,' as he calls it. But it is either a desperate or an over-sanguine student who promises at the end of the letter that, if he obtains the post :

> ' vertue shall therby be advanced, lernynge encreased, the churche of God in tyme better edified, my countreys expectacon satisfied and the glory of God celebrated.'[30]

The alternative to sending young Welshmen to the universities was to give them a sound education in law at the London Inns of Court. The intention was not only to prepare them for posts requiring legal knowledge, but also to equip them to deal with the complex problems arising out of landownership—entails, leases, marriage covenants, endowments and the like. It was generally the sons of the gentry and of the more affluent yeomen and merchants who registered as law students at the Inns. John Wynn, the son of Maurice Wynn of Gwydir, entered Furnival Inn and proceeded from there to the Temple, where his chambers cost him £5 a year. Some years later, he made a good match by marrying the daughter of the Lord Chancellor of Ireland.[31] Thomas Bulkeley, brother of Sir Richard, was a member of Lincoln's Inn, and amassed a considerable fortune as counsellor of the Inn. His death led to an ugly scene. He had converted his money into rubies and diamonds and, as the chambers at Lincoln's Inn were constantly being broken into, he had entrusted much of the treasure to his friends. Upon his death, Sir Richard travelled post haste to

London, and found—or imagined that he had found—some of the precious stones missing. He impetuously accused his brother's friends of transferring them to their pockets, only to be overwhelmed with a shower of malicious epithets.[32]

Sir Richard did not lack an answer for, like his brother, he was an adept in legal matters, and had proved on one occasion how a knowledge of law could be useful to a Welsh landlord. According to a contemporary report :

> ' being complay'd off at the Counsayle of Marches for breach of an Order of that Court, he drew his answer with his owne hand. That he could not bee evicted out of his possession but by order of the Common Law, pleaded the Statute of Magna Charta & demanded Judgment. Which answer being putt into the Court & Sir Richard Shuttleworth, knight then Chiefe Justice, being informed of it, called for a sight thereof & after perusall sayd to the Counsellours att the barre—"Looke, my masters, what a bone Sir Richard Bulkeley hath cast into the Court for you to tire & gnaw upon".'[33]

The cause concerned the possession of a house at Beaumaris, and Sir Richard won it. It was the sort of triumph that would impress the Welsh squires with the importance of acquiring a good legal education, in order to deal with property disputes of this kind and to hold their own in a court of law.

That the Welsh people passively accepted the imposition of the Protestant form of worship must have undoubtedly gratified the promoters of the new religion and disconcerted the defenders of the old. But it must have also mystified those who had anticipated a violent reaction to the forcible suppression of the Catholic creed and ceremonies, which had been indissolubly linked with the history of a proud and independent people for a thousand years or so. The dissolution of the Welsh monasteries, the abolition of the Catholic liturgy, the persecution of the papist recusants, clerical and lay, and the ruthless destruction of objects of reverence and the outward symbols of the faith, appear to have left the Welsh curiously unaffected. Where the stubborn Cornishman, the taciturn North Englishman, the intransigent Irishman—and for that matter the hard-headed Scotsman—took the religious reformation seriously to heart and demonstrated their approval or rejection in revolt and internecine struggle, the reputedly emotional Welshmen showed a singularly detached attitude towards the momentous upheaval in the religious evolution of the kingdom. They seem to have stood aside and capitulated without much protest to the new dispensat on whereby the same government that commanded their political allegiance demanded also their spiritual submission.

Their acquiescence can be partly attributed, of course, to their unreserved and undiscriminating support for the House of Tudor. Yet no Welshman was more loyal to the English throne than Robert Aske, the leader of the Pilgrimage of Grace, who opposed Henry VIII's pretensions as self-appointed head of the English Church, but proclaimed himself to be a faithful subject of the King before he suffered death. The imperturbability of the Welsh, when the very foundations of their ancient faith were being torn up one after another, seemed to be more expressive of apathy than of any conviction or feeling that what was being done was desirable or an improvement on the older order. And, with notable but few exceptions, the nation remained indifferent to religious matters until it was caught up in a paroxysm of spiritual experiences in the eighteenth century.

To unravel the reasons behind this strange apathy is no easy task, and the passivity of the Welsh, when the other Celtic nations were engaged in local or international wars of religion, is a fascinating problem. It is obvious, however, that Catholicism had become for many people an emasculated confession of faith, with little to maintain or commend it except traditional observances and a sentimental attachment to an ancestral form of worship. Its very inertness and complacency, induced by centuries of collective orthodoxy, made it vulnerable in any contest with an aggressive and individualistic creed like Protestantism, intolerant of authority, impregnated with nationalistic arrogance and ambitions, and seeking ways of acquiring property in this world without jeopardising an eventual claim to the promised mansions in the next. The materialistic twist given to the nature of the Welsh people by the economic pressure of the times, the abandonment of their old, leisured, even indolent, way of life, their preoccupation with the task of finding their place in the new social structure that was replacing the feudal compound of classes, may have been some of the factors that slowly but insidiously corroded their links with Catholicism and propelled them towards the new religion.

That the Welsh gentry should have accepted, for the most part, the new national Church was to be expected. They would hardly conceive it as a grievance, for example, that the religious houses should be destroyed, when they were allowed and encouraged to increase their own estates by leasing or purchasing the sequestrated monastic lands from the Crown. Neither did they resent the subordination of the Church to the Crown, for it curtailed the power and activities of the clergy, depressed their status, and opened the way for enlightened and capable laymen to take a more prominent part in national affairs and in the councils of the Government.

In general, however, the conformity of the squires was one of outward compliance with the ceremonies of the new Church. Some of them, it is true, showed energy and ruthlessness in prosecuting the opponents of the religious policy of the Government. Richard Vaughan, a Caernarvonshire Justice of the Peace, was hated :

' of all papists that knowe him for becawse he doth correct theire errores and goeth about to bryng them to amendment of leif.'[34]

His method of correction was to hale as many recusants as he could lay hands upon to the Quarter Sessions, and indict them for refusing to attend church services. But it is fairly evident that the new Protestant doctrines were not given an enthusiastic welcome. There were landed families in every shire in Wales who resolutely adhered to the old faith, and although the eventual conflict with Spain and the moderate conduct of Elizabeth's Government towards them drew many away from Catholicism, there remained a hard core of uncompromising recusants up to the end of the century and beyond. They were particularly conspicuous in North Wales, and it was their courage in facing the publicity and penalties of non-conformity that kept the spark of Catholicism alive in Flintshire, Denbigh-shire and Caernarvonshire, and, on one occasion at least, attempted to fan it into a flame of revolt.

It was in the hope of galvanising the more militant minority among the Welsh Catholics that a papist zealot wrote and circulated an appeal—or, more correctly, a call to arms—in the form of an *awdl*, a poem in the traditional strict metres. The anonymous poet may very well have been a member of the squirearchy, and his verses show him to have been intimately acquainted with classical literature and deeply impregnated with the theology, as well as the traditions and history, of the Catholic Church. His invocation to his co-religionists passion-ately denounced the persecution of the faithful and the dissemination of the new doctrines :

> ' The land is distracted by the Ammanite destroyer,
>   The Commandments and Justice are openly broken
>   By spurious and hollow casuistic assumptions,
>   By blasted doctrines ; the faithful are despoiled,
>   Robbed of homes and lands impiously ; and with
>   Ruthless hands are we put into bonds.'

There follows an impassioned call to initiate a religious crusade against the ministers of the new Church, and the poet did not hesitate to reanimate the dormant racial animosity between Welsh and English in the interests of his anti-Protestant campaign :

> ' Rout ! Rout out the spurious priesthood,
>   The illiterate drunken cures,
>   The unlearned Scripturists, blind leaders,
>   All and every heretic—unholy heathen,
>   Rout them with sword, ye true Cymric Brythons,
>   There's hatred to Jesus by traitorous Saxons ! '

The poem ends in a reminder of the essential doctrines of the old Faith, and a promise of superterrestial reward for those who joined the crusade :

> ' To Arms ! Now to the battle for the holy mysteries,
>   The bread of grace which holds the holy form of God,
>   His flesh and blood and wounds in mystic union,
>   Which by the sacred power and utterance of priests

Is brought from Heaven to earth and sacrificed anew.
'Tis now a favoured time to stay the offensive heretic.
Then Forward ! and you the unfading crown shall win.'[35]

The tenacity and integrity of the Catholic squires of North Wales, John Williams of Llansantffraid-yn-Rhos, Rees ap John Griffiths of Combe, Hugh ap Thomas of Whitford, Edward ab Ellis of Holywell, the Owens of Merioneth and a host of others, were matched by those of the South Walian recusants. Thomas Morgan and Owen Jones of Presteigne, the Buckes of Knighton, the Tubervilles in many Glamorgan parishes, and the Lloyds of Llandeilo, in Carmarthenshire, refused adamantly to renounce their faith.[36] They abstained from church services, although this laid them open to heavy fines, succoured priests in their homes, kept Catholic schoolmasters to educate their children, and organised the holding of Mass in secret. The house of Richard Lloyd at Erbistock, in Denbighshire, was a notorious rendezvous where priests met regularly to administer the sacrament to the faithful, and to baptise their children in Latin with salt, spittle and oil. At this ceremony, the officiating priest would take a little salt in his hand, spit on it and put some in the nostrils and ears of the child, and then annoint its breast and back with oil.[37] It was at these secret meetings also that Catholic literature, in Welsh and English, would be distributed from hand to hand to enlighten the scattered flock on the tenets of their faith and strengthen them in their adversity.[38]

The fact that many squires remained obdurate in their attachment to Catholicism, while others were lukewarm or indifferent towards the official religion, was not without its effect upon the common people. The gentry were expected to set the tone in this, as in other matters, and their inferiors were content to emulate the attitude and conduct of those set in authority over them ; not least, the Justices of the Assize :

' whose affection towards religion they note and are the redier to draw forwarde or backwarde as they shall perceve the temporall magistrate to be affected.'[39]

Encouraged by the behaviour of the recusant gentry, and by the general lack of enthusiasm among the conforming families—

and revolted, in some measure, by the calculated conversion of some for the sake of office and emoluments—the common folk paid lip service to the established Church while continuing to preserve and follow the ingrained habits of a thousand years of Catholic piety. The doors of the churches were closed to all traditional observances and customs, but there were sacred places outside the churches, and it was there that the ordinary people assembled to perform them.

No power on earth, it seemed, could prevent them from going on pilgrimages to various localities and shrines associated with their national saints. In North Wales, the times fixed for these pilgrimages were announced by Welsh minstrels known as ' Pencars ' (an anglicised form of *Pencerdd*—a member of the upper grade of bards in medieval Wales) :

> ' whoe at the direccon of some oulde gentle wooman doe orden-
> arilie geve the somons of the time certaine for suche meetings.'[40]

The shrine of Saint Beuno at Clynnog, in Caernarvonshire, was the scene of incessant supplication, backed up with offerings of bullocks and money. There was a common belief that some bullocks, when they were born, had certain marks which placed them under the special patronage of the saint and spelt prosperity for their owners. On the other hand, Beuno's vengeance was something to be feared and avoided, and it was only a foolhardy man, for instance, who would cut down a tree on ground hallowed by the saint's associations.[41] The well of Saint Trillo near Llandrillo, in Denbighshire, was another favourite haunt of pilgrims, and witnessed at least one secret marriage between Catholic communicants in 1590, where the service was conducted in Latin, an unknown language to the bridal pair, and officiated by a priest who also preferred to remain unknown to them.[42]

Other practices which reflected the religious temper of the common folk were the carrying of relics on one's person, the keeping of vigils in isolated chapels, and the telling of beads or ' knottes,' even in church, where the most fervent tellers often drowned the reading of the revised Prayer Book, and hotly alleged, when they were reprimanded, that ' they can read upon their beades as well as others upon their books.'[43] To make the sign of the cross was still prevalent and was done, for example, whenever the countryman shut the windows of his house, left his cattle in field or stable, and proceeded to his work in the morning. In fact, any tribulation or ill luck was invariably attributed to remissness in this outward expression of piety.

To many foreign observers, the tenacity with which the Welsh countryfolk clung to these practices seemed to postulate a deep desire for the restoration of the old Faith. In the mounting heat of the religious conflict between Catholic and Protestant Europe, it was perhaps inevitable that they should confound repugnance for doctrinal changes with active resistance to them. A papal agent informed His Holiness Pius V, in 1571, that :

> ' the province of Galia is a stronghold of the Catholics and the ancient enemies of the English.'[44]

The Irish rebel, Fitzgerald, was equally sanguine in his estimate of Welsh opposition to the forcible imposition of English Protestantism. In his declaration to the Irish people on the eve of his rebellion in 1569, he wrote that :

> ' All the chief and strongest of the Northern quarters (of England) as well as of Wales, which are next to us, are so Catholic that they long for nothing more than to see the Sacraments of Christ restored again in their country. The Queen can make no great army out of any part of England but that the greatest number of them must be husbandmen which usually are Catholics.'[45]

As far as Wales was concerned, it was a grievous misjudgment of the true relationship between husbandmen and throne, as the uninterrupted flow of Welsh soldiers to Ireland was to prove conclusively.

To all outward appearance, the Church in its Protestant guise showed little, if any, improvement on its previous Catholic trappings. After the first flush of reformist activities under Edward VI, and the abortive attempt under Mary to restore Papal supremacy, the ecclesiastical order was given a definitive shape under Elizabeth and sank into a dependence upon Royal supervision and the fruits of patronage and preferment. All the old abuses, which had discredited the reputation of the Catholic dispensation, reappeared in good measure. The most flagrant was the treatment of church property as marketable propositions. Parsonages, tithes, prebendaries, ecclesiastical offices were leased or farmed out as if they were pieces of rentable property, and it was generally the laity who entered into the deals and acquired church sinecures and emoluments as sources of personal income. For example, the Registrarship of the diocese of St. Asaph was in the hands of Humphrey Robinson of Oxford University :[46] that of the diocese of St. David's, worth £200 a year, was held by a Brecknock gentleman.[47] The Archdeaconry of St. Asaph, likewise, was leased to one of the sons of Sir John Salisbury—for sixty years if he wished it—on the condition that he paid the absentee archdeacon £100 a year either at the west door of the cathedral or at the west door of St. Paul's Cathedral in London.[48] These and many similar transactions roused no comment in that age. The Church in Wales was poor, and the members of its hierarchy hard put to make both ends meet, or so it was alleged. It was a natural solution that every available source of profit should be capitalised, and a regular income assured.

The effects of this system on the spiritual welfare of the people were disastrous. For one thing, it led to absenteeism on a large scale. The vicar of Hanmer, in Flintshire, who after much angling had finally procured for himself the cure of Islington in London, sold his interest in Hanmer to the highest bidder, a layman, and went off to the capital without a single thought for his parishioners.[49] The Dean of St. Asaph, who also lived in London, was content to draw his rents from church property in North Wales, which he had leased out to various people, more than half of it to Sir John Salisbury.[50] The law passed under Henry VIII, forbidding churchmen of every rank to be absent from their parish, church or office for an inordinately long time, was broken with impunity, and non-residence became, as in pre-Reformation times, an ineluctable habit of churchmen.

To escape the charge that they were neglecting their parishioners the clerical lessors generally laid down the condition that the lay impropriators should find substitutes to carry on church services, and to attend to such matters as baptism, marriage and burial. These requirements were met by hiring curates, and clerics at a loose end, for a miserable stipend, and without more than a very perfunctory examination of their qualifications and antecedents.

Few of these clerics, and of the parish priests in general, were capable of propounding Holy Scripture and of making even the simplest doctrines comprehensible to their flocks. Their ignorance and idleness were proverbial, and their lack of education painfully apparent in their uncouth ways and in the superficiality of their lives. For many, especially those who did not keep small farms to eke out their inadequate income, the problem of resisting the pressure of poverty appeared insurmountable, and led them to commit indefensible breaches of ecclesiastical discipline. Evicting people from their property through the unscrupulous detention of legal documents,[51] forging money,[52] keeping taverns,[53] and playing cards for money,[54] were resorted to, either out of desperation or a cynical indifference to the proprieties of their calling. The fact that they could claim benefit of clergy, and avoid the penalties of the secular law even for serious offences, rather encouraged their indulgence in them.

Benefit of clergy was one of those prerogatives enjoyed by churchmen which exasperated the laity beyond measure. To escape the consequence of their crimes, priests and clerics in holy orders had only to show that they were members of the established Church, to be transferred from the Royal Courts, with their severe punishments, to the spiritual courts and their lighter penances. What was particularly objectionable, in the eyes of the public, was that the system could be easily abused. A superficial knowledge of reading was usually accepted as sufficient evidence of association with the Church, inasmuch as learning was accounted synonymous with the ecclesiastical profession. It was a comparatively easy matter for intelligent criminals to profess an ability to read, and thus claim benefit of

H

clergy, the more so as so many clerics were unbeneficed and behaved, to all outward appearance, as ordinary laymen.

But even this unscrupulous method of cheating Royal Justice was not always successful, as was proved on one occasion in Radnorshire, where Thomas Bull was charged in 1602 with poisoning. His many friends who had attempted to hush up the case by bribing the whole judicial apparatus—Jury, Sheriff, Justices of the Peace and Gaoler, decided, as a last resort, to claim benefit of clergy for him :

> ' Hopinge to redeme the liffe of the said Thomas Bull by the benefytt of his clergie, being learned . . . and also the better to assure the saffety of the said Bull by the said benefitt of his clergie, they did bringe hym the said Bull a booke to assaye and to rede upon. Howbeit, the said Bull, beinge a man lettered as before, was so amazed by the secret worke of Nature, and the Judgment of Allmightie God, that he could not reede any Whitt, but said that there was a Miste before his eyes so that he could not decerne the letters or to that effect.'[55]

His unexpectedly defective vision dashed the hopes of his friends, for he was found guilty and executed for the crime.

Law-breaking clerics were rarely admonished, or assisted to mend their ways, by their ecclesiastical superiors. The Welsh bishops and other members of the Church hierarchy, many of them Englishmen or the sons of landed gentry, were too engrossed in their personal affairs to do much more than simulate an interest in the activities of the lower clerical orders. They occasionally, at the request of the Government, compiled reports in which they dutifully lamented the sad decay of Christian decorum and knowledge in their respective dioceses, but took few steps to rectify it. This might explain the incredible latitude allowed to the vicar of Llanrwst, Sir Griffith Kyffin, and to his incorrigible family whose bravado and brutality, about the year 1581, seem to have mesmerised the authorities into complete impotence.

Sir Griffith, blessed with a progeny as reckless as himself, was governed by no recognised or recognisable ethical code. He had appointed one of his sons and a son-in-law to be ministers, entrusted with the indelicate task of marrying couples, whether they favoured matrimony or not, and generally without licence.

Another son was a consummate card and dice sharper, who systematically cheated the servants of neighbouring gentlemen and forced them to pay their debts by stealing their masters' goods. Hunting and tippling were the daily physical exercises of the Kyffin family, and assaults and frays kept them in fighting trim. To meet current expenses, Sir Griffith forged and counterfeited wills and deeds of conveyance, and levied *comorthas* on his parishioners in return for ' saying new gospels,' whatever that may have meant. On one occasion he went so far as to kidnap the son and heir of a deceased gentleman, a boy of thirteen, and, with the threat of corporal punishment, forced him to marry his daughter, a libidinous wench who, moreover, had the unfair advantage of being eleven years older than the lad. Sir Griffith and his tribe might have enjoyed a longer lease of delinquency if they had not untimely attacked a servant of the Gwydir family, and found themselves exposed to the vengeance of Sir John Wynn and the Court of the Star Chamber.[56]

There was some excuse for the omission of the Welsh Church authorities in the matter of discipline, for they were not permitted to devote much time to the supervision and good regulation of their dioceses. The Government regarded the highest dignitaries of the Church quite as eligible for secular duties as any of the landed gentry, and certainly did not differentiate between them in their obligations to the state. The clergy of the diocese of Bangor, for instance, were ordered to provide soldiers and weapons at their own expense for the Irish wars, and made no attempt to evade this liability. In the same way, bishops and other high-ranking clerics were given, and loyally accepted, positions of authority which made them almost as much servants of the Government as of the Church, and interfered considerably with their pastoral and spiritual work.

A canon of Llandaff was a Justice of the Peace, and so were the Bishop and the Dean of St. Asaph. The Bishops of St David's were invariably members of the Council of the Welsh Marches, and were expected to attend its meetings regularly.

One of them, Richard Davies, was also given the invidious task of investigating the depredations of pirates, and identifying their aiders and abetters, on the coast of West Wales. The superior education and the wise statesmanship of many of the Welsh bishops fully entitled them to the Crown's confidence, but so many commitments must have interposed between them and the orderly administration of their dioceses, which they were obliged to delegate to less competent officials.

Their sedulous attendance on government work was not the sole obstacle to ecclesiastical reform. The pernicious system of pluralism was as congenial to Protestant bishops in Wales as it had been to their Catholic predecessors. Bishop Hughes of St. Asaph, for instance, was accused of holding fifteen livings in addition to the archdeaconry of the diocese and the rectory of Llysfaen. His maladministration of the bishopric was eventually made the subject of an official enquiry which revealed that he had leased church property on his own terms, and extorted money from his clergy during his periodic visitations. His successor, William Morgan, the translator of the Bible into Welsh, exercised more restraint, but he also kept the archdeaconry in his own hands. Another eminent churchman, Richard Davies, Bishop of St. David's, not only enjoyed the additional emoluments of three livings and a prebendary, but was guilty of simoniacal practices. He dealt arbitrarily with the property of the diocese, leasing it for long terms and drawing a sizeable income from the transactions. Yet these lucrative practices were not, and could not be, attributed merely to cupidity. The Welsh bishoprics were notoriously poor. That of St. Asaph could barely derive £200 a year from its temporalities, and St. David's was only richer by a hundred pounds. Expenses, both diocesan and personal, were heavy and had to be met out of revenue. But the methods used to balance episcopal budgets, although normal to the Elizabethan age, debarred the bishops from initiating any serious reforms among the lower orders of the clergy.

So did the ostentatious way of life of some of the bishops—Marmaduke Middleton, Bishop of St. David's, for instance, who tried to ape the manners and lavishness of a prince of the

Church. A chronic lack of money led him to bleed his clergy financially, but he died in debt, leaving his widow to face his creditors. She tried to placate them by selling the fine clothes that she had accumulated over many years, and her wardrobe was a fitting testimony to the Bishop's ideas of what his wife should wear. Among other choice items, it contained gowns of satin and silk grosgrain lined with squirrel and faced with marten, cloth of crimson and gold, crimson embroidered velvets and towels of damask.

The preponderantly secular outlook of the Church, its largely effete clergy and the many abuses that they committed, were bound to contribute towards the spiritual malaise that was afflicting the Welsh people. No one attempted to deny that it existed, although few were unduly perturbed by it. A lay observer recorded gloomily that whereas people over thirty years of age clung to certain papist ideas and tried to frame their lives according to them, those under that age had little or no conception of any religious faith or doctrine whatsoever.[57] This was corroborated by Bishop Richard Davies of St. David's who, much to his consternation, found ' a great nombre to be slowe and cold in the true service of God . . . some careles for any Relygion.'[58] If the criterion of layman and bishop was the general behaviour of the people towards the Church, they had every justification in assuming that there was profound apathy towards its message, and a corresponding lack of reverence for its institutions and ministers.

Possibly at no time in the history of the Welsh Church had so much hooliganism taken place within the parish churches. It was so prevalent that, as far back as the reign of Edward VI, the Government had found it necessary to promulgate a Statute to the effect that any person attacking another with weapons in a church or cemetery should lose an ear ; failing that, he should be branded in his cheek with the letter F, signifying fraymaker, and excommunicated.[59] As a deterrent the Statute had had, and continued to have, little success in Wales. It did not prevent Ieuan Gwyn, a priest, from drawing his rapier and dagger upon another member of the clerical fraternity in the chancel of Clyro church, in Radnorshire, and wounding him in the head ; nor Henry Thomas from striking Roger Phillip with a javelin in the churchyard of Llaneleu, in Brecknock.[60] And it certainly did not deter Sir John Wynn of Gwydir from assaulting another gentleman in Conway parish church, and barely managing to evade a vicious sword thrust in return.[61]

The theft of church goods became a commonplace incident. Silver chalices, surplices, Communion table cloths and even bells were stolen by people, who had little compunction in breaking into churches. A most outrageous and impudent larceny of this kind was committed at Wrexham. There the parish church, admired for its attractive tower, possessed another feature which drew the attention of visitors like the Englishman Fynes Morrison, who wrote in his Itinerary that :

' The town Wrexham, bewtified with a most fayre Tower called the Holy Tower, and commended for the musicall organes in the Church.'[62]

They also held an irrepressible fascination for a native of the town, James Myrick, who, in 1590, conceived the daring plan of extracting more than music from them. As many as twenty seven of the pipes were stolen by him and sold to a pewterer at Chester before he was finally detected.[63]

Such thefts and acts of desecration were deplored and punished, but the thieves could have reasonably pleaded that they were merely following precedents established by more exalted persons than they. It was the Government, in the reign of Edward VI, that had first organised the systematic spoliation of the goods and jewels of churches, often to the detriment of religious services. For instance, Gresford church had been so thoroughly rifled of its ornaments that divine service had been discontinued for a considerable time, and the parishioners had been forced to plead for the restitution of part of the looted ornaments in order to keep some semblance of religion alive in the district.[64] At Laugharne, in Carmarthenshire, the inhabitants had anticipated the rapacious officials of the Crown by appropriating the plate of the parish church, and selling some of it to procure a corporation charter for the town.[65] With these and other examples of sponsored thefts of church property occuring up and down Wales, it was not surprising that there should have been a widespread shedding of doubts about the propriety of stealing consecrated objects, which continued up to the end of the century.

The way was therefore made much easier for putting parish churches to more secular uses than those for which they had been originally designed. With the growth of local government, and the delegation of so much administrative and legal work to the regional and parochial officers of the Crown, it was found necessary to find some accommodation for them to perform their duties. The only buildings in the rural areas which were both convenient and commodious were the churches, and it became customary, for example, for the law courts of London to instruct their commissioners to hold enquiries, summon and interrogate witnesses and take down their depositions in churches, and for the neighbouring gentry to meet there to discuss the levying of subsidies on behalf of the Crown.[66] In time, other kinds of business were progressively added by the country people, who welcomed rather than resented this innovation. Churches became a useful rendezvous for meeting chapmen and dealers, inspecting and buying their wares,[67] and for debtors to meet their creditors furnished with ready money or excuses.[68]

The only remedy for the spiritual destitution of the people was enlightened religious instruction, but the Government took an uncommonly long time to realise this. It could not complain that it was ignorant of the situation, for the Welsh bishops had constantly deplored the lack of competent preachers in their reports,[69] and had stressed the desirability of appointing priests well versed in exegesis to counteract the growth of what they called atheism. They did not doubt that the irreverence and indifference of the common people would be gradually dissipated by a regular and intelligible exposition of Scriptural truths, for, as one of them wrote :

' The Welshman is not obstinate to heare nor dull to understand, nether carelesse in that he knoweth, but for want of knoleage now a long tyme seduced.'[70]

However, it was not only a matter of finding suitable preachers. It was equally indispensable that they should be able to expound the fundamental doctrines of the new Faith in the language of the people ; for if the Latin of the Catholic Liturgy had been incomprehensible to most of them, so was the English of the Prayer Book. And however much the people were prepared or resigned to accept English as the medium of law, administration and education, there were unmistakable signs that they preferred to worship in their own tongue. For example, at Llandrinio, in Montgomeryshire, where the absentee vicar had left the church in the charge of a unprepossessing and ignorant curate, the parishioners, led by the local gentry, sent a petition to the Archbishop of Canterbury demanding the appointment of a priest with an adequate knowledge of Welsh to minister to the parish. The Archbishop acceded to their request, and the choice fell upon John Williams, an Oxford graduate, who was also ' well seene in the Welsh tongue.'[71]

But the problem of providing competent clergymen to preach to the neglected church congregations was never seriously tackled by the Government. It may have considered that it had done enough by decreeing, through Parliament in 1562, that the Bible should be translated into Welsh. That of the New Testament had been printed, though in insufficient numbers, in 1567. Or it may have been indisposed to take further action after the short but bitter feud between John Penry and the Church authorities.

Penry, a sincere but uncompromising Welsh sectarian, had been roused to unbridled indignation by the indifference of the clergy in Wales towards their spiritual duties, and had conducted a campaign within and outside Parliament for the redressment of abuses and the provision of preachers. He never ceased to propagate his ideas for the betterment of religion in his native country. But his denunciation of ecclesiastical shortcomings and his clandestine polemical writings may possibly have persuaded the Government that evangelism, as conceived and exemplified by him, might constitute a danger for the established order.

In any case, there was a strong feeling in Church and Government circles that reforms should preferably be initiated from within the Church rather than imposed from without. The Archbishop of Canterbury, Whitgift, did not equivocate on this point, for he had Penry hanged on a dubious charge of treason, and so removed an importunate advocate of far-reaching reforms.

Yet it was Whitgift who helped to achieve one of Penry's immediate objectives. The reformer had demanded that the Old Testament should be, like the New, rendered into Welsh and placed at the disposal of the people. Already William Morgan, later Bishop of St. Asaph, was engaged on this momentous task, encouraged by the Archbishop who may have detested Penry but had a genuine respect for his native tongue. The translation, together with a revised version of the New Testament, appeared in 1588, and its publication was to have an immeasurable influence on the religious, social and educational life of the Welsh people during the centuries that followed.[72]

NOTES AND SOURCES

Abbreviations { P.R.O.—Public Record Office.
  B.M.—British Museum.
  N.L.W. National Library of Wales. }

CHAPTER I

[1] *Clenennau Letters and Papers in the Brogyntyn Collection.* Calendered and Edited by T. Jones Pierce. NLW Journal Supplement. Series 4. Part 1. 1947. pp. 134—135.
[2] W. Camden. *Britannia.* Translated by Philemon Holland. p. 665.
[3] Ibid. p. 676.
[4] W. Harrison. *An Historicall Description of the Islande of Britayne.* (Holinshed's First Volume of the Chronicles of England). 1577. fol. 73.
[5] Calendar of State Papers Venetian. Vol. IV. p. 294.
[6] Calendar of State Papers Spanish. Vol. III. p. 610.
[7] PRO. Gaol Files. Denbigh 5/1.
[8] NLW. MSS. 7602 D.
[9] PRO. Star Chamber Proceedings. Elizabeth. L 9/24. (Ifan ab Owen Edwards. *Star Chamber Proceedings relating to Wales.* p. 72).
[10] *Stradling Correspondence.* Edited by J. M. Traherne. p. 301. For a study of these aristocratic genealogists, see Francis Jones' ' Approach to Welsh Genealogy ' in the *Transactions of the Honourable Society of Cymmrodorion* 1948. pp. 378—386.
[11] BM. Harleian MSS. 3325. fol. 91b.
[12] BM. Additional MSS. 21435.
[13] BM. Harleian MSS. 473. fol. 10b. (Edward Owen. *Catalogue of MSS relating to Wales in the British Museum.* Part II. p. 153).
[14] NLW. MSS. 9091 D.
[15] PRO. Exchequer Q.R. Depositions. 38/39 Elizabeth. Mich. 33.
[16] Ibid. 42 Elizabeth. Trinity 5.
[17] *Clenennau Letters and Papers.* op. cit. p. 119.
[18] PRO. Proceedings of the Court of Requests. CCXXXIV/61.
[19] BM. Additional MSS. 9069. fols. 12—13. Owen. *Catalogue.* op. cit. p. 933.
[20] NLW. MSS. 9080 E. This MS has been edited by Mr. E. Gwynne Jones and published in the *Transactions of the Anglesey Antiquarian Society and Field Club,* 1948. pp. 11—99.
[21] There are instructive descriptions of sixteenth century houses in the Reports of the Royal Commission on Ancient Monuments for the counties of Flint, Denbigh, Anglesey, Carmarthen, Radnor and Pembroke. Other authoritative works on this subject are : Sir Cyril Fox. *A Country House of the Elizabethan Period in Wales.* National Museum of Wales. 1941 ; Sir Cyril Fox and Lord Raglan. *Monmouthshire Houses.* Cardiff. 1953 ; Iorwerth C. Peate. *The Welsh House.* Y Cymmrodor. Vol. XVII. London. 1940.
[22] PRO. Exchequer Q.R. Special Commissions. 3353.
[23] Ibid. 208.
[24] NLW. Derwydd MSS. 675.
[25] PRO. Exchequer Q.R. Special Commissions. 3400.
[26] PRO. Exchequer K.R. Inventory of Goods and Chattels. 3/41.
[27] PRO. Exchequer Q.R. Special Commissions. 208.
[28] PRO. Proceedings of the Court of Requests. LXXX/26.
[29] J. M. Traherne. *Historical Memoirs of Sir Mathew Cradock.* p. 15.
[30] PRO. Gaol Files. Denbigh 10/4.
[31] Ibid. 4/4.
[32] NLW. MSS. 9080 E.
[33] PRO. Gaol Files. Denbigh 7/3.

[34] PRO. Exchequer Q.R. Special Commissions. 208.
[35] *Stradling Correspondence*. op. cit. p. 162.
[36] PRO. Exchequer Q.R. Special Commissions. 3408.
[37] NLW. MSS. 9080 E.
[38] Ibid.
[39] PRO. Exchequer Q.R. Special Commissions. 208.
[40] PRO. Exchequer K.R. Inventory of Goods and Chattels. 3/41.
[41] PRO. Exchequer Q.R. Special Commissions. 3400.
[42] NLW. MSS. 9080 E.
[43] NLW. MSS. 7602 D.
[44] BM. Additional MSS. 36926. Norris Papers. Vol. III. fols. 8-9.
[45] PRO. Star Chamber Proceedings. Elizabeth. A 30/18. Edwards op. cit. p. 43.
[46] Ibid. Edward VI. 111/19.
[47] *Clenennau Letters and Papers*. op. cit. p. 14.
[48] Ibid. p. 125.
[49] BM. Lansdowne MSS. 21. fols. 64—65b. Owen. *Catalogue*. op. cit. Part I. p. 46.
[50] PRO. Star Chamber Proceedings. Elizabeth. L 2/10. Edwards. op. cit. p. 40.
[51] Ibid. Elizabeth. p. 20/11. Edwards. op. cit. p. 125.
[52] PRO. State Papers Domestic. 1547—1580. CVII/4—14.
[53] Ibid.
[54] *Clenennau Letters and Papers*. op. cit. p. 31.
[55] PRO. Proceedings of the Court of Requests. CXCVI/36.
[56] PRO. Gaol Files. Denbigh 4/4.
[57] PRO. Proceedings of the Court of Requests. LXXXII/6.
[58] PRO. Gaol Files. Brecon 331/1.
[59] *Clenennau Letters and Papers*. op. cit. p. 14.
[60] PRO. State Papers Domestic. 1547—1580. CVII/4—14. See *Bulletin of the Board of Celtic Studies*. Vol. VI. (1931). pp. 74—77. Also *History of the Gwydir Family*. 1927 edition. p. 60.
[61] PRO. Star Chamber Proceedings. Elizabeth. L 25/6. Edwards. op. cit. p. 79.
[62] The fewness of freeholders in Anglesey presented the authorities with the problem of finding enough of them to vote in elections and to serve on juries. It was solved by enrolling a number of people as freeholders, although they lacked the financial qualifications. (*Clenennau Letters and Papers*. op. cit. p. 60).
[63] PRO. Star Chamber Proceedings. Elizabeth. L 24/21. Edwards. op. cit. p. 138.
[64] Ibid. Elizabeth. S 51/14 ; T 15/14 ; T 15/33. Edwards. op. cit. p. 67.
[65] BM. Egerton MSS. 2222. fols. 25, 50b—53. Mr. E. Gwynne Jones describes the electioneering activities and rivalries of the Caernarvonshire squires in his ' Country Politics and Electioneering 1558—1625 ' in the *Caernarvonshire Historical Society Transactions*. Vol. I. 1939. pp. 37—46.
[66] PRO. Star Chamber Proceedings. Elizabeth. A 31/36 ; A 45/6 ; A 59/12 ; A 18/4. Edwards. op. cit. p. 53. In contrast with the rather taciturn and self-restrained burgess members, the Welsh knights of the shire became more vocal and active in the House of Commons as the years went by. Not only did they anticipate what was to become a national predilection in the fullness of time, by their enthusiastic participation in parliamentary committees, but some gained a reputation for their intervention and oratory in debates. Professor A. H. Dodd deals extensively with the whole subject of Welsh representation at Westminster during the Tudor period, and with the gradual emergence of a distinctly ' Welsh interest ' in the House in his ' Wales's Parliamentary Apprenticeship 1536—1625 ' in the *Transactions of the Honourable Society of Cymmrodorion*. 1942. p. 8—22.
[67] Sir John Stradling. *The Storie of the Lower Borowes of Merthyrmaure*. Edited by H. J. Randall and W. Rees. South Wales and Monmouthshire Record Society. Vol. I. pp. 70—71.

68 *Stradling Correspondence.* op. cit. p. 239.

69 BM. Additional MSS. 14905. fols. 3b—4.

70 Ibid. Additional MSS. 14872. fols. 172b—174.

71 *Stradling Correspondence.* op. cit. p. 315.

72 *Clenennau Letters and Papers.* op. cit. p. 23.

73 PRO. Exchequer Q.R. Special Commissions. 3437.

74 PRO. State Papers Domestic. 1547—1580. XVII/18.

75 PRO. Exchequer Q.R. Special Commissions. 3355.

76 *Calendar of State Papers Venetian.* Vol. V. p. 541.

77 PRO. Gaol Files. Denbigh 11/2. The loft in the lower end of the house was often used to preserve the hay crop over the winter, and was called the ' tavelott.'

78 PRO. Proceedings of the Court of Requests. IV/63.

79 NLW. MSS. 6020 E.

80 Higden. *Polycronycon.* fol. XXXIX.

81 PRO. Early Chancery Proceedings. 831/60. E. A. Lewis. *An Inventory of Early Chancery Proceedings concerning Wales.* p. 222.

82 PRO. Gaol Files. Flint 971/1.

83 Ibid. Denbigh 7/5.

84 Ibid. Pembroke 776/6.

85 Ibid. Flint 973/10.

86 PRO. Proceedings of the Court of Requests. CCXL/3.

87 PRO. Gaol Files. Denbigh 4/1.

88 PRO. Exchequer Q.R. Special Commissions. 3412. In Flintshire this communal ploughing of land was called 'merrow' (PRO. Gaol Files. Flint 971/1)

89 NLW. Kinmel MSS. 110 F ii.

90 PRO. Gaol Files. Denbigh 8/3.

91 Ibid. 10/4.

92 Churchyard. *The Worthiness of Wales.* p. 114.

93 PRO. Gaol Files. Flint 971/1.

94 Ibid. 968/13.

95 PRO. Early Chancery Proceedings. 1183/16. Lewis. *Inventory.* op. cit. p. 39.

96 BM Additional MSS. 39717. fol. 107.

97 PRO. Proceedings of the Court of Requests. XLVIII/53.

98 Ibid. CLXXXIII/36.

99 PRO. Gaol Files. Cardigan 883/8.

100 PRO. Proceedings of the Court of Requests. XXIX/112 ; CLXXI/11.

101 NLW. MSS. 6020 E.

102 NLW. St. Asaph MSS. Bishop's Register 1.

103 PRO. Star Chamber Proceedings. Henry VIII. XXIX/115.

104 PRO. Gaol Files. Denbigh 8/3.

105 Ibid. 4/2.

106 PRO. Proceedings of the Court of Requests. LXXXVIII/15.

107 NLW. MSS. 12358 D. p. 91.

108 PRO. Gaol Files. Carmarthen 716/1.

109 This appalling punishment was carried out on a lady and her maid at Smithfield in London in 1541. (BM. Additional MSS. 34751).

110 PRO. Proceedings of the Court of Requests. 1/38.

111 PRO. State Papers Domestic. 1581—1590. CXCIX/18.

112 BM. Harleian MSS. 368(a) fol. 1. Owen. *Catalogue.* Part II. p. 129.

113 *Memorials of Father Augustine Baker.* Edited by J. McCann and H. Connolly. p. 16.

114 PRO. State Papers Domestic. 1547—1580. CVII/4—14.

115 BM. Cotton Charters. XXV/6.

116 PRO. Gaol Files. Montgomery 135/1.

117 The Welsh bards of the period, however, in their elegies to lady patrons and lost loves, speak of their burial in coffins. See extracts from their poems in Professor Gwyn Williams's *Introduction to Welsh Poetry.* Chapter VII.

118 Gaol Files. Brecon 333/5.

[119] NLW. MSS. 7614 D.
[120] PRO. State Papers Domestic. 1547—1580. LXIX/14.
[121] Churchyard. op. cit. p. 52.
[122] NLW. Kinmel MSS. 1610/ F 11.
[123] PRO. Gaol Files. Denbigh 1/2.
[124] Ibid. 3/3.
[125] Ibid. 5/3.
[126] Ibid. Cardigan 883/8.
[127] *Stradling Correspondence.* op. cit. p. 172.
[128] PRO. Star Chamber Proceedings. Elizabeth. P 67/9. Edwards. op. cit. p. 111.
[129] PRO. Gaol Files. Denbigh 8/1.
[130] Ibid. Radnor 469/1.
[131] Ibid. Denbigh 10/2.
[132] Ibid. Radnor 475/2.
[133] Ibid. Brecon 326/2.
[134] Ibid. Cardigan 883/4.
[135] Ibid. Denbigh 6/1.
[136] George Owen. *A Description of Pembrokeshire.* pp. 270—280.
[137] PRO. Gaol Files. Denbigh 4/8.
[138] PRO. Star Chamber Proceedings. Elizabeth. R 10/8. Edwards. op. cit. p. 67.
[139] BM. Lansdowne MSS. 111. fol. 10. See also *Cymmrodor* XIX (1906). p. 69. David Mathew. *The Celtic Peoples.* p. 494. Hirsch Davies. *History of the Church in Wales.* p. 223. Owen. *Catalogue.* op. cit. Part I. p. 72.
[140] PRO. Gaol Files. Denbigh 4/1.
[141] PRO. Exchequer Q.R. Special Commissions. 5088.
[142] PRO. Gaol Files. Flint 968/9.
[143] Ibid. Denbigh 12/1.
[144] Ibid. 3/4.
[145] Ibid. Brecon 326/3 and 4.
[146] Ibid. Denbigh 7/3.
[147] Humphrey Llwyd. *Breviary of Britayne.* p. 69.
[148] PRO. State Papers Domestic. 1581—1590. CXCIII/14.
[149] PRO. Gaol Files. Radnor 474/1.
[150] PRO. Star Chamber Proceedings. Elizabeth. P 13/18. Edwards. op. cit. p. 124.
[151] BM. Egerton MSS. 2203. fol. 2.
[152] BM. Additional MSS. 15047. p. 414.
[153] PRO. Gaol Files. Denbigh 3/5.
[154] NLW. Peniarth MSS. 377 B.
[155] PRO. Gaol Files. Denbigh 7/4.
[156] NLW. Plas Nantglyn MSS. 1.
[157] PRO. State Papers Domestic. 1601—1603. CCLXXXV/48.
[158] NLW. Plas Nantglyn MSS. 1.
[159] BM. Lansdowne MSS. 99. fol. 27. Owen. *Catalogue.* op. cit. Part I. p. 67.
[160] PRO. Gaol Files. Denbigh 4/1.
[161] PRO. Star Chamber Proceedings. Elizabeth. K 10/8. Edwards. op. cit. p. 79.
[162] Ibid. W 37/29 ; W 58/6. Edwards. op. cit. p. 52.
[163] PRO. Gaol Files. Flint 973/10 ; Denbigh 5/1.
[164] PRO. Proceedings of the Court of Requests. CCLXI/53.
[165] PRO. Gaol Files. Denbigh 8/4. A bankrupt pedlar had no alternative but to go to prison. In this respect, he was at a disadvantage compared with a merchant or private person, who, if they had influential friends, could present such a woeful tale of bad luck to the Council of the Welsh Marches that they would sometimes obtain letters authorising them to solicit financial aid from well-disposed people, especially among the gentry. A letter of recommendation from a gentleman,

attached to the official permit, would serve as an extra inducement. (*Stradling Correspondence*. op. cit. p. 198).

166 PRO. Records of the High Court of Admiralty. 13/7.

167 PRO. Proceedings of the Court of Requests. LIII/44.

168 PRO. Exchequer K.R. Inventory of Goods and Chattels. 3/17. Records of the High Court of Admiralty. 13/3.

169 NLW. Castle Hill MSS. 2640—2644 and 2645.

170 PRO. Gaol Files. Denbigh 8/1.

171 Ibid. 3/2.

172 PRO. Star Chamber Proceedings. Elizabeth. C 2/29. Edwards. op. cit. p. 43.

173 PRO. Gaol Files. Montgomery 140/2.

174 Humphrey Llwyd. op. cit. fol. 73.

175 PRO. State Papers Domestic. 1581—1590. CLXV/33.

176 *Clenennau Letters and Papers*. op. cit. pp. 42—43 ; 47 ; 48.

177 *Stradling Correspondence*. op. cit. p. 203. The equipment and dress of the Anglesey men left little to be desired, and on one occasion it almost caused a wholesale military defection at the port of Chester. Writing to the Privy Council, the Mayor of that city declared that, ' the 50 soldiers levied within the country of Anglesea came to this city very well apparelled with caps, cassocks, doublets, breeches, netherstocks, shoes and shirts, which gave great discontentment to the residue of the soldiers which had no apparel, and to us some trouble for their pacification.' (*Calendar of Hatfield MSS*. Part II. p. 474).

178 PRO. Gaol Files. Denbigh 12/3.

179 Ibid. 8/1. An Act of Parliament passed in 1593, however, authorised maimed soldiers to seek relief from parish officials.

180 PRO. Gaol Files. Montgomery 140/2.

181 PRO. Star Chamber Proceedings. Elizabeth. J 6/7 ; J 1/20. Edwards. op. cit. p. 45.

182 The division of an inheritance by gavelkind did not prevent its reconsolidation as a single property. The co-heritors could, if they wished, sell or convey their shares to one of their number as long as they did not alienate them to someone outside the family. But this was only a temporary reintegration, for on the death of the owner the land would once more be divided among the immediate heirs. It should be added that in Pembrokeshire, the abolition of gavelkind was welcomed because it opened the way to the enclosure of fields and the sowing of winter corn in them. (George Owen. *The Description of Pembrokeshire*. p. 61). It would be no less welcome to families who had property in both England and Wales. Where the eldest son would automatically inherit the English estates, he would have to share the Welsh property with his brothers. (PRO. Chancery Proceedings. Elizabeth. R 2/26).

183 PRO. Exchequer. Miscellania. 15/9.

184 BM. Egerton MSS. 2222. fols. 183b—184b.

185 PRO. Duchy of Lancaster Records. Miscellaneous Books. Vol. 122. Abolition led to many court cases in later years revolving round the question whether lands in variance had been subject to gavelkind. (BM. Harley Rolls. D 26).

186 For instance, at the manor of Court Hendre in Monmouthshire, a widow holding by this lease could only lose her property if she were guilty of incontinence, or neglected her holding, or married the second time. (PRO. Proceedings of the Court of Requests. XXXVIII/83).

187 *Stradling Correspondence*. op. cit. p. 112.

188 George Owen. *A Description of Pembrokeshire*. p. 190.

189 PRO. Gaol Files. Flint 971/1.

190 NLW. *Calendar of Wynn Papers*. p. 11.

191 PRO. Exchequer Q.R. Depositions. 10 Elizabeth. Hilary 2.

192 For instance, on the manor of Sully in Glamorgan, days work on the lord's harvest had been commuted into an annual rent of 10d. (PRO. Land Revenue. Miscellaneous Books. 238. fols. 37—105).

[193] BM. Additional Charters. 41276.
[194] BM. Additional MSS. 19713. fol. 34b.
[195] NLW. Bodwyryd Deeds and Documents. 8.
[196] PRO. Exchequer. Miscellania. 15/9.
[197] Camden. op. cit. p. 675.
[198] Churchyard. *The Worthiness of Wales.* op. cit. pp. 51—52.
[199] NLW. *Calendar of Wynn Papers.* p. 25.
[200] PRO. Gaol Files. Denbigh 3/5.
[201] Ibid. 8/1.
[202] PRO. Proceedings of the Court of Requests. XLVI/44.
[203] PRO. Gaol Files. Radnor 465/2.
[204] Ibid. Denbigh 8/1 and 8/2.
[205] Ibid. 10/3. In South Wales, there were yearly droves of wethers, young sheep and lambs to England. (George Owen. op. cit. p. 57).
[206] Ibid. 11/1.
[207] PRO. Proceedings of the Court of Requests. CCXVII/23.
[208] PRO Land Revenue. Miscellaneous Books. 238. fols. 37—105.
[209] Harrison. op. cit. fol. 15.
[210] PRO. Miscellaneous Books relating to the Wogan family. 163/1. fol. 55.
[211] PRO. Land Revenue. Miscellaneous Books. 238. fols. 20—36.
[212] NLW. Bronwydd Documents. Vairdre Book.
[213] PRO. Land Revenue. Miscellaneous Books. 238. fols. 20—36.
[214] PRO. Chancery Proceedings. Elizabeth. W 11/61.
[215] NLW. Chirk Castle MSS. 547 D.
[216] PRO. Duchy of Lancaster. Miscellaneous Books. Vol. 120. fol. 27b.
[217] Ibid. fol. 98b. Ostensibly the profits from this enclosure were to go towards the maintenance of a free school in Carmarthen.
[218] NLW. Bronwydd Documents. Cemaes Supra Estreat Rolls. Gaol Files. Carmarthen 716/2 ; Flint 967/3 ; Glamorgan 591/6.
[219] PRO. Exchequer Q.R. Special Commissions. 3367.
[220] PRO. Star Chamber Proceedings. Elizabeth. N 10/34 ; N 6/34. Edwards. op. cit. p. 91.
[221] Ibid. V 1/29. Edwards. op. cit. p. 26.
[222] Ibid. P 54/4. Edwards. op. cit. p. 83.
[223] Ibid. H 76/17. Edwards. op. cit. p. 119.

CHAPTER II

[1] There had been a certain amount of Welsh infiltration into these towns. See E. A. Lewis. *The Medieval Boroughs of Snowdonia.* p. 254 seq.
[2] Leland. *Itinerary.* p. 96. Humphrey Llwyd. *Breviary of Britayne.* p. 67.
[3] Leland. op. cit. pp. 72 and 86.
[4] Harlech, however, made some effort to shake off its stagnation by insisting that where property was leased by the corporation the leaseholder should undertake to erect a house. (BM. Additional Charters 8486). Its burgesses were sufficiently proud of their ancient but now insignificant borough to criticise the Crown when it inadvertently leased Harlech to an Englishman, and to protest that it had been paying an annual rent to the Royal Exchequer for its liberties since the days of Edward I. That the financial officers of the Crown could have been so careless or ignorant as to treat a Royal Borough in this manner shows how Harlech had shrunk in importance since the thirteenth century. (PRO. Chancery Proceedings. Elizabeth G 25/30).
[5] BM. Harleian MSS. 3325. fols. 19b, 21, 64b. Owen. *Catalogue.* op. cit. Part III. p. 390.
[6] NLW. Plas Nantglyn MSS. 1.
[7] *Memorials of Father Augustine Baker.* op. cit. p. 56.

8 BM. Additional MSS. 22623. fol. 25.

9 Leland. op. cit. p. 34.

10 PRO. Star Chamber Proceedings. Elizabeth. L 38/22. Edwards. op. cit. p. 59.

11 BM. Harleian MSS. 595. The smallness of town population can be better appreciated when it is related to the total population of Wales. Professor David Williams estimates that during the sixteenth century the number of inhabitants, excluding those of Monmouthshire, was between 301,000 and 351,000. See the *Bulletin of the Board of Celtic Studies*. Part IV. pp. 359—363. 1937. Owen. *Catalogue*. op. cit. Part II. p. 158.

12 Churchyard. op. cit. p. 58.

13 PRO. Land Revenue. Miscellaneous Books. No. 238. fol. 20. Assizes were held in the castles of Harlech, Brecon, Kidwelly and Monmouth.

14 PRO. Gaol Files. Denbigh 8/3.

15 PRO. Exchequer Q.R. Special Commissions 3413.

16 Ibid. 109.

17 In Denbigh this lane was called the ' Privy.'

18 PRO. Gaol Files. Denbigh 6/4.

19 Leland. op. cit. p. 43.

20 Towns which retained their walls intact included New Radnor, Cowbridge, Cardiff, Chepstow, Monmouth, Abergavenny, Old Kidwelly, Carmarthen, Haverfordwest, Brecon, Tenby, Aberystwyth, Denbigh, Conway, Caernarvon and Beaumaris.

21 PRO. Gaol Files. Denbigh 10/4.

22 BM. Additional MSS. 19714. fol. 13b.

23 PRO. Star Chamber Proceedings. Elizabeth. G. 13/21. Edwards. op. cit p. 31.

24 PRO. Exchequer. Miscellania. 12/21 B.

25 PRO. Gaol Files. Denbigh 6/2.

26 PRO. Exchequer Q.R. Special Commissions 3484. NLW. MSS. 235.

27 PRO. Gaol Files. Denbigh 5/1.

28 NLW. MSS. 7618 D.

29 PRO. Proceedings of the Court of Requests. CLXV/205.

30 PRO. Exchequer Q.R. Depositions. 3 James 1. Trinity 5.

31 Ibid. 6 James 1. Hilary 25.

32 The municipal gaol of Cardiff was a chamber under the Town Hall, andknown by the Welsh name of 'Kwchmoel' (Merrick. *Antiquities of Glamorganshire*. p. 54).

33 PRO. Gaol Files. Pembroke 775/4.

34 The oligarchical composition of Brecon Corporation may be judged from the fact that two of its members held the office of Bailiff four times, and a third occupied it as many as eight times between 1564 and 1584. (N.L.W. MSS. 235).

35 PRO. Land Revenue. Miscellaneous Books No. 238. fol. 20.

36 NLW. MSS. 235.

37 PRO. Gaol Files. Denbigh 1/5.

38 Ibid. 8/2.

39 PRO. Star Chamber Proceedings. Henry VIII. XXI/10.

40 NLW. MSS. 12358 D. p. 82.

41 NLW. Plas Nantglyn MSS. 1. Published in *Archaeologia Cambrensis*, 1915.

42 NLW. MSS. 9082 D.

43 BM. Additional MSS. 19714. fol. 14.

44 NLW. MSS. 12358 D. The dreadful smells associated with medieval streets were partly neutralised when the Corporation decided, in 1580, to pave the main thoroughfare of the town.

45 B. G. Charles. ' Records of Haverfordwest 1563—1620 ' in *NLW. Journal*. Vol. IX. No. 2. 1955. p. 176.

46 H. Owen and J. B. Blakeway. *A History of Shrewsbury*. p. 350.

47 Charles. op. cit.

48 PRO. Gaol Files. Montgomery 139/2.

49 Ibid. Brecon 333/2.
50 PRO. Chancery Proceedings. Elizabeth. L 9/11.
51 NLW. *Calendar of Wynn Papers.* op. cit. p. 7. See *English Historical Review.*
1929. p. 672.
52 BM. Egerton MSS. 2222, fol. 28.
53 Ibid. fol. 77b.
54 PRO. Star Chamber Proceedings. Elizabeth. H 78/35 ; H 54/30. Edwards.
op. cit. p. 96.
55 Ibid. Elizabeth. C 54/53. Edwards. op. cit. p. 55.
56 Ibid. Elizabeth. L 38/22 ; L 19/4. Edwards. op. cit. p. 59.
57 Dislike of 'foreigners' was so ingrained that at Harlech a burgess was leased
a small piece of turbary on the condition that he would not alienate or farm it out
to any person outside the borough. (BM. Additional Charters 45961).
58 PRO. Star Chamber Proceedings. Elizabeth. V 9/37 ; W 28/29. Edwards.
op. cit. p. 26.
59 Ibid. Elizabeth. D 11/3. Edwards. op. cit. p. 136.
60 A favourite device at Carmarthen for electing personal friends to office was for
their supporters to hoist them on their shoulders and declare vociferously that
they had been chosen. (NLW. MSS. 22358 D. p. 15).
61 PRO. Star Chamber Proceedings. Elizabeth. p. 33/19. Edwards. op. cit.
p. 49. A former Carmarthen mayor had avoided this state of affairs by distributing
pieces of land among receptive and sympathetic electors, thus securing a reliable
majority in borough elections. On the other hand, a mayor of Bala, in Merioneth,
popularly known as ' Maor y Bala ' had to deal with more timorous burghers. It
was enough for him to threaten them with death or detention of property by his
servant, *Morgan y Gwas*, to be elected for six successive years without opposition.
(PRO. Star Chamber Proceedings. Elizabeth. G 9/31. Edwards. op. cit. p. 88).
62 PRO. Gaol Files. Denbigh 11/3.
63 BM. Additional MSS. 38823. fol. 27b.
64 BM. Harleian MSS. 3325. fols. 66b, 67. Owen. *Catalogue.* op. cit. Part II.
p. 391.
65 PRO. Star Chamber Proceedings. Elizabeth. M 40/38. Edwards. op. cit.
p. 24.
66 NLW. MSS. 22358 D.
67 NLW. Miscellaneous Documents. Glamorgan. No. 1589.
68 NLW. MSS. 8496 D. An authoritative study on the evolution of a Welsh
town, Pwllheli, from medieval to Tudor days has been contributed by Professor
T. Jones Pierce in his ' A Caernarvonshire Manorial Borough '—see the *Caernarvonshire Historical Society Transactions.* Vol. 3. 1941. Pp. 9—32 ; Vol. 4. 1942. pp
35—50 ; Vol. 5. 1943. pp. 12—40.
69 PRO. Gaol Files. Denbigh 7/4 ; 7/5.

CHAPTER III

1 PRO. State Papers Domestic. 1547—1580. CXXIV/11.
2 Ibid. XXXIX/29.
3 Ibid. XXXVIII/30.
4 Ibid. CXXVII/35.
5 PRO. Gaol Files. Pembroke 775/4.
6 PRO. State Papers Domestic. 1547—1580. XXXIX/27.
7 BM. Additional MSS. 38823. fol. 24b.
8 NLW. MSS. 585. This document has been edited by Professor T. Jones
Pierce, and published in the *Caernarvonshire Historical Society Transactions.* Vol. 6.
1945. pp. 60—63.
9 PRO. Records of the High Court of Admiralty. 13/15.
10 Ibid. 13/16.

I

[11] PRO. State Papers Domestic. 1547—1580. CXXVI/49.
[12] *Stradling Correspondence*. op. cit. p. 158.
[13] PRO. State Papers Domestic. 1547—1580. LXXVII/36.
[14] Ibid. CLXXV/88.
[15] See Introduction to E. A. Lewis. *Welsh Ports Books. Cymmrodorion Record Series* No. 12.
[16] George Owen. op. cit. p. 124.
[17] BM. Additional MSS. 22623. fol. 28.
[18] PRO. Exchequer Q.R. Port Books. 1298, 1299. See E. A. Lewis. op. cit. pp. 61—109, 154—196.
[19] Leland had recorded that Merioneth 'bredith good horses'. *Itinerary*. op. cit. Part VI. p. 78.
[20] George Owen. op. cit. p. 57.
[21] PRO. Exchequer Q.R. Port Books. 1270, 1271. (Lewis. op. cit. pp. 1—5, 18—21, 23—40, 42—48).
[22] PRO. Exchequer Q.R. Depositions. 25 Elizabeth. Easter 5.
[23] Ibid. 35 Elizabeth. Hilary 9 ; 22/23 Elizabeth. Mich. 13 ; 25/26 Elizabeth. Mich. 15 ; 22/23 Elizabeth. Mich. 11 ; 36/37 Elizabeth. Mich. 4 ; 10 Jas. 1. Easter 2 ; 16 Jas. 1. Mich. 13.
[24] PRO. State Papers Domestic. 1547—1580. XXI/48, 48(1), 48(2).
[25] BM. Harleian MSS. 4776. fol. 129b. Owen. *Catalogue*. op. cit. Part II. p. 430. This is the 'Record of Caernarvon' edited by Sir Henry Ellis in *Record Commission*, 1828.
[26] This illicit traffic in corn with Spain had begun as far back as the reign of Henry VIII. (PRO. Star Chamber Proceedings. Henry VIII. XXIII/208).
[27] PRO. Exchequer Q.R. Special Commissions. 3345 ; Depositions. 19/20 Elizabeth. Mich. 14.
[28] PRO. Exchequer Q.R. Special Commissions. 3445.
[29] Ibid. 2895.
[30] Ibid. 4143.
[31] This clandestine traffic was not unknown in the reign of HenryVIII either. When a ship owned by Walter Herbert, a Monmouthshire gentleman, was captured by Breton pirates, her cargo contained a number of falcons, handguns, crossbows and other artillery. (PRO. Records of the High Court of Admiralty. 1/33).
[32] PRO. Exchequer Q.R. Special Commissions. 3345.
[33] For Ffetiplace's activities on the Welsh coast, see Records of the High Court of Admiralty. 1/36 fol. 154 and 1/37 fols. 81b—87.
[34] His name was Edward Buckley. Any distant connection of Sir Richard's ?
[35] Records of the High Court of Admiralty. 1/43. fols. 217—218.
[36] Ibid.
[37] Ibid. 1/36. fol. 154.
[38] Ibid. 1/43. fols. 61—62.
[39] Ibid. 1/36. fols. 245—298, 364—391.
[40] Ibid. 1/45. fols. 84—88. 114—118.
[41] Ibid. 1/46. fol. 41.
[42] Ibid.
[43] *Acts of the Privy Council*. Vol. 9. 1575—1577. p. 267.
[44] PRO. Records of the Court of the Admiralty. 1/40. fols. 22—25, 31b. But not for long ! The extraordinary case of Callice's escape from the execution dock, where the more unfortunate Hicks was soon to end his career, has been investigated by C. L'Estrange Ewen in his *The Golden Chalice*. The pirate seems to have turned Queen's Evidence against his fellow buccaneers, but later his irrepressible habits reasserted themselves. He took to his nefarious practices once more, and after many adventures and escapes, met his death near the coast of Barbary sometime in hte year 1587.
[45] PRO. Ibid. 13/16.
[46] PRO. State Papers Domestic. 1581—1590. CLVII/4, 5.

47 PRO. State Papers Domestic. 1581—1590. CLVII/4.

48 Ibid. XV/67.

49 Historical MSS. Commissions. *MSS. of Shrewsbury Corporation.* p. 62.

50 George Owen. op. cit. p. 57.

51 PRO. Proceedings of the Court of Requests. CLIX/38. It was to keep the poor employed in this kind of work that merchants were prohibited in 1602 from buying wool in North Wales and exporting it without licence. (*Clenennau Letters and Papers.* op. cit. p. 58).

52 PRO. Duchy of Lancaster Records. Miscellaneous Books. 120. As early as 1529, Sir Rice Mansell had leased the 'Coles' near Swansea from the Crown. (Traherne. op. cit. p. 15).

53 PRO. Chancery Proceedings. Elizabeth. U 1/50.

54 PRO. Proceedings of the Court of Requests. XXV/103.

55 NLW. Carreglwyd Papers. 1750 and 2191.

56 PRO. Exchequer Q.R. Special Commissions. 3325.

57 PRO. Gaol Files. Denbigh 6/5.

58 Ibid. Flint 970/3.

59 Ibid. Denbigh 3/3, 4/5, 5/1, 5/3, 6/2, 7/4, 8/2 ; Flint 969/1, 969/5, 970/1, 970/3, 970/4, 971/1, 973/5.

60 Ibid. Denbigh 10/4.

61 Unlike the 'sulphurous' fumes of the coal brought from Newcastle to London and other towns in England which gave an impetus to the building of chimneys. G. M. Trevelyan. *English Social History.* p. 189.

62 George Owen. op. cit. p. 87.

63 PRO. Gaol Files. Pembroke 775/6.

64 Boys were set to work in mines at the age of ten or under. (PRO. Exchequer Q.R. Special Commissions. 3493).

65 George Owen. op. cit. p. 91.

66 PRO. Exchequer Q.R. Port Books. 1298 and succeeding books. (Lewis. op. cit. P. 61 seq.) Coal dust cost 20/- per cwt at the pithead and culm 20d. per cwt. (PRO. Exchequer Q.R. Special Commissions. 3493).

67 George Owen. op. cit. p. 91.

68 PRO. Exchequer Q.R. Depositions. 12 Elizabeth. Easter 1.

69 Merrick. op. cit. p. 6.

70 PRO. Exchequer Q.R. Special Commissions. 3441.

71 *Calendar of Hatfield MSS.* Part XIV. p. 330.

72 There had been copper mines in existence before this. A list of 33 mines in Wales surveyed by a German expert in the reign of Henry VIII included three where copper was worked. (PRO. Letters and Papers. Henry VIII. Vol. 236. fol. 31).

73 PRO. State Papers Domestic. 1581—1590. CLXXI/36 ; CLXXIX/2 ; CLXXXIII/55 ; CXCIX/18.

74 NLW. Additional MSS. 465 E.

75 BM. Lansdowne MSS. 55. fols. 81—82. Owen. *Catalogue.* op. cit. Part I. p. 116.

76 BM. Additional Charters. 25744.

77 PRO. Exchequer Q.R. Depositions. 32/33 Elizabeth. Mich. 6.

78 One of the witnesses testifying in this case was a former Somerset lead miner. The migration of workers from one enterprise to another was a marked feature of the Elizabethan age.

79 NLW. Bettisfield MSS. 872.

80 BM. Additional MSS. 36926. Norris Papers. Vol. III. fol. 16.

81 PRO. Proceedings of the Court of Requests. VI/214.

82 PRO. Exchequer K.R. Depositions. 19 Jas. 1. Easter 17.

83 Ibid. 6 Jas. 1. Mich. 7.

84 Ibid. 9 Jas. 1. Easter 3.

85 PRO. Chancery Town Depositions. Bundle 6.

86 PRO. Chancery Proceedings. Elizabeth. A 2/50.

[87] PRO. Proceedings of the Court of Requests. CCLV/77.
[88] Their names were John and Walter Ramsden.
[89] PRO. Proceedings of the Court of Requests. CCLIX/6. The usual phraseology was, ' as wind and weather would permit ', but in this case there was either an attempt at a joke or a slip of the pen.
[90] Ibid. CCXXXIX/31.
[91] PRO. Chancery Proceedings. Elizabeth. M 6/53 ; M 8/36. NLW. Bute Collections. Box 88 C.
[92] He also mined ore on the waste and mountain land of the manor of Ebbw Fawr. (NLW. MSS. 76461).
[93] PRO. Proceedings of the Court of Requests. CCXIX/13 ; CCLXVIII/63.
[94] PRO. Exchequer Q.R. Special Commissions. 1512.
[95] PRO. Exchequer Q.R. Depositions. 21 Elizabeth. Easter 16.
[96] PRO. Proceedings of the Court of Requests. CCXXXII/28.
[97] NLW. MSS. 7618 D.
[98] PRO. State Papers Domestic. 1547—1580. XL/63.
[99] BM. Lansdowne MSS. 76. fols. 72—72b. Owen. *Catalogue*. op. cit. Part I. p. 61.
[100] PRO. Exchequer Q.R. Depositions. 2 Jas. 1. Hilary 12.
[101] BM. Lansdowne MSS. 76. fols. 72—72b. Owen. *Catalogue.* op. cit. Part I. p. 61.
[102] PRO. State Papers Domestic. 1547—1580. XLVIII/43.
[103] PRO. Exchequer Q.R. 632/39. Her share of the profits was 34/8.
[104] PRO. Exchequer Q.R. Depositions. 39 Elizabeth. Hilary 23.
[105] PRO. Exchequer Q.R. Special Commissions. 1518.
[106] PRO. Exchequer Q.R. Depositions. 39 Elizabeth. Hilary 23.
[107] Ibid. 2 Jas. 1. Hilary 12.

CHAPTER IV

[1] Ortelius. *Theatrum Orbis Terrarum*. fol. 13.
[2] PRO. Proceedings of the Court of Requests. CL/43.
[3] Ibid. LXCV/7.
[4] PRO. Gaol Files. Denbigh 10/4.
[5] Ibid. Brecon 331/1.
[6] Ibid. 327/2.
[7] Ibid. Denbigh 1/1.
[8] Ibid. Brecon 324/1.
[9] Ibid. Denbigh 5/1.
[10] Ibid. Brecon 330/4.
[11] Ibid. Flint 969/5.
[12] Ibid. Brecon 327/3.
[13] PRO. Exchequer Q.R. Special Commissions 3395.
[14] *Stradling Correspondence*. op cit. pp. 99—100 ; 120.
[15] PRO. Star Chamber Proceedings. Elizabeth N 12/21. (Edwards. op. cit. p. 91).
[16] PRO. State Papers Domestic. CVII/4—14.
[17] G. M. Trevelyan. op. cit. p. 169.
[18] NLW. Peniarth MSS. 377 B.
[19] PRO. Records of the High Court of Admiralty. 1/45.
[20] PRO. Gaol Files. Denbigh 12/1 ; 12/3.
[21] Ibid. 8/2.
[22] NLW. Peniarth MSS. 410 D. Part 2.
[23] George Owen. op. cit. pp. 401, 544, 584, 691.
[24] PRO. Gaol Files. Brecon 332/4.
[25] Ibid. Flint 970/1.

[26] Ibid. 968/13.
[27] Ibid. Montgomery 136/4.
[28] Ibid. 138/2.
[29] Ibid. Denbigh 6/3.
[30] Ibid. Pembroke 775/4.
[31] Ibid. Denbigh 2/5.
[32] Ibid. 1/5.
[33] Ibid. 4/6.
[34] Ibid. 5/2.
[35] Ibid. 4/2.
[36] NLW. Kinmel MSS. 1610/F ii.
[37] PRO. Gaol Files. Radnor 465/6. The tenants of Chirk were liable to a fine of 2/6 if they accommodated vagabonds in their homes. (NLW. Chirk Castle MSS. 547 D).
[38] Ibid. Denbigh 6/4.
[39] Ibid. 2/1 ; 3/1 ; 5/3.
[40] Ibid. 10/4.
[41] *A Minute Account of the Social Condition of the People of Anglesey* (1612—1613). Edited by J. A. Halliwell. pp. 15—17.
[42] PRO. Gaol Files. Brecon 323/1.
[43] NLW. Peniarth MSS. 332 A.
[44] NLW. Peniarth MSS. 410 D.
[45] NLW. MSS. 7611 D.
[46] NLW. MSS. 7614 D.
[47] BM. Additional MSS. 39713, 39717.
[48] NLW. Bodwyryd MSS. Documents No. 13.
[49] PRO. Exchequer Q.R. Depositions. 30 Elizabeth. Easter 13 ; 30/31 Elizabeth. Mich. 29.
[50] NLW. St. Asaph MSS. Bishop's Register 1.
[51] NLW. Kinmel MSS. 1610/ F ii.
[52] NLW. Carreglwyd Papers II. No. 352.
[53] PRO. Gaol Files. Denbigh 7/2.
[54] Ibid. 8/1.
[55] PRO. Star Chamber Proceedings. Elizabeth. O 5/31. (Edwards. op. cit. p. 124).
[56] PRO. Gaol Files. Denbigh 8/1.
[57] Ibid. Flint 973/10.
[58] Ibid. Denbigh 6/4.
[59] Ibid. 5/3.
[60] Ibid. 8/1.
[61] Ibid. Brecon 323/1 ; 328/5 ; 332/2.
[62] PRO. Proceedings of the Court of Requests. CLXXIX/45.

CHAPTER V

[1] BM. Cleopatra MSS. E IV. fol. 141. Owen. *Catalogue.* op. cit. Part I. p. 38.
[2] PRO. Exchequer Q.R. Depositions 37/38 Elizabeth. Mich. 60.
[3] Ibid.
[4] Churchyard. op. cit. p. 71.
[5] L. S. Knight. *Welsh Independent Schools to 1600.* Appendix XII. Mr. A. H. Williams has written an authoritative account of the early history of Ruthin Grammar School in Volume II (1953) of the *Denbighshire Historial Society Transactions.* pp. 31—44.
[6] *Calendar of Hatfield Papers.* Part V. p. 164.
[7] NLW. Bodwyryd Correspondence. No. 37.

8 Ortelius. op. cit. fol. 13.
9 BM. Additional Charters 8360 and 39708. NLW. MSS. 7602 D and 7614 D.
10 PRO. Chancery Proceedings. Elizabeth U 3/19.
11 NLW. *Calendar of Wynn Papers.* p. 72.
12 PRO. Exchequer K.R. Depositions. 10 James 1. Easter 2.
13 NLW. *Calendar of Wynn Papers.* p. 34.
14 BM. Additional MSS. 24632. Richard Watkyns of Abergavenny became Headmaster of Eton ; John Merrick of Anglesey was elected Bishop of Sodor and Man ; Hugh Lloyd of Carnarvon was appointed Headmaster of Winchester School itself ; and Thomas Leyson of Neath acquired a reputation at Bath as an excellent Latin poet and a capable surgeon.
15 *Memoirs of Father Augustine Baker.* op. cit. p. 56.
16 PRO. Gaol Files. Montgomery 138/2.
17 Ibid. Denbigh 4/2.
18 Ibid. Flint 973/10.
19 NLW. MSS. 7615 D.
20 PRO. Star Chamber Proceedings. Elizabeth L 33/18 ; L 10/7 ; L 10/9. Edwards. op. cit. p. 73.
21 NLW. MSS. 6020 E. BM. Additional MSS. 39717.
22 *Clenennau Letters and Papers.* op. cit. p. 126.
23 E. G. Hardy. *Jesus College.* p. 401.
24 *Clenennau Letters and Papers.* op. cit. p. 120.
25 PRO. Early Chancery Proceedings 1377!59. E. A. Lewis. *Inventory of Early Chancery Proceedings concerning Wales.* p. 22.
26 PRO. Proceedings of the Court of Requests. CCLVI/63.
27 The richer class of students were prone to overdress themselves. See Trevelyan. *English Social History.* p. 183.
28 PRO. State Papers Domestic. 1547—1580. CXXVII/17 and 18 ; CXXVI/48.
29 NLW. Bodwyryd Correspondence. No. 40.
30 *Stradling Correspondence.* op. cit. p. 331.
31 NLW. *Calendar of Wynn Papers.* pp. 7 and 13.
32 PRO. Proceedings of the Court of Requests. CLXXXII/72.
33 NLW. MSS. 9080 E. A Monmouthshire gentleman left his collection of law books to his heir. (NLW. MSS. 7613 D).
34 PRO. Star Chamber Proceedings. Elizabeth O 7/22. Edwards. op. cit. p. 33.
35 PRO. State Papers Domestic. Addenda 1557—1558. VIII/127.
36 The gentry around Raglan and Abergavenny were conspicuous for their loyalty to Catholicism. At one time, over 160 people in these parts were outlawed for recusancy. (PRO. State Papers Domestic. 1581—1590. CXCV/86). Despite persecution and intimidation, the number of North Wales Catholics actually increased after the accession of James I. (See E. Gwynne Jones. ' Catholic Recusancy in the Counties of Denbigh, Flint and Montgomery, 1581—1621 ', in the *Transactions of the Honourable Society of Cymmrodorion,* 1945. For a more comprehensive study of recusancy in Wales during this period, see *Cymru a'r Hen Ffydd* by the same author).
37 PRO. Gaol Files. Denbigh 5/4.
38 In an action brought against John Games, J.P. of Brecon, he was accused of reading Welsh superstitious (Catholic) books which contained songs and rhymes. (PRO. Star Chamber Proceedings. Elizabeth W 69/19. Edwards. op. cit. p. 28).
39 PRO. State Papers Domestic. 1547—1580. LXVI/26.
40 BM. Lansdowne MSS. III. fol. 10. Owen. *Catalogue.* op. cit. Part I. p. 72.
41 PRO. State Papers Domestic. 1581—1590. CCXXIV/74.
43 PRO. Gaol Files. Denbigh 8/2.
43 PRO. State Papers Domestic. 1581—1590. CCXXIV/74.
44 Calendar of State Papers. Rome. Vol. I. p. 389.
45 Carewe MSS. Vol. I. p. 398.
46 PRO. Proceedings of the Court of Requests. XLXX/18.

47 PRO. Gaol Files. Brecon 329/5.
48 BM. Additional MSS. 36926. Norris Papers. Vol. III. fol. 13.
49 PRO. Proceedings of the Court of Requests XLIX/33.
50 Ibid. CCI/50.
51 Ibid. LXXIV/84 ; CIX/28.
52 PRO. Gaol Files. Brecon 332/1.
53 Ibid. Glamorgan 592/2.
54 Ibid. Radnor 465/6.
55 PRO. Star Chamber Proceedings. Elizabeth. V 6/14. Edwards. op. cit.
p. 140.
56 Ibid. J 22/2. Edwards. op. cit. p. 32.
57 BM. Lansdowne MSS. III. fol. 10. Owen. *Catalogue*. op. cit. Part I. p. 72.
58 PRO. State Papers Domestic. 1547—1580. LXVI/26.
59 PRO. Gaol Files. Radnor 476/1.
60 Ibid. Brecon 324/1.
61 PRO. Star Chamber Proceedings. Elizabeth W 27/23. Edwards. op. cit. p. 38.
62 Fynes Moryson. *Itinerary*. Part III. p. 143.
63 PRO. Gaol Files. Denbigh 8/3.
64 PRO. Early Chancery Proceedings. 1375!72. E. A. Lewis. *Inventory*. op. cit.
p. 99.
65 Ibid. 1222/34. E. A. Lewis. *Inventory*. op. cit. p. 53.
66 PRO. Proceedings of the Court of Requests. CLXXI/12.
67 PRO. Gaol Files. Denbigh 7/2.
68 PRO. Proceedings of the Court of Requests. LXXXII/11.
69 In 1583, there were only 14 preachers in the diocese of St. David's. (PRO.
State Papers Domestic. CCXV/1). Prof. Glanmor Williams throws much light
on the conditions obtaining in this diocese in his ' Richard Davies, Bishop of St.
David's 1561—1581 ' in the *Transactions of the Honourable Society of Cymmrodorion*
1948. See also his *Bywyd ac Amserau'r Esgob Richard Davies*.
70 PRO. State Papers Domestic. 1547—1580. XLIV/27.
71 PRO. Star Chamber Proceedings. Elizabeth. A 19/31. Edwards op. cit.
p. 94.
72 Professor David Williams stresses that the survival of the Welsh language was
primarily due to the translation of the Bible and the Book of Common Prayer into
the vernacular, and that, 'in view of the smallness in number of the Welsh people
and their close proximity to England, it is doubtful if, without this difference in
language, the consciousness of a separate Welsh nationality would have endured.'
For an instructive evaluation of the religious changes in Wales during this century,
see his *A History of Modern Wales*. pp. 46—78.

BIBLIOGRAPHY

A.—ORIGINAL SOURCES

PUBLIC RECORD OFFICE

Chancery Records. Early Chancery Proceedings (C.1).
                 Chancery Proceedings. Elizabeth (C.2).
                 Chancery Town Depositions (C.24).
Proceedings of the Court of Star Chamber. Elizabeth (St. Ch. 5).
Proceedings of the Court of Requests. Elizabeth (Requests 5).
Records of Wales and the Palatinate. Gaol Files (Wales 4).
Exchequer Records. Special Commissions (E.178).
               Depositions (E.134).
               Inventory of Goods and Chattels (E.154).
               Port Books (E.190).
               Licences to go beyond the Seas (E.157).
               Miscellania of the Exchequer (E.163).
               Ecclesiastical Documents (E.135).
               Church Goods (E.117).
               Parliamentary Surveys (E.317).
Land Revenue. Miscellaneous Books (L.R.2).
Rentals and Surveys (Sc. 12).
Duchy of Lancaster Records. Miscellaneous Books (D.L.42).
State Papers Domestic (1547—1580, 1581—1590, 1601—1603).
Records of the High Court of the Admiralty. Oyer and Terminer
                                  Records (HCA 1).
                                  Examinations (HCA
                                  13).
Published Calendars : Calendars of State Papers Venetian, Spanish,
  Rome, Carewe MSS, and Hatfield MSS. Letters and Papers of
  Henry VIII.

BRITISH MUSEUM

Additional MSS 9069, 14872, 14905, 19713, 19714, 21435, 22623,
                 24632, 34751, 36926 (Norris Papers), 38823,
                 39713, 39717, 15047.
Additional Charters 8360, 25744, 39708, 41276, 45961.
Cotton Charters XXV/6.
Cleopatra MSS E. IV.
Egerton MSS 2222, 2203.
Harleian MSS 368(a), 473, 596, 3325, 4776.
Harley Rolls D.26.
Lansdowne MSS 21, 55, 76, 99.

NATIONAL LIBRARY OF WALES

Bettisfield MSS 872.
Bodwyryd Correspondence 37, 40.
Bodwyryd Deeds and Documents 8, 13.
Bronwydd Documents, Vairdre Book, Cemaes Supra Estreat Rolls.
Bute Collections Box 88C.
Carreglwyd Papers I 1750, 2191 ; II 352.
Castle Hill MSS 2640—2645.
Chirk Castle MSS 547 D.
Derwydd MSS 675.
Kinmel MSS 110 F ii, 1610 F 11.
Miscellaneous Documents. Glamorgan 1589.
NLW MSS 235, 465E, 585, 6020E, 7602D, 7611D, 7613D, 7614D,
        7618D, 8496D, 9080E, 9082D, 9091D, 22358D.
Peniarth MSS 332A, 377B, 410D.
Plas Nantglyn MSS 1.
St Asaph MSS. Bishop's Register.

B.—PUBLISHED WORKS

Calendar of Wynn (of Gwydir) *Papers* 1515—1696. Cardiff, 1926.
CAMDEN, W. BRITANNIA (tr. Philemon Holland). London, 1610.
CHURCHYARD, THOMAS. *The Worthiness of Wales.* London, 1587.
DAVIES, D. J. *The Economic History of South Wales Prior to 1800.*
    University of Wales Press, Cardiff, 1933.
DODD, A. H. *The Industrial Revolution in North Wales.* University of
    Wales Press, Cardiff, 1933.
DODD, A. H. *Studies in Stuart Wales.* University of Wales Press,
    Cardiff, 1952.
EDWARDS, IFAN AB OWEN. *Catalogue of Star Chamber Proceedings
    Relating to Wales.* University Press Board, Cardiff, 1929.
EDWARDS, A. G. *Landmarks in the History of the Welsh Church.* John
    Murray, London, 1912.
EWEN, C. L'ESTRANGE. *The Golden Chalice.* Paignton, 1939.
FLENLEY, R. *Calendar of the Register of the Council in Wales* (Cymmr.
    Rec., Series No. 8), 1916.
FOX, SIR CYRIL and LORD RAGLAN. *Monmouthshire Houses.* Welsh
    Folk Museum Pub., Cardiff, 1941.
FOX, SIR CYRIL. *A Country House of the Elizabethan Period in Wales.*
    National Museum of Wales Pub., Cardiff, 1941.
HALLIWELL, J. O. *A Minute Account of the Social Condition of the
    People of Anglesey.* London, 1860.
HARDY, E. G. *History of Jesus College, Oxford.* Oxford, 1899.
HARRISON, W. *An Historical Description of the Island of Britayne.*
    London, 1577.

HIGDEN, R. *Polycronycon.* London, 1497.

JAMES, J. W. *Welsh Church History.* A. H. Stockwell, Ilfracombe, 1945.

JONES, E. GWYNNE. *Exchequer Proceedings (Equity) Concerning Wales.* University Press Board, Cardiff, 1939.

JONES, E. GWYNNE. *Cymru a'r Hen Ffydd.* Gwasg Prifysgol Cymru, Caerdydd, 1951.

JONES-PIERCE, T. (ed.). *Clenennau Letters and Papers in the Brogyntyn Collection.* NLW Journal Supplement, 1947.

KNIGHT, L. S. *Welsh Independent Grammar Schools to 1600.* Welsh Outlook Press, Newtown, 1926.

LEWIS, E. A. *The Medieval Boroughs of Snowdonia.* Henry Sotheran & Co., London, 1912.
An Inventory of the Early Chancery Proceedings Concerning Wales. University Press Board, Cardiff, 1937.
Port Books (Cymmr. Rec. Series No. 12), 1927.

LELAND, JOHN. *Itinerary* (ed. Toulmin Smith). George Bell & Sons, London, 1906.

LLOYD, SIR J. E. and JENKINS, R. T. *Y Bywgraffiadur Cymreig Hyd 1940.* London, 1953.

LLWYD, H. *The Breviary of Britayne.* R. Johnes, London, 1573.

MATHEW, DAVID. *The Celtic Peoples and the Renaissance in Europe.* Sheed and Ward, London, 1933.

Memorials of Father Augustine Baker (ed. J. MacCann and H. Connolly). Catholic Record Society Publications, 1933.

MENDENHALL, T. C. *The Shrewsbury Drapers and the Welsh Cloth Trade in the Sixteenth and Seventeenth Centuries.* Oxford University Press, London, 1953.

MERRICK, R. *The Antiquities of Glamorganshire.* 1578.

MORYSON, FYNES. *Itinerary.* J. Beale, London, 1617.

NEALE, J. E. *Queen Elizabeth.* Jonathan Cape, London, 1934.

OWEN, GEORGE. *Description of Pembrokeshire* (ed. Henry Owen). C. J. Clark, London, 1892—1906.

OWEN, H. and BLAKEWAY, J. B. *A History of Shrewsbury.* Harding, Lepard & Co., London, 1825.

PEATE, IORWERTH C. *The Welsh House* (Y Cymmrodor, Vol. 47), London, 1940.

PARRY, THOMAS. *A History of Welsh Literature* (tr. H. Idris Bell). Clarendon Press, 1955.

PEEL, ALBERT (ed.). *The Notebook of John Penry.* Camden Third Series. Vol. 67. 1944.

PIERCE, W. *John Penry, His Life, Times and Writings.* Hodder & Stoughton, London, 1923.

PHILLIPS, JAMES. *The History of Pembrokeshire.* Elliot Stock, London, 1909.

REES, J. F. *Studies in Welsh History.* University of Wales Press, Cardiff, 1947.

RHYS, J. and JONES, D. BRYNMOR. *The Welsh People.* T. Fisher Unwin, London, 1900.

SKEEL, C. A. J. *The Council of the Marches of Wales.* Hugh Rees Ltd., London, 1904.

SMITH, W. J. *Calendar of Salusbury Correspondence.* University of Wales Press, Cardiff, 1954.

STRADLING, SIR JOHN. *The Storie of the Lower Borowes of Merthyr-Maure* (ed. H. J. Randall and W. Rees). South Wales and Monmouthshire Record Society No. 1, Cardiff, 1932.

TRAHERNE, J. M. (ed.). *Stradling Correspondence.* 1840.

TRAHERNE, J. M. *Historicall Notices of Sir M. Cradock.* Llandovery, 1840.

TUCKER, NORMAN. *Conway and its History.* Gee & Son, Denbigh, 1960.

WILLIAMS, DAVID. *A History of Modern Wales.* John Murray, London, 1950.
  John Penry's Three Treatises Concerning Wales. University of Wales Press, Cardiff.

WILLIAMS, D. TREFOR. *The Economic Development of Swansea and the Swansea District.* University of Wales Press Board, Cardiff, 1940.

WILLIAMS, GLANMOR. *Bywyd ac Amserau'r Esgob Richard Davies.* Gwasg Prifysgol Cymru, Caerdydd, 1953.

WILLIAMS, GWYN. *An Introduction to Welsh Poetry.* Faber & Faber, London, 1953.

WILLIAMS, PENRY. *The Council in the Marches of Wales Under Elizabeth I* University of Wales Press, Cardiff, 1958.

WILLIAMS, W. LLYWELYN. *The Making of Modern Wales.* Macmillan & Co., London, 1919.

Note. A more exhaustive guide to published material on this period is provided by the new edition of the *Bibliography of Welsh History,* prepared by the History and Law Committee of the Board of Celtic Studies, and published by the University of Wales Press, Cardiff, 1962.

INDEX

Abercarn, 159, 161.
Aberdare, 160.
Abergavenny, 93, 94, 99, 200, 204.
Abergele, 12, 40.
Abergwili, 199.
Abermenai, 192, 193.
Aberthaw, 131.
Aberystwyth, 33, 92, 93, 108, 123.
Acts of Livery and Maintenance, 31.
Act of Union, 27, 33, 75, 76, 91, 102, 107, 175, 176, 198.
Admiralty, Court of the, 136, 142.
Agriculture, improvements in, 79-81 ; open field husbandry, 85.
Agricultural Labourer, 45, 72.
Agricultural Produce, export of, 128, 131 ; smuggling of, 131-132.
Alehouses, 53, 58, 101.
Algiers, 143.
Almer, John, 35.
Almshouses, 51.
Ambassador, Venetian, 11, 39 ; Spanish, 11.
Amsterdam, 132.
Angle, 131.
Angle Bay, 131.
Anglesey, 24, 37, 70, 79, 84, 85, 121, 130, 136, 155, 158, 187, 188, 192, 193, 204, 213.
Antwerp, 69.
Apprentices, 69, 101, 114, 115, 118, 119, 205.
Archery, 56, 201 ; shooting at the butts, 57.
Armada, Spanish, 124, 125.
Aske, Robert, 216.
Assize of Bread, 101.
Atkinson, Jenkin, 113.
Aubrey, Dr. 108.
Azores, the, 144.

Babington Plot, 24.
Bagillt, 150.
Bagnall, Sir Nicholas, 150.
Bala, 174.
Bangor, 200, 201, 202, 205, 206, 225.
Bangor, Bishop of, 52, 192.
Bangor on Dee, 207.
Bankruptcy, Statute of, 160.
Barbary, coast of, 143.
Barbary States, 167.
Barber, John, 54.
Bardsey Island, 125, 135, 137.

Barlow, William, Bishop of St David's, 199-200.
Barnet Fair, 84.
Barnstaple, 127, 128, 132.
Barry, 131.
Barry Island, 11.
Bartholomew Fair, 84.
Beaumaris, 25, 52, 94, 104, 109, 121, 129, 135, 136, 141, 142, 143, 192, 193, 200, 205, 215.
Beddows, John, 208.
Bedford, 206.
Beddgelert, 205.
Begelly, 151, 152.
Beggars, 70, 72, 185-187.
Benefit of Clergy, 223-224.
Berkshire, 69.
Berw, 150.
Betws Bledrws, 47.
Bible, Welsh translation of the, 230, 231.
Blaenllyfni, 111.
Bodwyryd, 213.
Bôn y Don, 192.
Bosworth, Battle of, 9.
Bowls, 56.
Brecon, 60, 94, 102, 107, 114, 115, 171, 190, 196, 199.
Brecon, lordship of, 13.
Brecknock, 13, 46, 47, 50, 52, 56, 72, 82, 89, 107, 111, 172, 173, 179, 190, 222, 228.
Brentwood Fair, 84.
Bristol, 106, 126, 127, 128, 129, 132, 159, 160.
Bristol Channel, 126, 128, 129, 160.
Brittany, 127, 128, 154.
Bromfield, lordship of, 23, 58.
Broughton, 150.
Browne, Launcelot, 119-122.
Bryghan, Hugh, 62.
Bryghan, Rhys, 63.
Brymbo, 150.
Brynkir, William, 210.
Bucke, family of, 219.
Buckley, —, 211, 212.
Bulkeley, Sir Richard II, 17, 18, 22, 23, 24, 25, 138.
Bulkeley, Sir Richard III, 135, 136, 139, 141, 142, 143, 144, 206, 214, 215.
Bulkeley, Edward, 142, 143-144.
Bulkeley, Thomas, 214.
Bull, Thomas, 224.

Great Sessions, the, 169, 171, 172, 173, 174, 182.
Greenland, 25.
Gresford, 228.
Griffith, John, 137-138.
Griffith, John, 141.
Griffith, Hugh, 139-143.
Griffith, Meredudd ap, 184.
Griffiths, family of, 15.
Griffiths, Rees ap John, 219.
Grosmont, 99.
Guilds, the, 68, 93, 114-118.
Guinea, 133.
Guns, for hunting, 55 ; smuggling of, 132-133, 139.
Gunter, Philip, 190.
Guto, Evan, 46.
Gwendraeth, valley of, 153.
Gwentcoed, wood of, 161.
Gwragedd Cawsa, in Anglesey, 188.
Gwyn, David, 126.
Gwyn, Ieuan, 227.
Gypsies, 62.

Hanbury, Richard, 160-162, 165, 166.
Hanmer, 208, 222.
Hare, Sir William, Master of the Rolls, 62.
Harlech, 94.
Harps and Harpists, 36, 57, 58.
Harri, Morgan, 74.
Harrison, William, 11.
Haverfordwest, 94, 95, 102, 105, 145, 146, 152.
Haverfordwest, lordship of, 87.
Hawking, 55.
Hawkins, Sir John, 73.
Hay, 92.
Haynes, the pirate, 135, 136, 137.
Hebb, Richard, 84.
Henry VII, 9, 10, 92, 117.
Henry VIII, 29, 30, 54, 170, 216, 222.
Herbert, Edward, 178, 208.
Herbert, Sir George (Newport), 132.
Herbert, Sir George (Swansea), 38, 149.
Herbert, Sir George (Glamorgan), 32.
Herbert, Sir Walter (Monmouthshire), 76.
Herbert, Sir William (St. Julians), 13, 25.
Herbert, Sir William (Swansea), 137.
Herbert, Sir William, Earl of Pembroke, Lord President of the Council of the Marches, 26, 28, 31.
Herefordshire, 112, 132.
Hewett, Thomas, 139, 140.
Hicks, Robert, 145.
Holland, Owen, 150.

Holland, Piers, 12, 30.
Holt, 101.
Holywell, 61, 150, 156, 157, 219.
Hope, 74.
House of Commons, 26, 33, 35, 75, 76, 108, 109.
Howel, David ap, 173.
Huet, Thomas, 200.
Hugh, William ap, 172.
Hughes, William, Bishop of St Asaph, 226.
Humfrey, William, 163.
Humphreys, Gilbert, 195.
Hunting, 55.

Ilfracombe, 127.
Interludes, 105.
Inquisition, House of the, 126.
Ireland, 61, 68, 73, 119, 124, 126, 127, 135, 148, 153, 157, 192.
Ireland, military service in, 27, 32, 34, 69, 72, 185, 221.
Iron Industry, 159 ; speculation in, 160 ; leads to destruction of woods, 161, 165.
Islington, 222.
Italy, 104, 148.

James I, 93.
Jeffreston, 151.
Jesus College (Oxford), 209.
Jevons, James, 71.
John, Griffith ap, 139.
John, Robert ap, 186.
Johns, family of, 15.
Johnston, 151.
Jones, Charles, 69.
Jones, Edward, 24, 25.
Jones, —, 211.
Jones, Owen, 219.
Jones, Sir Thomas, 26.
Jones, William, 207.
Jones, William, 43.
Juries and Jurymen, 171, 172, 173-175, 180, 181, 193.
Justices of the Peace, 27, 28, 45, 67, 70, 71, 72, 89, 110, 112, 114, 123, 124, 145, 173, 176-179, 183, 186, 187, 188, 189, 190, 195, 225.
Justices of the Assize, 54, 95, 171, 219.

Kent, 69, 76, 84, 159.
Kidwelly, 133.
Kidwelly, lordship of, 88, 149.
Knappan, game of, 56.
Knighton, 218.
Kyffin, Griffith, 224, 225.